Midlife Eating Disorders and Body Image

Midlife Eating Disorders and Body Image offers a unique view of potential causes of midlife eating disorders and provides clinicians with practical applications for treatment.

The purpose of this book is to inform and support eating disorder professionals who work with clients in midlife, a phase spanning the late 30s to mid-60s that is predominately overlooked in the eating disorder field. This book emphasizes the intersection of sociocultural demands to meet Western beauty ideals with the shifting roles and expectations of midlife to provide an understanding of the complexity and treatment of midlife eating disorders. Based on the author's experiences as a psychologist, this comprehensive clinical resource will provide numerous case examples of individuals from an array of identities and genders. These cases throughout this book as well as the end-of-chapter reflections will facilitate discussions of real-life applications of the material.

This book is essential reading for practicing clinicians and advanced clinical students in the fields of eating disorders and mental health.

Heidi J. Dalzell is a psychologist, specializing in eating disorders and trauma. Dr. Dalzell has a busy private practice. Her areas of interest include midlife eating disorders, the intersection of trauma in eating disorders and addictive behaviors, and gender/gender identity as it relates to body image.

"Dr. Heidi Dalzell's, *Clinician's Guide to Midlife Eating Disorders and Body Image* is an informative, comprehensive and practical new resource for treating eating disorders in this often-neglected age group. She shares both research and her own clinical experiences treating midlife eating disorders, both identifying and delineating critical factors to consider in individualizing treatment for clients in this age group. It is a must-read for any clinician in the field and includes practical exercises to use in treatment sessions. Treating eating disorders in midlife is not 'one size fits all' and with the knowledge gained from this guide, clinicians will be able to provide informed care with a sensitivity to the treatment needs for this age group."

Betsy Brenner, *author of* The Longest match: Rallying to Defeat an Eating Disorder in Midlife *(Stillwater River, 2021)*

"Dr. Heidi Dalzell, Ph.D., has provided an invaluable resource for clinicians, clients and anyone interested learning more about the long-overlooked needs of older adults struggling with recovery with Eating Disorders and related Disordered Eating and body image distress at Midlife and Beyond! This "invisible, but in plain sight" population often feel left out and overlooked, so thank you for this much needed addition.

A Clinician's Guide to Midlife Eating Disorders and Body Image should be on the bookshelf for anyone involved in the field of Eating Disorders. I look forward to recommending this to those who have longed for more understanding and guidance in their journey to recovery! Dr. Dalzell has melded a thoughtful relational perspective with many stories of healing that highlight the many ways later life is a vital time to learn and grow towards making peace with their relationship with their aging bodies. It's NEVER too late!"

Karen Samuels, *PhD, CEDS psychologist and specialist in midlife eating disorders*

"In *A Clinician's Guide to Midlife Eating Disorders and Body Image*, Heidi Dalzell shares her wisdom, gained from decades of working with eating disorders and trauma and she is able to support her clients through a new lens specifically designed for those who are in mid-life. Most importantly, Heidi instills hope that recovery is possible at any age. She thoughtfully weaves in her clients' stories throughout, and I really felt like I got to know them and understand their struggles through her treatment lens. These diverse stories reflect the unique challenges of living in a body in midlife as well as working toward eating disorder recovery.

Heidi defines the eating disorders most prevalent in clients in midlife, the most common comorbidities as well as other unique challenges, including medical concerns. I learned about the challenges faced when a client has a lifetime of trauma as well as the body image concerns that present at midlife. Heidi highlights what is missing in treatment today for midlife clients and offers solutions. Heidi offers tangible tools in her Clinician Resources at the end of each chapter! These are creative, tangible skills you can use with your clients today, whether that is in the assessment process, or an activity to do in a therapy session. Heidi also asks you, the clinician, to self-reflect with thoughtful questions.

Personally, as a woman in midlife, I feel incredibly seen by Heidi in this book. I have lived experience with an eating disorder, sobriety, trauma, and chronic illness. Thank you for giving voice to so many things that have gone unspoken."

Tamie Gangloff, *MA, MFT, author of* Chronic Illness and Eating
Disorders: Assessments, Clinical Skills and Lived Experiences
(Routledge, 2015)

"*A Clinician's Guide to Midlife Eating Disorders and Body Image*, by Heidi Dalzell, does a great service to the mental health field.

Heidi Dalzell presents a compelling and thorough understanding of eating disorder and body image concerns that are specific to the midlife population. She explores added complexities of trauma, identity, age range within midlife, timelines of eating disorder onsets, and a broad variety of circumstances.

Dalzell demonstrates how this population tends to get overlooked, misunderstood, or treated without discernment. In addressing this population's needs, Heidi adapts existing concepts, tools, frameworks, and modalities toward midlife-specific concerns. She highlights treatment protocol considerations that I believe all professionals should have at their disposal.

This book is succinctly, clearly, and practicably organized. Heidi incorporates case examples, diagrams and charts, and applicable practices. She includes prompts for professionals to reflect on themselves and their clients. This reflection renders client work meaningful and sustainable.

A Clinician's Guide to Midlife Eating Disorders and Body Image paves a novel path toward meaningful eating disorder recovery for the midlife population. It is certain to enrich the breadth of knowledge and wisdom of those who read it, and it is guaranteed to have a profound impact on the mental health field. Dalzell's care and compassion reverberates throughout her book, as she gently and directly guides the reader through her understanding of this topic. I felt like both a professional and a student as I was reading."

Jenn Friedman, *LMHC – Mental Health Counselor, author of*
Veganism and Eating Disorder Recovery *(Routledge, 2022)*

Midlife Eating Disorders and Body Image

A Clinician's Guide

Heidi J. Dalzell

Routledge
Taylor & Francis Group

NEW YORK AND LONDON

Designed cover image: Getty Images

First published 2026
by Routledge
605 Third Avenue, New York, NY 10158

and by Routledge
4 Park Square, Milton Park, Abingdon, Oxon, OX14 4RN

Routledge is an imprint of the Taylor & Francis Group, an informa business

© 2026 Heidi J. Dalzell

For Product Safety Concerns and Information please contact our
EU representative GPSR@taylorandfrancis.com. Taylor & Francis
Verlag GmbH, Kaufingerstraße 24, 80331 München, Germany.

ISBN: 978-1-032-61573-8 (hbk)
ISBN: 978-1-032-60383-4 (pbk)
ISBN: 978-1-032-61574-5 (ebk)

DOI: 10.4324/9781032615745

Typeset in Times New Roman
by codeMantra

Contents

Acknowledgments

To my clients – especially those who have faced midlife eating disorders: thank you for allowing me into your most vulnerable moments and for trusting me with your stories. Your strength, wisdom, and resilience have deeply touched my heart. You've shown me that recovery is not bound by age. May your stories inspire readers and future therapists working with clients with midlife eating disorders.

To my teachers, mentors, and pioneers in the field of eating disorders: your dedication has shaped the way I understand healing and recovery at all ages and stages of life. Your commitment to advancing knowledge, challenging stigma, and supporting those in need has inspired me and countless others.

To those people in the background asking, "How's that writing going?" Thank you, Betsy Brenner, who courageously shared her own story of a midlife woman with an eating disorder. Thank you to my advance readers, Betsy Brenner, Tamie Gangloff, Jenn Friedman, and Karen Samuels. You read the whole book – I was so touched by your kind words (despite some small typos).

Thank you to my steadfast supporter and life partner, Michael Dalzell. Whether it's stepping in to feed a hoard of hungry cats, cooking a great meal, or reading my work, he is always there as a support.

With deepest gratitude,

Heidi

Introduction

I started working with eating disorders in the mid-1990s as a teacher on a hospital-based inpatient unit. We'd hold class after lunch, resulting in less teaching and more informal meal support. This was a unique window into the struggles and hopes of younger to older teen clients. It was, overall, a homogeneous group, like the one author and psychoanalyst Hilde Bruch described in her works on eating disorders: young, white, middle class, and female.

As a young clinician, I eagerly consumed books such as *The Golden Cage* and *Eating Disorders: Obesity, Anorexia and the Person Within*. In these, Bruch shared the struggles of young, white, affluent women given every material privilege but lacking love and emotional nurturance. The culprit: the mothers, of course. As a field, we've come a *long* way in debunking some myths about eating disorders, but others die hard. I would never have imagined I'd specialize in working with the very mothers, fathers, and other middle-aged persons we'd implicated in these disorders. While midlife eating disorders have their differences, the struggles can be similar.

I focus on midlife eating disorders. In this book, we define *midlife* as the period spanning from the late 30s to the late 60s. I have a unique lens into the lives of my clients – their histories, hopes, dreams, and struggles. Though each person I treat is unique, the commonalities among them are the struggles around food, eating, body image, and self-esteem. Other common themes are the sadness, shame, and desperation driving them to reach out for support.

Jocelyn (name and identifying details changed) was one such client. This 68-year-old, vibrant, and artistic woman struggled with what she called "too muchness" – too much food (including food binges), too much drink, too much smoking. Her self-esteem was at an all-time low. While I immediately connected with her personality and expressiveness, she could not acknowledge *any* strengths, focusing instead on her weight and aging process. Jocelyn's daughter and grandchildren, once the center of her world, had moved across the country. Their busy lifestyles made for limited contact. In our initial conversation, Jocelyn made an interesting observation. During a recent visit with her family, she felt great. "I didn't overeat or drink," she said. "I even smoked less." We both were quick to recognize the

DOI: 10.4324/9781032615745-1

relationship between eating disorders and lack of connection – whether to family, friends, religious communities, or sources of support.

Therapy provided a needed bridge for Jocelyn to learn other ways to manage her sadness, to work on her deeply held feelings of not deserving more than she had in her life, and to assess her own goals for the next chapter of her life. Jocelyn ultimately went on to move closer to her daughter and grandchildren, something she'd resisted in the past. She was careful to also seek out other opportunities for herself: volunteering at a local school with an adopt-a-grandparent program, joining a local church, and learning Mah Jongg. "I can't believe how busy I am now," she shared in a recent email. "While I still overeat occasionally, the binges are a thing of the past. And no more drinking." She went on to share that she had not realized how much focus she'd put on not being "a burden." Much of this conflict was because she'd felt so burdened by her own mother. "My daughter loves me, and I love her," she shared. "But I also love the life I've created."

Jocelyn's story, and many others, show that midlife eating disorders are treatable. People who struggle with them are not doomed to live an unsatisfying life focused on calories and exercise. Nor is everyone with a midlife eating disorder someone who has struggled for years. Eating disorders are unique, which is part of the challenge of decoding them.

Why, then, does the counseling field so often fail clients like Jocelyn – people who seek eating disorder treatment at midlife – or worse yet, promote in these potential clients a sense of shame? It's often due to misunderstanding what midlife eating disorders look like, a lack of developmentally appropriate models ("adult" programs often begin at the age of 18), and an unwillingness to challenge the messages of diet culture, a multimillion-dollar diet industry that shapes our perception of ideal and acceptable bodies.

Fortunately, the eating disorder field *is* shifting. It has begun to acknowledge the diversity of people affected by eating disorders. Despite this shift, the public – and some therapists – think of eating disorders as a "teenage problem." This may prevent adult men and women from seeking needed treatment. When they do bravely seek out outpatient therapy and program options, the care they receive may not be developmentally appropriate. Worst of all, they may be met with a lack of understanding or empathy. I have had clients tearfully reach out from eating disorder programs where they are the oldest person in the community – and this includes the staff as well. "I caught a therapist referring to me as a 'frequent flyer,'" one client reported. There are both a knowledge gap and an empathy gap.

This book will bridge that gap, providing a unique lens into the challenges that lead to midlife eating disorders.

Midlife itself is a broad developmental phase. It is a time of changes – family transitions, relationships that look dramatically different, and body changes, to name a few. Understanding these factors can help us to develop more effective treatment approaches and to reduce stigma. A key message of this book is that there is hope at every age. With appropriate, collaborative support, eating disorder recovery *is* possible at midlife and beyond.

While the scope of this book is intended to support clinicians with a range of theoretical perspectives, its overarching perspective is that of relational psychology. Thus, this book emphasizes the intersection of sociocultural demands to meet Western beauty ideals and the shifting roles and expectations of midlife, all of which are buffered through compassion and connection.

What is the scope of the problem? It's far-reaching. Midlife "maturity" was once considered a protective factor for body image and disordered eating, but this is not the case. Eating disorders can both begin and recur at midlife. A study of women aged 60–70 years found that 60% of those surveyed reported body dissatisfaction (Mangweth-Matzek et al., 2006). A study of 1,800 women, aged 50 and older, yielded similar results. More than 60% of the women experienced daily thoughts about their weight and said that weight and body shape negatively affected their lives (Gagne et al., 2012). Physical changes, such as menopause, can intensify negative body image.

While aging men appear to be more satisfied with their bodies overall, there are things they lament. One study of men found that the stomach and midsection were prominent body concerns (Forrester-Knauss & Zemp Stutz, 2012). Another small study of middle-aged men found that between 8% and 17% expressed concerns about their bodies (Matsumoto & Rodgers, 2020).

If you are working with midlife clients, there's a good likelihood that they feel bad about themselves from time to time. Most therapists I know, whether they specialize in eating disorders, trauma, depression, or something else, are privy to conversations lamenting cellulite, wrinkles, or other indications of aging and "imperfection."

As you've likely noted, research often forces us to take a gendered view of body image. Body dissatisfaction can affect people of all genders and those who do not identify in a binary way. Current studies show that body dissatisfaction is rampant in LGBT persons. Many of these studies are cited in an earlier work (Dalzell & Protos, 2020). Anecdotally, one challenging factor is that midlife clients may not seek gender-confirming treatments. This is an area which definitely needs further study.

Facebook, Instagram, and magazines feature images of middle-aged (and older) people that are photoshopped, enhanced through fillers or cosmetic surgeries, or created by artificial intelligence. These are not the faces or bodies of the average adult. Nor do we see some of the common signs of aging: wrinkles, widening hips, and cellulite. Mainstream media would have us believe that these normal changes are unacceptable. Even more often, such advertisements lack images of people at midlife, leading to a sense of invisibility. Many of our clients seek "perfection" or "youth" or a way to stay relevant.

At 81, Martha Stewart recently became the oldest *Sports Illustrated* swimsuit model. Despite her own comments meant to demonstrate the "health," to prepare for the shoot, Stewart followed a keto diet. "I didn't starve myself, but I didn't eat any bread or pasta for a couple of months," Stewart shared on the *Today Show*. "I went to Pilates every other day and that was great." My own mother, at 81, is *not* going to Pilates daily, nor is she striving for a swimsuit cover. Stewart clearly does not resemble most octogenarians out there.

In addition to the role of media and its views of "aging" (lack of aging is probably more accurate), midlife eating disorders and body image are influenced by stress. And what do people seek when they are stressed? Numbing, control, self-esteem. Dieting and weight loss can promote these things, but the research shows that weight loss is rarely sustainable, leading to a cycle of weight loss and regain.

Those of us who have reached midlife intimately know these stresses: body changes, menopause/andropause (Mangweth-Matzek et al., 2023), increased competition at jobs, financial stress as we prepare for retirement – and that's just scratching the surface. It is important to look at these life transitions and how they affect each person. What function(s) do eating disorder symptoms serve for each person?

Feminist relational psychology (Jordan, 2017; Miller, 1976) has been a long-standing underpinning of my work with clients. Feminist approaches point out that eating disorders may be due to the changing relationships and disconnections so prominent in our society. Many of these observations are just common sense. Connections with others are life-affirming and promote positive emotional wellness. Disconnections, however, are destabilizing. Midlife is a time of transition: children going to college, newly empty nest, losses of parents or friends, and other changes in relationships. Such changes can lead to connection or disconnection. For example, an empty nest may bring partners closer to one another – or reveal just how distant they have become. Another common disconnection is one's disconnection from a changing body. And such transitions play out against the backdrop of a culture obsessed with youth and thinness.

While theories help guide us, much of my inspiration for the work I do comes directly from my own experience as a person in eating disorder recovery and from the people I work with. While my eating disorder occurred in college, it's never far from my mind. As a woman at midlife, I face the same stresses as my clients. While we share commonalities, there are also differences. Many of the remarkable people I work with weekly have allowed portions of their story to be used in this book. To preserve their confidentiality, none of the clients described in this book represent a person in my practice; rather they represent the many themes they share. You will read about struggles and triumphs, what's worked, and what has not. This has led to best practices that I will share throughout this book and the Clinician Resources that conclude each chapter. Please feel free to edit or adapt these resources to your own practices and needs. Almost all can be easily adapted to individual or group therapy.

I hope this inspires you in your own work with people at midlife.

Chapter 1

The face of midlife eating disorders

In this chapter, we meet several clients who share very little beyond age. All are what we would consider midlife. The people we meet in this chapter have different histories, past experiences of eating disorders, and different goals and dreams. All struggle, however, with midlife eating disorders.

Eating disorders include a range of symptoms and presentations. They affect men and women (and people whose inner genders are not readily categorized in this way), people who are gay, straight, or bisexual, and people of all religions, ethnic groups, body sizes, and identities. With this in mind, let's meet a cross-section of adults struggling with food and body-image concerns. Perhaps you will identify with their situations, empathize with their struggles, or know a client who shares some similar factors.

Meet Sasha

We'll begin with 38-year-old Sasha. When meeting Sasha, who is usually decked out in Disney attire, you'd likely think she is much younger. Sasha has struggled with an eating disorder most of her life. Sasha lives in Philadelphia in a neighborhood that reflects her roots as a transplant from Russia. Her family came to the United States when Sasha was 5, and they maintain a strong connection to their culture. Resettling in a new country was difficult, and her family has never achieved the financial success they enjoyed in Russia.

Sasha started dancing at an early age. She felt "pushed into this" by her mother, a classically trained ballerina. Sasha's mother maintains the bearing and discipline of a ballerina even now, and Sasha often feels like she can never measure up to that standard. Sasha cannot recall a time when she had a healthy relationship with food or with her body. Sasha's family is burned out by the many years of struggle, although they continue to support her financially. "It's like watching my daughter die a slow death," her mother once commented.

Sasha's eating disorder began in high school, where Sasha thought the key to popularity was being thin. "The thinner the better," she laughs. "It seemed like my only talent." Sasha has not achieved the goal of having a large group of

DOI: 10.4324/9781032615745-2

friends. "I feel really alone a lot of the time," she says. Sasha's main "friends" are people she met in eating disorder treatment.

"There's Mimi, who has had an eating disorder longer than I have," she shares. "And Abby, who can't stop binging. And Tara, whose self-esteem is awful." With these friends, Sasha becomes a quasi-therapist. "I know what to do and say to help *them*," she says. "I just can't help myself."

While church was a respite when she was younger, Sasha now also feels distant from her church community. Others her age are married and have children. "I just can't relate to their lives," she says. "And they probably can't relate to mine." Sasha is closest to her mother, despite the criticism. "I know she'd never leave me," Sasha says. "And she needs me too. She and my dad have not been close in years."

Sasha graduated from college but has never worked in her field, mainly because of her eating disorder. "At a real job, I'd need to sit at a desk and do projects," she says. "At the daycare I can run after the kids. It's good exercise." While Sasha knows she can do more with her life, she shies away from change. With her long-standing eating disorder and more limited earnings, Sasha qualifies for Medicare and Medicaid coverage, which is a must given her complex medical situation. Her medical history isn't always clear, but some of the things she's noted include gastroparesis, a condition that causes severe bloating after meals and further affects her body image, osteoporosis, and kidney disease from dehydration.

The daycare center where she works is coming under new ownership, and the owners have been making changes. They already have cut back her hours, and Sasha is terrified she may lose the one job that allows her plenty of time to focus on her food and body.

Sasha has alluded to a sexual assault in high school but has never been able to share more than the slimmest of details in therapy. With her malnutrition, therapy sessions can feel meandering and unproductive, and Sasha breezes through therapist after therapist.

Recently, Sasha's mother has been falling, and while they've ruled out some of the obvious possibilities, no one is sure what's been going on. Sasha is very worried, and she tries to help, but her mother often rebuffs her.

The possible change in jobs and her mother's failing health have caused Sasha to think more about aging. She's scared. Lately her eating disorder pattern has begun to change – she's finding less comfort in restricting her food and has started binging. It's a vicious cycle – one in which Sasha feels "constantly at war" with her body. Her binging quickly gives way to guilt. Sasha then "gets rid of" the calories by vomiting. Sasha is terrified of gaining weight and desperately wants to stop binging. She has tried to restrict during the day, which only causes her to binge more. In desperation, Sasha has recently started to cut herself, and her stomach is now covered in cuts and gouges. "I know it's awful," Sasha says. "But punishing myself in this way actually helps me to feel a little better about the binging and purging.

With the increase in symptoms, Sasha and her treatment team made the decision to seek out a non-eating disorder partial hospital program. "I feel like I've actually learned some things," she says. The lack of focus on her eating disorder has been positive, and Sasha is beginning to consider that recovery may mean more than gaining weight. It may mean creating a more fulfilling life.

Meet Susan

Susan is 45 and is a biracial woman. Susan's parents lost contact with one another when she was a toddler, and Susan was raised by her mother and grandparents in a predominately white neighborhood. "I feel a void at times," Susan shares. "Like part of me is missing." Despite this, Susan has not sought out contact with her birth father or his family. Her mother, grandmother, and grandfather have all died. She is unsure if her father is still alive.

Susan has been a homemaker, raising twin daughters. Susan desperately misses her daughters who are sophomores at college. Her husband, Ted, works long hours and travels frequently. "We've grown apart," she says. "Even when he is home, we don't really spend time together." As Susan shares more of herself, the loneliness and isolation are evident.

Throughout her life, Susan has maintained an average weight. While she previously "accepted" her weight, this has changed. "Since my kids have left, I am more aware of how I look," she says. "And my body is different than it used to be," she says. "Frumpy."

The supermarket tabloids have provided the key: keto. Keto seems to be all the rage, and Susan can see why. Since she has started keto, Susan's weight has plummeted. Her goal of "losing five pounds" soon became 10. At first, Susan felt good about her weight loss. Acquaintances commented on how she looked, and she got more attention from men. Her husband has been much less complimentary. "To me she just looks sick," Ted shared. Ted was initially supportive of Susan's recovery, but as the realities of needing to be at home more have set in, his support has wavered. "My eating disorder is the only thing that gives me a sense of purpose," Susan says. "It feels like my only friend." As her weight has continued to dip, all the compliments have stopped. "I still think I look great," Susan says.

Things came to a head when Susan blacked out at church. At her pastor's urging, Susan was hospitalized for her eating disorder. Susan was mortified. "I feel like I have a teenage problem," she said. This idea was further reinforced by the young 20s cohort in the hospital unit. "The staff – everyone – treats me like a child," she said. "I felt like one of my kids." Susan ultimately discharged herself from the hospital and did not initially seek support.

She has subsequently found an outpatient team that specializes in midlife. The progress is slow, and she is reluctant to "give up something that gives me a sense of purpose." Susan has been a reluctant "joiner," but has found a puzzle

Meetup she enjoys. Recently, Susan has been considering Ancestry or another DNA program to contact her wider birth family. "I'm scared," she shared. "But my girls deserve to know their relatives – and maybe I do too."

Meet Carla

Carla is a 50-year-old photographer and graphic designer. She loves her career. Carla has always been very successful, and clients and coworkers rave about her work. "I love what I do," she shared. "It's my life."

Lately, her company has hired several younger designers, and while they do not have the technical knack Carla has, she often compares herself to them physically. "I look at these twentysomethings and just feel so old," she says. This is especially evident in work gatherings, and Carla has been passed over for several recent promotions.

Carla is gay and has always hoped to find that "special someone," settle down, and have a family. "You'd think I'd have come to terms with not having children," she says. "But the struggle is real. And my erratic [menstrual] cycles only remind me more of what I never had. It's a constant sadness."

Carla has experienced several past traumas, including parents who were functional alcoholics with little time for their child. She also experienced a date rape in college. Carla left home following her senior year, and never returned. The rape affected her greatly. In college, Carla struggled with bulimia. Carla was fortunate to find support at college, including some good friends and a skilled trauma therapist.

Carla's eating disorder symptoms have remained largely in remission since college, although Carla considers herself a "serial dieter." "Up 5, down 5," she jokes. "I keep thinking that's the magic bullet, but I guess not." While Carla acknowledges the absurdity of her situation, she's quick to reach for supermarket tabloids touting the latest quick fix diet and has spent countless dollars on diet pills and other remedies.

Carla's mother has recently shown signs of cognitive decline. The change has been rapid. Carla has tried to help but is resentful. "She didn't take great care of me growing up," she says. "And now I'm expected to somehow be the parent."

Carla uses her workload and other responsibilities to beg off caretaking as much as possible and has offered to pay for some in-home supports. Her father refuses. "Your mother just wouldn't want strangers in the house," he says. Carla is angry at how poorly her parents have aged and blames their alcohol abuse. "They were young when they had me," she says. "And at 75 they shouldn't need so much of my attention and focus." Carla knows this situation is not sustainable, and she is overwhelmed by anger, frustration, and fatigue.

As she's become more aware of the severity of her parents' needs, Carla has started skipping breakfast to stop by before work. She knows "too busy" is an excuse and that skipping breakfast helps numb her anger. "It works. And the scale is finally moving downward," she says.

Her job often precludes a lunch break – and while she'd at least eaten at her desk in the past, Carla now skips lunch as well. Coffee – and too much of it – does a fabulous job of suppressing her hunger cues. Carla has recently started to binge on food and wine after work. The steady diet of alcohol, food and stress has taken a toll. Her weight has crept back up, which makes her feel even worse about herself. She then turns to food and alcohol for comfort. Carla feels helpless and ashamed: "It's a vicious cycle," she says, "I don't see a way out. But this stress – it's killing me."

The final straw for Carla was a recent work evaluation. Her previously stellar evaluation is now lukewarm at best, and the alcohol and emotional eating are the likely culprits. Carla knows that she needs to shape up or risk more formal performance counseling at work.

In her first meeting, Carla was met with some hard facts. Her alcohol consumption had crossed a line from problem drinking to alcoholism. "Nothing changes if nothing changes," her therapist stated. And Carla's first change was attending a women's Alcoholics Anonymous (AA) meeting. "It felt like coming home," she said. "I was surrounded by people who understood not only the drinking but also what it feels like to deal with parents like mine." Carla has taken steady steps toward caring for herself and her needs, and she is working on the effects of being raised in a family of emotionally immature parents.

Meet John

John is an active 69-year-old who lives with his partner of 40 years, Rick. They have a grown son who lives close by. The couple has many fascinating stories about their activism within the LGBT community and are well known and liked in these circles. Rick tends to be the more social of the two, and John the quieter one. While John tries to be social for Rick, he is more of a homebody. John does not have contact with his family of origin, who rejected his sexuality, but is close to Rick's more accepting family. Rick's mother recently passed away, a major heartbreak for them both. John and his mother-in-law were especially close, and "I am devastated by her death." Shirley was diabetic and had been in poor health for many years, but the death was still unexpected.

Rick has been talking with John about relocating to Florida. John was excited about this possibility, though reluctant to leave his son and grandchildren. Recently, John has been experiencing some puzzling health concerns. No one can diagnose the vague symptoms of Gastrointestinal (GI) distress, fatigue. John has tried to make dietary changes and has cut out carbs, fat, and sugar. He's lost weight. "I know I'm too skinny," he shared. "But on the bright side I probably won't get diabetes." Rick has lost 20 pounds over the past three months, weight that he could not afford to lose.

Friends – and even Rick – have made negative comments about his changing appearance. "I've started avoiding people now," John shared. "Every time I see someone I know, it's 'You look awful,' or 'Where has the rest of you vanished to?' It's much easier to just be on my own." Worse yet, the dietary changes have not helped him feel better. John has started to become convinced that he may have a terminal illness. "I've been to just about every doctor," he says. "No one can seem to pinpoint what's wrong with me. It must be something pretty bad – and rare."

Lately, John's obsession with "healthy eating" and "food purity" has ramped up. John spends hours each day thinking about food and planning meals. He had a similar, although short-lived, preoccupation as a teen. "It was something like this, right after I came out to my family," he says. "But that went away when I really accepted myself." Even though he can see the similarity to what he's currently experiencing, he's skeptical. "Shirley's acceptance helped me then," he says. "But she's no longer here to tell me things are ok."

John was initially nervous about asking for help and ashamed to be seeking therapy. His fears were quickly put to bed, and John was relieved to learn that his struggles have a name: orthorexia. John's psychologist explained that orthorexia, an obsession with "healthy eating" and food purity, was something that he could work on – and change – with support. The first step? Slowly add some things back into his eating. John fearfully agrees that sweet potatoes may be a good first challenge. When his therapist asked if he was still grieving Shirley's loss, John broke down in tears, and her empathic response to his grief felt healing.

What do these cases tell us?

These cases are representative of midlife eating disorders, including common stresses and manifestations. Some people with eating disorders have struggled for many years, a manifestation known as severe and enduring eating (SEED) disorders. Others had eating disorders at an early age and have recovered, only to relapse at middle age. Still others develop a late-onset eating disorder.

Other substance use disorders – particularly alcohol use disorder – also commonly co-occur with eating disorders (Devoe et al., 2021; Gregorowski et al., 2013). Other co-occurring disorders include anxiety and depression.

While on the surface these cases look very different, there are several themes among them:

- Pressures to look/appear a certain way, with the belief that life will change for the better
- Feelings of not meeting these beauty standards
- Relational disconnections, which precede or accompany the eating disorder
- Illness or death of significant people
- Normal age-related body changes

- Presence of dual addictions or recent recovery from another substance, such as alcohol
- Reluctance to ask for help and shame about having an eating disorder

While clinicians working with eating disorders are certainly aware of some of these themes, the field lacks guidance on how to work with and treat midlife eating disorders. We will look at current research and explore the above themes more fully as we continue. We will also look at the many functions that eating disorders serve for midlife clients. While there will be many cases in these pages, we will return to many of these clients throughout the course of this book.

For further reflection and application

The clients in this chapter share struggles with eating disorders. They reflect a range of ages, from early midlife to older ages. They demonstrate differing clinical courses, beliefs, and eating disorder symptoms.

1 Think over your roster of past and current clients. How are your clients similar to Sasha, Susan, Carla, or John? Are there themes you notice that do not seem to be represented in these stories?
2 Of the clients described in this chapter, pick the client you most identify or connect with. What about his/her/their story resonates with you? If this was your client, what would you like to know or further explore? Take a few moments to jot down your reflections.
3 Based on your current knowledge of eating disorders, develop an initial treatment plan. What are your goals and objectives? What strategies will support your goals? How is your approach similar or different from how you would work with a teen or young adult?

Clinician resource 1: assessment cheat sheet for midlife eating disorders

As you read through the cases in this chapter, you've likely noted many of the key themes we see when working with midlife eating disorders. Most therapists are very familiar with assessment, although perhaps less so with some of the areas specific to midlife eating disorders. Let's tackle this right away in the form of the following "cheat sheet."

This resource provides a breakdown of areas to cover when assessing midlife eating disorders. As with any assessment, you would also cover relevant psychosocial history. This assessment provides an overview of eating disorder symptoms and related medical and psychiatric conditions. Feel free to use only the sections that apply to the client you are assessing and to be conversational.

CLINICIAN RESOURCE 1: ASSESSMENT CHEAT SHEET FOR MIDLIFE EATING DISORDERS

In meeting with a new client, it's helpful to have some guidelines for assessment. These areas are presented for awareness, not as a checklist you read to a new client. If something obviously does not fit, skip it and move on.

1   **Physical symptoms and behavioral indicators**

- Assess for the presence of the following (National Eating Disorders Association):

  - Intense fear of gaining weight
  - Restricting food intake
  - Need to change the body (such as size or shape)
  - Counting calories or restricting food groups, such as fats/carbs
  - Compulsive exercise or exercising to compensate for food
  - Vomiting after eating (purging)
  - Using diet pills
  - Diuretics or laxative abuse
  - Body checking (e.g., spending time in front of the mirror or pinching fat)
  - Hoarding food
  - Binge eating (or binge/restrict cycle)
  - Shame after eating
  - Fear of eating around others
  - Weighing oneself frequently
  - Focus on the purity of food
  - Fad diets, extreme dieting, serial dieting
  - Chewing and spitting
  - Poor or unrealistic/distorted body image (belief in being "fat" even when very thin)

2   **Psychological factors**

- Self-esteem: assess current self-esteem and how this may be related to eating
- Perfectionism, rigidity, overcontrol
- Emotional instability, impulsivity
- Obsessive-compulsive personality traits

3   **Comorbid mental health issues**

- Does the client show signs of the following:

  - Mood disorders: depression, anxiety, or bipolar disorder

- Obsessive-compulsive tendencies or obsessive-compulsive disorder (OCD)
- Trauma-related symptoms (especially with a history of past trauma)
- Substance use/abuse

4 Personal history

- History of dieting or eating disorders
- Past trauma: list any past traumas and/or "difficult life events"
- Assess for losses (personal, loss of job, etc.)
- Family history: assess family history of eating disorders

5 Age-related biological changes

- Hormonal fluctuations: perimenopause and menopause; other
- Changes in metabolism, weight gain
- Performance-related concerns (balance, slowing down)

6 Social and cultural influences

- Cultural pressure: assess buy-in to societal ideals of youth, beauty, thinness
- Changes in social roles (e.g., empty nest, caregiving for aging parents)
- Isolation or loneliness

7 Lifestyle and environmental factors

- Work stress: assess job-related stress
- Relationship dynamics: have there been changes in relationships
- Financial strain

8 Support systems

- Lack of social support
- Family or relational conflict

9 Impact on overall well-being

- Physical health complications: complications of eating disorder symptoms, such as malnutrition, dehydration, and heart conditions
- Quality of life: mental and emotional quality of life can be deeply impacted by eating disorder behaviors, affecting overall satisfaction with life and relationships

10 Medical history

- Chronic conditions: certain conditions like diabetes, hypertension
- Medication use: including prescribed medications

11 Treatment history and access to care

- Previous treatment: assess for prior history of treatment for eating disorders

12 Spiritual

- Beliefs and resources: assess openness to spiritual approaches and protective factors
- Negative experiences: assess any negative messages in a person's spiritual background

Chapter 2

What the research says

The clients I have worked with through the years are a diverse bunch, spanning all genders, races, and ages. Many of those I see today are in the period of life we call midlife. Supporting these clients means expanding our understanding of "midlife" or "middle age." It also challenges us to increase our perceptions of who is affected by eating disorders.

There is no universally agreed-upon age range for midlife. For the purposes of this book, I'll define midlife as the period that spans the ages from the late 30s to the late 60s. Thanks to the Baby Boomers, midlife today looks very different than it did years ago. Today's Millennials are following the Boomer's lead, starting families at later ages, with women having more "geriatric pregnancies." Many are choosing not to retire until their 70s. Middle-aged folks may be tasked with dual caretaking roles, caring for older parents and children simultaneously. With these realities comes a shift in what it means to be middle-aged. Many people in their 40s, 50s, and 60s live on the fast track. It's a different demographic than a generation prior. But for all the people in this age demographic, research on this developmental time is sorely lacking.

If the research on midlife is underwhelming, research on midlife eating disorders is even more scant – although this seems to be slowly changing. This chapter will summarize current research findings on eating disorders, body dissatisfaction, and stresses associated with midlife. We'll expand on the themes in this research in subsequent pages of this book.

Developmental approaches to psychology

Most of us have taken one or more developmental psychology classes, so this section is meant to be a quick review.

When I refer to *developmental stages*, I mean a series of distinct and typically sequential phases through which people pass as they grow and mature. Each stage is characterized by specific physical, cognitive, emotional, or social changes. These stages help explain how people develop over time, typically from infancy to adulthood. Developmental stage theories suggest that individuals

DOI: 10.4324/9781032615745-3

must successfully navigate the challenges or tasks of each stage to move on to the next, and failure to do so can impact later development (Berk, 2018). The hope is that through navigating the key developmental tasks, people "graduate" to the next stage of their development. Failure to navigate any of these tasks results in a kind of "stuckness" or lack of healthy forward movement. Sounding at least vaguely familiar? Read on.

Some of the most influential stage theorists include Sigmund Freud, Jean Piaget, Erik Erikson, and Lawrence Kohlberg. Piaget is known for his theory of cognitive development, which primarily focuses on children. Piaget outlines how children's thinking evolves through four stages: sensorimotor, preoperational, concrete operational, and formal operational (Piaget, 1952). Freud is best known for his psychosexual theory (more soon). Erikson expanded on Freud's theory to propose eight psychosocial stages of development, each marked by a central conflict such as trust vs. mistrust or identity vs. role confusion (Erikson, 1963). Kohlberg built on Piaget's work to propose a stage theory of moral development, where individuals progress from basic obedience to advanced ethical reasoning (Kohlberg, 1981). These theories have profoundly shaped the understanding of human development in psychology and education.

Sigmund Freud is probably the most well known (and maligned) of these developmental theorists. While his theory of psychosexual stages is a product of Victorian times, I have heard many an eating disorder therapist joke (or maybe not joke) about certain clients being stuck in the oral stage of development. In Freud's view, children and adults navigate the world through a pleasure-seeking behavior connected to various erogenous zones (such as the mouth, anus, and genitals) (Freud, originally published in 1915).

Freud would likely view eating disorders as expressions of unconscious conflicts, rooted in early childhood experiences. According to Freud, unresolved issues during the oral stage (birth to 18 months), when pleasure centers on the mouth through activities like sucking and eating, could lead to fixations that manifest later in life. An eating disorder might thus reflect an oral fixation resulting from inadequate or overly indulgent feeding practices during infancy (Freud, 1905/1953). Freud might also interpret eating disorders as symbolic attempts to exert control over internal conflicts, especially those involving identity, autonomy, and sexuality. For example, in anorexia, the refusal to eat and extreme control over the body could be seen as an unconscious rejection of emerging adult sexuality. It could also be a way to assert control in response to repressed emotions, parental dominance, or parents who provide for material but not emotional needs. Hilde Bruch, one of the earliest people to describe eating disorders, used Freud's theories (Bruch, 1978; Freud, 1915/1957) in her work.

Erikson, the German-American psychoanalyst, was the first developmental theorist to focus on midlife *per se* (1982). Erikson approached development not from a sexual or pleasure-seeking lens, but through the lens of social experiences.

Life is a series of challenges and mastery connected to the larger social fabric. He called the period preceding midlife, the young adult stage, *intimacy vs. isolation*. This period spanning the ages of 19–40 is the time in which people develop relationships, fall in love, and create their own families.

By the time people reach middle adulthood – age 40–60 – their attention shifts. Erikson calls the midlife stage *generativity* (making one's mark) *vs. stagnation* (failure to find a way to contribute). Erikson said that people in middle adulthood should "take care of the persons, the products, and the ideas one has learned to care for" (Erikson, 1982, p. 67). Being generative can include a range of pursuits: parenthood and grandparenthood, work and professional activities, volunteering, and participation in religious or political organizations (McAdams & de St. Aubin, 1992). It includes a desire to give back to society and contribute in one's own unique way. Generative people also can empathize with the struggles of others or recognize a need for assistance. One of the factors in midlife eating disorders involves a feeling of not having made one's mark in life or regrets about a "road not taken" to quote Robert Frost. Stagnation, the opposite of generativity, involves feeling empty and unproductive.

We can also thank Erikson's theory for the notion of the midlife crisis, a transition of identity and self-confidence brought about by events that highlight a person's growing age, inevitable mortality, and lack of accomplishments in life. Midlife crisis is said to result in feelings of depression and desires to achieve youthfulness or make changes in lifestyle through stereotypical behaviors such as buying a sports car or dating someone much younger.

So how common are the kinds of midlife crises such as those depicted in popular films such as *City Slickers*, the iconic *Wild West* comedy, or *Thelma and Louise's* infamous identity crisis?

While the midlife crisis is widely recognized in popular culture, research has shown that it is not a universal experience. Some studies suggest that only a minority of people experience a profound crisis or emotional upheaval during middle age (Blanchflower & Oswald, 2008). While feelings of disillusionment or dissatisfaction may be common in middle adulthood, they do not necessarily lead to the dramatic upheaval often depicted in the media (Lachman, 2004). That's not to say that emotional upheaval does not occur – it does – but it's more to say that buying a sports car is rarely the path or solution. The midlife crisis, then, appears to be more of a stereotype than a common psychological event.

Research on life satisfaction has found a U-shaped pattern of happiness across the lifespan. A study by Blanchflower and Oswald (2008) found that people report lower levels of happiness in their 40s and 50s, which could contribute to the perception of a midlife crisis. However, life satisfaction tends to increase again in later years, suggesting that midlife dissatisfaction is part of a broader, normal life trajectory.

Several factors have been identified as contributing to midlife concerns, although no single factor explains the phenomenon entirely. These factors include:

- **Age-related changes:** physical aging, awareness of mortality, and declines in health or physical vitality can trigger a reevaluation of life goals (Rowe & Kahn, 1997). The onset of midlife often brings reflections on time and the realization of aging, which can prompt anxiety or crisis-like feelings. However, this realization of aging can spur people to action and allow them to make shifts that bring them great satisfaction.
- **Life events:** major life transitions, such as the "empty nest syndrome" (when children leave home), career changes, or the death of parents, are often associated with midlife dissatisfaction or crisis (Lachman, 2004). Others navigate transitions such as empty nest, fully embracing the freedom and independence this period can bring.
- **Cultural and societal expectations:** Western societies often have high expectations for career success, family stability, and personal achievement by midlife. The failure to meet these expectations can lead to feelings of disappointment or frustration (Lachman & James, 1997). While these expectations can be challenging, midlife can be a time when people decide to be truer to their own needs and goals, rather than bound by societal dictates.
- **Gender differences:** there are also gender-related differences in experiencing midlife crises. The predominant experience of midlife for women involves changing roles, such as motherhood. They also experience societal pressures around aging, beauty, and maintaining a youthful look (Matud, 2004). Men, however, might face crises tied to career accomplishments or the loss of physical vitality (Levinson, 1978). These are older studies, and newer ones may not be as influenced by gender norms.

The final backdrop for thinking about midlife is the Midlife in the United States (MIDUS) study, a comprehensive longitudinal study. And comprehensive it was, filling a book with data on the 7,189 people the study followed. It's difficult to summarize this comprehensive study, but there are some notable takeaways:

- Midlife remains a pivotal developmental period
- In midlife, psychological and physical well-being is influenced by modifiable factors, including relationships, lifestyle, attitudes, and socioeconomic resources – more than by aging itself
- Resilience and personal control are significant buffers against stress and decline
- Socioeconomic inequality has lifelong effects. Individuals from lower socioeconomic backgrounds tend to have worse health outcomes, including higher rates of chronic disease and shorter life expectancy

- Positive psychological traits (e.g., purpose in life, optimism, autonomy) are associated with lower inflammation, better immune function, and reduced risk of chronic diseases (e.g., heart disease)
- Contrary to popular belief, midlife is often a time of stability or growth, not crisis. Many people experience increased emotional regulation, life satisfaction, and deeper relationships
- Family history, early life adversity, and cultural context play lasting roles in health and well-being

Midlife eating disorders epidemiology

If this chapter does nothing more than further debunk the myth that eating disorders and body dissatisfaction *only* occur in teens and young adults, it has accomplished its goal. While the research and interest in midlife eating disorders waxes and wanes, it provides solid evidence that eating disorders occur at all ages and are not limited to women and girls. And while midlife is a common time to develop or relapse into an eating disorder, several studies included even participants in their 70s and 80s. My oldest client, a youthful 92, often lamented her shifting weight and the carbohydrate-rich food at her assisted living facility.

Mitchison and colleagues (2014) were some of the first researchers to note the changing demographic of eating disorders. This was a longitudinal study, conducted over ten years and looked at both men and women. The researchers found that eating disorder behaviors increased across all demographic groups over the decade. Notably, the rise was more pronounced among men, particularly in extreme dieting and purging behaviors, individuals aged 45 and above, especially in purging behaviors, people with below-median household incomes, where binge eating and extreme dieting behaviors were more prevalent and residents of regional areas, who reported greater physical health-related quality of life impairment associated with binge eating. The study suggests a "democratization" of disordered eating, indicating that eating disorders are no longer confined to young, white, upper-class women but are increasingly prevalent across various demographic groups.

More recently, Mangweth-Matzek (2023) and colleagues reviewed the literature on the epidemiology and treatment of eating disorders in middle age. This must have been a daunting endeavor due to the diversity of diagnoses and differing criteria. The studies they reviewed spanned from 2017 to 2023 and included search terms such as "eating disorders," "eating behavior," "disordered eating," "middle age," and "older age." Most seasoned clinicians working with eating disorders recognize that there can be a vast difference between "eating disorders" – typically reflecting the DSM diagnostic criteria – and "disordered eating," the latter being an almost normative experience.

While drawing prevalence data from literature reviews is difficult, Mangweth-Matzek et al. (2023) drew some conclusions, estimating that midlife eating problems affect about 7.7% of women and 10% of aging men. For women, eating disorders tended to peak at adolescence and again around menopause. Menopause seemed to be a time of increased vulnerability. Those women with more acute menopausal symptoms were most vulnerable to developing an eating disorder (Mangweth-Matzek et al., 2021).

While men do not go through menopause *per se*, hormonal shifts, especially changes in testosterone, may also be a factor in men's eating disorders (Morley et al., 2006). Prevalencewise, about 10% of men experience "disordered eating," verbiage ascribed to less severe eating problems. Reas and Stedal (2015) found that midlife men are especially vulnerable to stigma, shame, and stereotypes portraying eating disorders as disorders of youth and the female gender. The research on male eating disorders remains limited.

Diagnostic profile. When we consider full DSM diagnoses, Binge Eating Disorder seems to be the most common diagnosis among those at midlife (APA, 2013). Anorexia and "atypical anorexia" (in which the person is not severely underweight) are also quite prevalent. Chronic anorexia is dangerous, with high mortality rates (Gaudiani et al., 2022).

In many cases, individuals in midlife may not meet the traditional diagnostic criteria for eating disorders or may have developed symptoms later in life, which complicates the clinical picture. Therefore, the prevalence of eating disorders in midlife may be underestimated, as these conditions may not always align with stereotypical presentations seen in younger individuals. Other Specified Feeding and Eating Disorder (OSFED) – is a catch-all for diagnoses that do not fit cleanly into other categories – may be the largest bucket, although specific prevalence is difficult to identify. One study published in the *International Journal of Eating Disorders* suggested that OSFED accounts for 39.5% of eating disorder cases among males, and 44.2% of cases among females in the United States across all age groups (Streatfeild et al., 2021).

Body image and midlife research

Body dissatisfaction is a risk factor for pathological dieting and eating disorders. No one living in Western society escapes its ideals: what beauty means; a focus on remaining "youthful"; and most of all, thinness. Many people exposed to such ideals become preoccupied with meeting them. This can lead to an endless cycle of serial dieting and, eventually, an eating disorder.

Preoccupation with one's body can be very limiting. It affects many people, not only those with clinical eating disorders. Body dissatisfaction affects people of all ages. Several studies attempted to look at just how prevalent body dissatisfaction actually is. Mangweth-Matzek et al. (2006), for example, looked at men and women aged 60–70 and found that well over half of the group reported body dissatisfaction. Keith and Midlarsky (2004) studied an even older cohort, finding that women as old as 92 were dissatisfied with aspects of their bodies. And Hooper et al. (2023) found that men were similarly affected by critical body talk. We can draw at least one conclusion from these studies. People of all ages are affected by such unrealistic cultural standards, and aging does not halt the pursuit of thinness.

People seem to be willing to go to significant lengths to correct perceived body imperfections. One route? Cosmetic surgery. The market for surgeries such a liposuction, gynecomastia (male breast reduction), fillers, and other cosmetic procedures is booming (Milothridis et al., 2016). People seeking these procedures span Generation Z through Baby Boomers. In fact, older people often opt for more expensive and intensive procedures. The hope? Those changes in their bodies will improve self-esteem and overall well-being. The reality is that while there may be some small gains in self-esteem due to cosmetic procedures, overall results have not been dramatic or lasting (Honigman et al., 2004).

One of the trends we find in looking at the cosmetic surgery literature is that there seems to be a trend away from the idea of "aging beautifully" to the idea of "appearing not to age at all" (Westwood, 2023). The stress of appearing youthful at all costs is one of the biggest drivers of low self-esteem and of eating disorders.

Research on causal/triggering factors

The discussion in this chapter thus far has outlined several factors that play a role in the development of midlife eating disorders. Midlife eating disorders are influenced by a range of causal factors spanning biological, psychological, social, and cultural domains. This section outlines some of the research, and we will expand on these ideas in subsequent chapters.

Midlife is a time of significant biological changes in both men and women. For women, hormonal changes can impact metabolism and lead to weight gain, which may provoke negative body image and eating disorders (Bulik et al., 2007). As with younger clients, control is also a factor in midlife eating disorders – in this case, control over midlife weight gain. This is somewhat of a slippery slope – people go on diets to lose weight, but diets are rarely successful. For many people, such diets become more extreme and even less sustainable.

While anyone is susceptible to messages to lose weight, men's experiences of aging and poor body image are also due to losses in muscle mass and athleticism. While men may diet to achieve a toned look, they may also "bulk up" or engage in compulsive exercise (Pope et al., 2000).

In transgender individuals, hormone replacement therapy (HRT) or the lack thereof may further complicate body image issues, as they navigate physical changes that do not always align with their gender identity (Budge et al., 2013).

Psychologically, midlife is often associated with increased stress, due to life transitions such as career changes, caregiving responsibilities, and the loss of a partner or loved one. These stressors can contribute to feelings of loss of control, which some individuals may cope with by controlling their food intake, using it as a way to manage emotions or alleviate distress (Grabe et al., 2008). Additionally, individuals in midlife may experience a sense of identity crisis, as they reflect on their life achievements or unmet goals, potentially leading to a heightened preoccupation with appearance and body image. The pressure to maintain a youthful appearance in the face of aging can be overwhelming, particularly given the widespread societal emphasis on youthful beauty (Cash & Smolak, 2011). This psychological strain is compounded by the increasing normalization of diet culture, which often dictates unrealistic standards of beauty and can promote unhealthy eating behaviors, especially when individuals are seeking to conform to these ideals.

Socially, people at midlife often face role-related challenges, such as empty nest syndrome or shifts in family dynamics, which can trigger feelings of isolation or self-worth tied to caregiving or parental identity. These changes may lead to emotional eating or restrictive eating patterns as individuals try to reclaim a sense of purpose or control (Grabe et al., 2008). Moreover, peer influence and social media have exacerbated the pressure to maintain a "perfect" body, even at older ages. While traditional media have long propagated idealized body images, social media platforms have intensified these pressures by providing a constant stream of curated, edited images that contribute to unrealistic standards of beauty and aging (Tiggemann & Slater, 2014). The rise of the "fitspiration" trend, which promotes a combination of fitness and weight-loss ideals, has further fueled body dissatisfaction among midlife individuals, often exacerbating feelings of inadequacy or prompting unhealthy attempts to conform to these ideals.

Another prevalent causal factor in younger clients of all genders, including gender-diverse clients, is the effects of trauma (Dalzell & Protos, 2020; Dalzell et al., 2022). While not explicitly found in the midlife literature, it appears likely that past and present traumas are related to eating disorders and negative body image. A traumatic foundation for eating disorders may be particularly true for those clients with severe and enduring eating disorder presentations.

Together, these diverse biological, psychological, and sociocultural factors interact to create a particularly complex landscape for the development of eating disorders during midlife. This age period, marked by significant life transitions and societal pressures, often triggers or exacerbates underlying vulnerabilities to disordered eating behaviors. Understanding the multifaceted nature of these causal factors is crucial for the development of effective prevention and intervention strategies for midlife eating disorders.

Research summary

Overall, research findings suggest:

• Eating disorders can have their onset in older age (sometimes called late onset), can be a relapse into symptoms seen earlier in life, or may be a chronic condition.
• Body dissatisfaction continues throughout the lifespan.
• Weight is a global source of discontent including for people of all ages, including midlife.
• Changing roles and responsibilities may play a role in midlife eating disorders.

Treatment implications of research

As we delve more fully into our conversation about midlife eating disorders, an overarching theme is the need to widen our definition of recovery or better yet allow people to define recovery in a way that is achievable and satisfying.

While midlife eating disorders are less stigmatized than they once were, at least by professionals who keep up with the literature, there continue to be few developmentally appropriate treatment options, particularly when there is a need for a higher level of care. Mature adults are often reluctant to attend programs in which the average age of the adult cohort skews toward their 20s. There is a palpable sense of desperation when people know they need more help and are not comfortable in a program with predominately younger people.

Clinicians must often be creative in developing treatment plans. Most people over age 40 are treated using a combination of outpatient therapy and medication (Mulchandani et al., 2021).

For further reflection and application

After reading this chapter, take some time to consider these research findings in the context of your current client caseload.

1 How did the research dovetail with what you've observed in your clients? Was any of the research unexpected? Lacking?
2 Think about the research in terms of your current client assessment. Does anything stand out as something you would like to add to your intake materials? Is there anything that surprised you?
3 Consider your strengths. Pay close attention to those strengths that are not connected to physical appearance. How can you use this list of strengths to guide and support clients?

Clinician resource 2: embracing the positive aspects of aging

Midlife comes with a multitude of changes, many of which are connected to our physicality. The following resource can be used as a handout or for discussion within sessions. It allows clients to identify the strengths they have developed as middle-aged adults. It can be given for homework to support reflection and a focus on things other than the physical. Shifting focus to the positive can be extremely helpful.

CLINICIAN RESOURCE 2: EMBRACING THE POSITIVE ASPECTS OF AGING (CLIENT HANDOUT)

This exercise allows you to explore some of the positive aspects of aging. It can be used to journal or to simply consider what's been positive about getting older. We often look only at the negatives. What's been positive?

Wisdom: bringing your years of learning forward
Think about the life lessons you've learned. Reflect on prior life stages (adolescence, early adulthood, midlife). What wisdom have you gained over the years?

Spirituality: deepening connection and purpose
Aging offers the opportunity to deepen your connection to yourself, the world, and sometimes the Divine. Do you notice personal growth that feels sacred or spiritual? A renewed sense of purpose? A gratitude practice? Something else? Please describe that here.

Stronger relationships: building bonds over time
Aging allows us to nurture our relationships. What meaningful connections have you made in your life? What's been positive about these relationships?

Self-acceptance and confidence
As we age, we tend to become more comfortable with who we are. Do you agree with this? Disagree?

Time for personal growth and hobbies
Aging can bring more time for personal growth. What new interests or hobbies have you developed? What old hobbies and interests have you nurtured?

Freedom and flexibility
As we age, there are often fewer obligations (like work or raising children), which can create a sense of freedom. Do you have more time for yourself? Time to pursue passions? Describe that here.

Chapter 3

What's really different about midlife eating disorders?

In Chapter 1, we met Susan, a 45-year-old mother of two with an initial onset of anorexia. Susan is a composite of many middle-aged women and men seeking treatment for an eating disorder. Significant in Susan's story is the embarrassment of having a "teenage problem." This was reinforced by the staff at the eating disorders program, and by the comments of extended family and friends. A common theme was that midlife is supposed to be a time of increased wisdom, which leads to the myth of "maturing out" of many types of problem behaviors, including eating disorders and alcohol use disorders. Another common myth is that midlife men and women don't care what they look like, which we've already debunked in Chapter 2.

These myths, more than anything, render people like Susan invisible, often leaving them to struggle silently. Instead of seeking support and validation that some of the toxic messages of diet culture – beliefs about food, weight, and health – perpetuated by media and based on the ideal of thinness are ubiquitous and do not only affect those under 40. Our profession, however, sometimes shames people struggling with midlife eating disorders. This prevents them from seeking the help they desperately need. Following Susan's flight from hospital-based treatment, it was months before Susan was able to seek support – and then only reluctantly. We will dive further into Susan's story shortly.

The myth of "maturing out"

Susan is a trooper – there's no denying that. On the surface, Susan's first-time eating disorder looked similar to those we see in younger people, including the sense of isolation, the eating disorder becoming a "friend," and reliance on it as a way to fit in and become happier. Following the disastrous hospitalization on a unit filled with people in their young 20s, and whose "level system" – tokens earned for phone calls and privileges – intensified her sense of regression and powerlessness, Susan gamely tried to seek another treatment option. Her experience at an intake for a partial hospital program was no less traumatic.

DOI: 10.4324/9781032615745-4

The partial program was one in which others of my clients had done well and felt respected. While it was not a midlife program *per se*, the range tended to skew older. I was taken aback when Susan reached out, in tears, following the meeting with a nurse practitioner who'd assessed her suitability for admission. The NP listened to Susan's background and questioned dismissively, "how do you even have an eating disorder at *your* age?" Needless to say, Susan did not admit there, and my conversation with the medical director, who was apologetic but ineffective, has kept me from referring others to this program.

Do people really mature out of problem behaviors? The literature on the question would suggest that the answer is "no." Charles Winick (1962) proposed that addiction was a time-limited process – an idea that has stuck. Winnick thought that most people stopped abusing substances once the stress of developmental transitions ended. This is also the idea behind the natural recovery movement, which further suggests that most alcoholics move past their addiction without formal treatment and due to maturation.

Lee and Sher (2018), for example, found an overall decrease in binge drinking[1] as people age. In a meta-analysis of 27 longitudinal studies, Johnstone et al. (1996) found a peak in alcohol consumption by age 20, followed by a decreasing and stabilizing pattern after 30. While no one offers a definitive explanation for these decreases, the researchers offer various theories, including that the transition from teen roles to adult responsibilities is a protective factor. Developmental researchers further offer that adolescents exhibit "normal impulsivity" and that decreases in risk-taking are part of the developmental trajectory due in large part to the prefrontal and limbic networks. There is more to this picture, however.

While Lee et al.'s (2018) study showed that substance use decreased or stabilized, it did *not* disappear entirely. While binge drinking decreased every decade from the 20s onward, the prevalence rate in their sample of problem drinkers was still 22% of the sample for people who were in their late 40s and 14% of the sample for people in their late 50s. While these are less than the adolescent numbers, a significant number of people continued drinking heavily.

Other studies have found that upward of 50% of seniors in the United States consume alcohol at levels that are considered risky, especially in the context of co-occurring medical conditions (Moore et al., 2006).

The idea of "maturing out" is a complex and nuanced topic that, under scrutiny, does not bear out. Drawing the conclusion that maturity is a substantially protective factor for midlife eating disorders perpetuates a harmful stereotype that persists beyond the addiction field.

While midlife clients I have treated are definitely more mature than younger teens, this is not a factor that protects them from developing eating disorders. Maturity instead comes with the ability to do the deeper work of therapy – work that supersedes symptoms. I often use the analogy that symptoms are the tip of the eating disorder iceberg, and it's what's below the surface that often allows for greater change. The downside of this maturity, however, is that people at midlife are often keenly aware of how these problems affect not only themselves but also others in their lives. This insight can result in shame. Add that to the stigma of having what Susan termed a "teenage problem," and we have our second theme in what's different about midlife eating disorders.

Eating disorders historically and in mental health sources

A recent search of memoirs and books about eating disorders spanning many years featured 15 books in the popular press. Of these, 14 were memoirs or fictionalizations of teens; the other was a parent memoir. While the author may have been writing for a specific audience, it was not apparent that this was the case and appeared to be more of a reflection of the popular notions linking eating disorders to adolescence.

So, how did this myth that eating disorders are teenage problems originate? While it's hard to say definitively how this occurred (and a full history of eating disorders is beyond the scope of this book), a couple of thoughts do occur. These have to do with our insights and understanding in the mental health field itself.

Eating disorders have been around for millennia. Self-starvation as a religious practice goes back to 12th–14th centuries – young women who would starve themselves as a show of godly devotion. St. Catherine of Sienna is the most famous of these young women. These practices continued into Victorian times with the so-called "fasting girls," whose ability to live without sustenance was considered miraculous. For a fascinating history of the religious aspects of "holy anorexia," I highly recommend Joan Jacobs Brumberg's (2000) *Fasting Girls*.

Fascination aside, we seem to have somehow incorporated these ideas into the mental health world. I started working as a clinician in one of the first local eating disorders programs in the United States. The treatment team there often talked about the idea of "parentectomy" – removing young women from their families as a cure for anorexia. As appalling as that is nowadays, it was considered a legitimate treatment for what was seen as an adolescent who could not otherwise individuate. Psychoanalyst Hilde Bruch espoused similar ideas in her early texts on eating disorders, essentially blaming parents for disorders we now know to be multifactorial. With Karen Carpenter's death came an increasing awareness of eating disorders, including criticisms of Carpenter's mother's overprotectiveness.

Anorexia was included in the earliest *Diagnostic and Statistical Manual of Mental Disorders* (DSM) as a "neurotic illness," later moving it to the chapter on "feeding disturbances," which included pica and rumination. Perhaps most significantly, earlier editions of the DSM categorized eating disorders as "disorders of childhood or adolescence." The criteria also included problematic and narrow descriptors, for example percentage of ideal body weight and loss of menstruation, to make a diagnosis of anorexia. These criteria suggest that eating disorders are about food and weight and are younger, female issues. Women at midlife often have erratic or nonexistent monthly periods, and while they may significantly restrict food intake, their weight may not decrease to the level indicated by these early (DSM III, DSM IV) criteria. Earlier DSM descriptors also suggest that men do not develop eating disorders, which is a fallacy as well.

The DSM-5 was a step forward, although the current chapter on "feeding and eating disorders" includes disorders such as pica and rumination disorders and illnesses that are very different from anorexia, bulimia, and other specified eating disorders. Eating disorders are not about food but about the concerns that underlie them (often difficult life situations, past and present) and the way a person copes.

Lack of role models for recovery

Another difference with people at midlife is the lack of role models of people in recovery from eating disorders. This has been changing with some celebrities speaking about their own struggles and sharing recovery stories. Often, there is also a lot of secrecy within families, especially from older generations, about past family history of any eating-related concerns. Consider, for example, Marianna's story:

> As a child and young woman, I saw my mother on various diets, her weight increasing and decreasing – sometimes by a lot – never eating with us, always aware of my weight. But I never knew she was struggling with just what I am: binging and purging. Diets just seemed so normal, and her "nervous stomach" was a daily problem. After she'd died, I read some of the journals she left behind, and it hit me. She'd been binging and purging all these years and had never gotten help. I wish she would have, or at least shared that she's been struggling. Just knowing that she also had bulimia, and not wanting to pass this on to my own daughter is what motivated me to seek help.

Absence of treatment settings specific to midlife adults

At midlife, relational approaches emphasize the importance of connection in healing. Many therapeutic settings use a group therapy approach, one of the best ways to enhance connection within the healing realm. Eating disorder inpatient and partial hospital programs often delineate teen programs (often due to licensure), but "adult" programs range from age 18 onward.

While some middle-aged people are fine with a mix of age ranges, including these very young adults, others like Susan may not feel as comfortable when surrounded by younger clients. For Susan and others, this reinforced the shame of having a problem they "should" have never developed or outgrown. Additionally, group dynamics within inpatient cohorts often mirrors the roles that people play in families, and many middle-aged adults report being the group parent, focusing on solving everyone else's problems and distracting from their own. This is hardly an effective way to be treated for one's own severe illness.

Another concern about the lack of targeted programs involves the approach used in many eating disorder inpatient programs. The "level system" is a behavioral approach based on completing specified goals (such as eating the entire meal they are given, participating in groups, and completing therapy assignments). Those who complete the goal(s) receive privileges, such as the ability to use their phones and call home. While this may be motivating to a young adult, it's demotivating, and in fact demeaning, to older clients who have responsibilities such as work and family.

At the time of this writing, there are no treatment programs specializing in midlife adults and eating disorders. This gap leaves many who need treatment with few resources – or worse, trying to manage a difficult illness on their own.

Traditional treatment programs are often geared toward anorexia and bulimia. This may be because they are based on a symptom-reduction or weight-restoration approach, which is more readily quantifiable to insurers.

As an example, the Magellan insurance medical necessity guidelines state that in order to be admitted to an inpatient hospital program, clients must demonstrate physiologic instability such as low blood pressure, impaired liver function, or electrolyte imbalance or have a body mass index (BMI) of 16 or below. The criteria also consider admission for clients with bulimia if they require constant supervision to interrupt binging and purging that would lead to serious medical complications. It's less typical that middle-aged people will meet these criteria.

The eating disorders field is beginning to take more of a lifespan approach to diagnosis. The inclusion of two diagnoses – binge eating disorder (BED) – and other specified feeding and eating disorder (OSFED) is an important change that came with DSM-5.

Binge eating disorder at midlife

Mark is a police officer who, after years on the job, is looking forward to his upcoming retirement. As a divorced father, he sees his boys only on the weekends, and he often feels alone. His ex-wife is remarried, and while he still carries a torch for her, he knows that the relationship was unhealthy. During the workday, Mark often gets so distracted by the seemingly endless tasks he's doing that he often skips lunch (he's never enjoyed breakfast.) By the time Mark gets home at night, he is very hungry and often stops to pick up takeout. Most of the binging occurs later at night, starting with the decision to have "just a little bit more" and as a way to get to sleep. Mark is often surprised by the amount he has eaten and vows nightly to "do better" the next day. He carries shame about the binging, calling himself "weak" and "a glutton." Prior to seeking outpatient treatment, Mark briefly considered a hospital program but was told that his insurance would not pay for treatment, a decision in large part due to Mark's current weight.

Mark's story encapsulates some of the struggles of BED. BED is common among midlife men and women. In BED, people consume large amounts of food in one sitting. They often feel a loss of control and significant shame around the binging. While some people with BED have larger bodies, others do not.

Research estimates that BED affects 1.5% of women and 0.3% of men worldwide. Many adults with BED report longstanding symptoms; less than half are recognized in healthcare settings (Keski-Rahkonen, 2021). This suggests numbers that are actually much higher, likely due to the shame associated with binging. The cycle of overeating followed by self-recrimination can create a vicious loop that is difficult to break. Shame is one of the most challenging aspects of working with BED.

Many people with BED have a similar pattern to Mark – they eat very little during the day and binge in the evening. This restrict-binge cycle is in part physiological, which emphasizes the importance of teaching clients to eat meals consistently. It's also helpful to have a trusted dietician who can further assess nutritional intake and support clients in this way.

Another physiological connection involves hormones. BED may increase during peri-menopausal and menopausal years, when hormonal fluctuations affect appetite, metabolism, and emotional regulation (Berent-Spillson et al., 2017). As with psychology as a whole, it's difficult to tease out the role of hormones as we consider the increased psychosocial stresses during this time. During the menopausal years, many women find themselves facing other challenges such as responsibilities of caregiving or career shifts. All of these differences are important to note when looking at how eating disorders are different at midlife.

While BED has traditionally been thought to affect women more than men, recent research demonstrates that BED also affects middle-aged men. The rates for men are lower than for women, estimated to be between 0.8% and 2.0% (Spiegel & Kelly, 2005). These are older studies but represent what is available at this time.

Men develop BED for many of the same reasons as women: binging as a response to emotional distress, body dissatisfaction, or various stress related to aging. While the issues are the same, body image is different. Women tend to want to lose weight, and while men may experience concerns about weight gain, their focus is often a desire to build muscle mass or change the shape of their body (Grucza et al., 2007). Several examples from my own practice come to mind: a male client in his 70s who had been overweight as a teen and routinely ran outdoors even with injuries and another who despite marital difficulties could not conceive of skipping days at the gym to spend more time with his wife. Men may not seek help as readily as women (Grucza et al., 2007), although this changes with age (Devlin et al., 2007).

Other specified feeding or eating disorder (OSFED) at midlife

Another common difference between working with teens and young adults and working with middle-aged adults is that the latter often do not fit into clear diagnostic categories. DSM-5 introduced the field to a new diagnosis: OSFED, which is one of the most common diagnoses among middle-aged adults.

OSFED is a catch-all category that describes eating disorders that do not meet the specific criteria for disorders like anorexia nervosa or bulimia nervosa but still involve significant disordered eating behaviors. There is a misperception that OSFED is a less severe problem than other eating disorders. This is *not* the case for most clients. An illustration may be helpful here.

Lara first developed disordered eating patterns in her early 20s, struggling with body image and weight fluctuations after a period of stress during college. However, her eating behaviors got better over time. She maintained a healthy weight and body image through her 30s and into her early 40s.

Lara had experienced a significant deterioration in her physical and mental health over the past two years. Chronic work stress, an empty nest, and increasing dissatisfaction with her personal life have reignited her eating disorder symptoms. Her weight has dropped about 10 pounds, and while she is still within a normal weight range, she appears much thinner due to her athletic frame. Lara exercises 3–4 hours a day. She also shared that she vomits 2–3 times a week, a strategy she developed to manage her emotional distress. While Lara knows she needs help, she often minimizes the seriousness of her symptoms. Lara's fear of gaining weight was the biggest barrier to her seeking help, and it was only after an intervention of sorts from her husband and daughters that she was willing to enter therapy.

Lara was eventually admitted to a partial hospital program, which helped her to get back to healthier patterns. This was an example where the empty nest worked to her advantage, and she was able to "mother" the younger clients attending with her. It also gave her some space to focus on herself and her needs. This was a success story, a relative rarity when older adults attend higher-level-of-care programming.

Lara's case demonstrates some of the many behaviors we find in people with OSFED: distorted body image, abnormal eating patterns, and harmful weight control behaviors. People with OSFED may or may not recognize the need for help and often minimize their own struggles (a situation that can inadvertently be reinforced by medical providers). While Lara failed to recognize how much these patterns had affected her, her family was worried and confused.

While the OSFED umbrella includes many variations of food, body image, and symptomatic concerns, one of the more prevalent OSFED presentations is *atypical anorexia*. This is the most prevalent diagnosis among women in their 40s and 50s. Most people with atypical anorexia nervosa cases meet all the criteria of anorexia nervosa, with the exception of low body weight. In fact, many people with atypical anorexia are in significantly larger bodies, or they may be of average weight. People diagnosed with atypical anorexia often report can be subject to weight stigma and lack of access to care. They are also more likely to have a longer duration of illness and less likely to receive inpatient care (Eiring et al., 2021).

Atypical anorexia is just as debilitating as classic anorexia nervosa. People with this illness often experience psychological distress, such as severe anxiety about eating, constant self-monitoring of food intake, and distorted body image. These symptoms can interfere with daily functioning, relationships, and overall quality of life. People with atypical anorexia need to be met with a supportive environment free of judgment.

There are many reasons that people with atypical anorexia do not seek treatment. One significant factor is the high value placed on thinness in today's society. Restrictive eating behavior and "dieting" are so commonplace, which can promote trivialization, or even reinforcement, of weight loss by friends or family.

Other examples of OSFED include:

- Purging disorder (without binge eating): people with purging disorder are stuck in a cycle of purging after meals. This may include self-induced vomiting and the use of laxatives or diuretics. What differentiates purging disorder from bulimia is that such purging occurs in the absence of binge eating. People who are stuck in this cycle may purge even small amounts of food in an effort to take in fewer calories.
- Night eating syndrome: in this variation of OSFED, a person frequently wakes up in the middle of the night and eats large amounts of food, such as entire meals. This often occurs in a dissociated state. Salman and Kabir (2022) estimate this incidence of night eating syndrome at 1.5% across all age groups.
- Orthorexia: this refers to an obsession with eating "healthy" or "pure" foods to the exclusion of other foods. This is often seen as socially desired or virtuous. People with orthorexia are often opposed to eating anything that does not fall into their rigid standards of acceptable foods. This may lead to severe dietary restriction, malnutrition, and distress. Severe orthorexia may look similar to anorexia in terms of intentionally restricting food, but the motivation is different. People with orthorexia are rarely motivated by weight, a key difference from anorexia. John, whom you met in Chapter 1, struggles with orthorexia.
- Chronic dieting: while dieting is something we see in this diet-obsessed culture, chronic dieting can become a problem when it becomes obsessive. Chronic dieting may lead to calorie counting, restricting food groups such as carbs and fats, and frequent weight fluctuation. While people who diet chronically may not have a clinical eating disorder, it can often appear similar – thus falling under the OSFED category.

- Chewing and spitting (formally known as rumination syndrome) – some people with eating disorders engage in the behavior of chewing food and then spitting it back out, with the goal of tasting the food without taking in the calories.

Weight stigma

We have already touched on the idea of *weight stigma*, an important consideration for the diagnoses we have discussed. Mark, who struggled with BED, was one example, as are many other clients. Probably the most ridiculous case I've heard involves a colleague who went to the doctor with what turned out to be a nasty cold, only to be lectured on her weight.

Weight stigma refers to the negative attitudes, beliefs, and discriminatory behaviors directed toward individuals based on their body size or weight. It manifests in many forms, such as social exclusion, judgment, verbal harassment, and biases within healthcare settings (Ryan et al., 2023). Weight stigma is such a pressing concern that an international group of experts recently released a consensus statement aimed at ending stigma (Rubino et al., 2020).

Weight stigma is deeply embedded in cultural ideals that equate thinness with health, beauty, and success, while associating larger body sizes with laziness, poor self-discipline, and lack of control.

One of the most harmful aspects of weight stigma is its impact on mental and physical health. Research shows that individuals who experience weight-based discrimination are at an increased risk for mental health problems, such as depression, anxiety, and eating disorders (Pearl & Puhl, 2018). The stress caused by frequent negative encounters can also contribute to poor physical health outcomes, including high blood pressure, cardiovascular disease, and difficulty managing chronic conditions like diabetes (Prunty et al., 2023; Westbury et al., 2023). In fact, weight stigma can deter people from seeking medical care, as they may fear judgment from healthcare professionals or avoid consultations altogether due to previous negative experiences (Prunty et al., 2023).

The root causes of weight stigma are complex and multifaceted, but they are largely influenced by societal norms and media representations of the "ideal" body. These ideals often promote unrealistic beauty standards that favor slimness and marginalize those who do not conform. The increasing prevalence of dieting culture, along with the rise of weight-loss industries, perpetuates these standards, creating an environment where weight discrimination is normalized. Achieving such standards is difficult for most, let alone for people at middle age when physiological changes occur naturally (Hurtado et al., 2024). Many experts recommend that the optimal BMI for older adults may be in the range of 24–29, a range previously thought of as "overweight" (Lavie, 2014).

This discussion encourages a brief segue into the discussion of BMI. BMI is a relatively simple concept to understand. Simply put, BMI is a calculation that compares a person's weight and height, then places an individual into ranges (e.g., *underweight* is ≤18; *healthy weight* is 18 to <25; *overweight* is 25 to <30; *obesity* is ≥30).

It is in this simplicity that BMI is problematic. Because BMI takes *only* a person's weight and height into account, without considering factors like muscle mass, bone density, or fat distribution, it can falsely categorize people as overweight. For example, individuals with a high muscle mass, such as athletes, may be classified as overweight or obese even though they have low body fat and are in excellent physical condition. Similarly, someone with a higher percentage of body fat could have a normal BMI but still be at risk for health issues like heart disease or diabetes. Moreover, BMI doesn't account for differences between individuals in terms of age, sex, or ethnicity, which can influence how fat is distributed and how it affects health. Therefore, while BMI can offer a rough estimate of potential health risks, it doesn't provide a complete picture of an individual's overall well-being.

Combating weight stigma requires a shift in how society views and discusses body size. It includes eliminating words like "obesity" from how we approach treatment. It involves promoting body acceptance, encouraging diversity in media representations (including age diversity), and fostering environments where people of all sizes can thrive without fear of judgment. Additionally, healthcare providers must be trained to approach weight-related issues with sensitivity and a focus on overall well-being, rather than just weight as a sole indicator of health. Ultimately, weight stigma does more harm than good. By fostering inclusivity and respect for all body types, we can create a healthier, more compassionate society where individuals are not defined or judged by their size, but rather by their overall worth and capabilities. Promoting body neutrality and acceptance is one of the key goals of working with midlife adults.

Severe and enduring eating disorders (SEED)

Severe and enduring eating disorders (SEED) represent a subset of eating disorders that persist over a long duration, often despite treatment attempts, and are characterized by their severity and resistance to standard therapeutic interventions (Kotilahti et al., 2020). By its very nature, people with SEED typically fall within the age range considered midlife. While we've discussed this diagnosis, we have not talked about the therapeutic differences and treatment needs.

Sasha, whom you met in Chapter 1, has a severe and enduring eating disorder. At 38, she has been through years of treatment programs (at last count, at least 20). More recently, Sasha had agreed to hospitalization because of her failing kidneys, a complication of chronic dehydration and purging.

Sasha's medical concerns and her insurance, Medicare disability, limited her options to a very few eating disorder programs that are connected to medical hospitals. All of the available options are programs that Sasha has previously attended, and when it comes to Sasha, the therapists there are burned out by her needs. This is understandable; she has been hospitalized there many times, and each time appeared to be doing well, only to return again for some complication. The biggest obstacle has been the deeply entrenched nature of Sasha's symptoms: severe food restriction, weight control behaviors, and an intense fear of gaining weight. The therapeutic lore that SEED patients are "difficult" and cannot change is rooted in this rigidity. Over time, this leads to more complex psychological and medical conditions, including comorbid mental health disorders like depression, anxiety, and personality disorders (Treasure et al., 2010).

Let's face it: many of our current eating disorder programs are woefully unprepared to work with a client like Sasha (who, frankly, could be running the groups better than some of the clinicians). This is less a critique of the clinicians and more a commentary on how therapeutically savvy many people with SEED can be. Despite that insight, patients' fears run so deep that traditional treatment approaches fail again and again.

Treating SEED presents unique challenges. While these may not apply to all midlife clients, they are worth noting. Traditional interventions, including cognitive behavioral therapy (CBT) and family-based therapy (FBT), while helpful for more acute (less longstanding) eating disorders, are largely unsuccessful for people with SEED. Why? People with longstanding eating disorders often find it difficult to engage with therapy – especially if the end result is weight gain – let alone to follow discharge plans. Long-term outcomes for SEED are often poor, with high relapse rates and continued psychiatric comorbidities (Fichter & Quadflieg, 2016).

I've noted that a common theme is that intensive treatment may *initially* be successful – helping to stabilize weight or resolving depression. Having a nourished brain and feeling better emotionally is great. These gains are often fleeting, however, and when clients leave the safety of highly structured inpatient or residential environments, the fears intensify and relapse occurs.

Sasha actually had more long-lasting success in a general psychiatric rather than an eating disorder-specific program. This program emphasized other aspects of recovery, such as accepting what cannot be changed (a dialectical behavior therapy (DBT) skill), values clarification, and family work. While it did little to support weight gain, Sasha has been able to focus on hydration, which has slowed the progression of her kidney disease. She is also more engaged in life and has made several friends who enjoy socializing.

Sasha's story illustrates that part of the equation in treating SEED and other midlife eating disorders lies in redefining "recovery" as something that is different than a number, BMI, or the amount a person eats – the common metrics in many eating disorder settings. Many of the things that helped Sasha can support an array of clients and may be more developmentally appropriate than restrictive, reinforcement-based programming (especially seen in inpatient settings). Such paradigm changes are sorely needed.

Substance and alcohol use disorders

Midlife eating disorders often co-occur with substance and alcohol use disorders, presenting complex challenges for diagnosis and treatment. Individuals in midlife with eating disorders are at elevated risk for developing substance use disorder (SUD), especially alcohol use disorder. The link between midlife eating disorders and SUD is partly explained by the shared underlying factors of eating disorders and SUD: emotional dysregulation, trauma history, and mental health issues like depression and anxiety (Bulik, 2000). Such shared vulnerabilities may increase the likelihood of "maladaptive coping strategies," such as the use of substances or disordered eating behaviors, as a means of managing psychological distress. Individuals with both eating disorders and SUD often display more severe forms of each condition, leading to greater clinical complexity and a higher risk of poor long-term outcomes (Lozano-Madrid et al., 2020; Holderness et al., 1994).

Carla, the 50-year-old photographer, is a composite of a client in the early stages of comorbid SUD and OSFED. The trauma of her family history – functionally alcoholic parents and a lack of love – contributes to the picture.

Among clients like Carla, who abuse both alcohol and food, we often see greater functional impairment, including disruptions in relationships, employment, and overall quality of life (Fairburn & Harrison, 2003). Such clients are often highly motivated, especially when they have had prior treatment successes or have hit their proverbial rock bottoms. The latter can be different for everyone. Carla's declining work performance has scared her and motivated her in equal measure.

While Carla benefitted from traditional outpatient care, some people need more. Individuals with these co-occurring conditions may find accessing effective care challenging, due to the complexity of treating both disorders simultaneously. Many eating disorder programs are not equipped to work with SUD (at best, some offer a "track" with a few targeted groups weekly); similarly, most drug and alcohol programs do not have the expertise or resources to address the eating disorder.

Research suggests that the presence of one disorder can exacerbate the symptoms of the other, leading to a cycle of worsening behaviors. For example, individuals may use alcohol or drugs to cope with the distress caused by their eating disorder, while the negative effects of substance use may further fuel the disordered eating behavior (Keski-Rahkonen, 2021). Therefore, addressing both conditions in a coordinated and integrated treatment plan is critical to improving outcomes for individuals with this dual diagnosis.

Other psychological comorbidities

Another factor related to the complexity of midlife eating disorders is that they rarely occur alone. Instead, they present alongside other comorbidities, such as depression, anxiety, and obsessive-compulsive disorder (OCD). While younger people with eating disorders may also struggle with these issues, such comorbidities are especially prevalent among those at midlife.

Middle-aged depression and anxiety are among the most common comorbidities. Depression, for example, occurs in up to 50% of individuals with anorexia nervosa and 80% of those with bulimia nervosa (Keski-Rahkonen, 2021) – very high incidences indeed. Anxiety disorders, including generalized anxiety disorder (GAD), OCD, and social anxiety disorder, are also prevalent in this population (Kaye et al., 2004). The interplay between these psychological disorders and eating behaviors is bidirectional: eating behaviors may serve as a coping mechanism for managing negative emotions, while the disorder itself can exacerbate feelings of guilt, shame, and hopelessness (Fairburn & Harrison, 2003).

It may be helpful to pause here and return to John, whom you met in Chapter 1. John's struggles with depression surrounding the loss of his surrogate mother and an unhealthy obsession with food choices and purity.

People with midlife eating disorders are at higher risk for personality disorders, with borderline personality disorder (BPD) being especially prevalent. About 30%–50% of individuals with anorexia nervosa or bulimia nervosa meet the criteria for a co-occurring personality disorder (Zanarini et al., 2004). The emotional instability characteristic of BPD can amplify the challenges of managing eating disorders, requiring more specialized and tailored treatment approaches as well as a knowledgeable treatment team.

Providers should be prepared to offer treatment that can support a range of concerns and to be able to refer to medical colleagues when needed.

Trauma

Trauma also frequently co-occurs with midlife eating disorders. The Sidran Institute, an agency that provides trauma resources to survivors and families, defines *trauma* as "an individual's experience of an event in which a person's ability to integrate emotional experience is overwhelmed, or the individual experiences a subjective threat to life or bodily integrity. Trauma, then, is the norm, not the exception, for many people who develop or continue to struggle with midlife eating disorders. Examples of such traumas include physical, emotional, or sexual violence, family disconnection and abandonment (especially common among LGBTQ persons), religious traumas, microaggression/marginalization, and sudden or devastating losses. While this is hardly an exhaustive list, it provides a sense of the array of experiences people bring to treatment.

How common is this intersection of trauma and eating disorders? The span of prevalence estimates across all age groups is considerable, ranging from 37% to 100% (Dalle Grave et al., 1996; Mitchell et al., 2012). Some of this variability can be explained by studies which define trauma differently or include or exclude subthreshold symptoms.

Unprocessed trauma remains trapped in the body. As Bessel van der Kolk (2015) sagely remarks: "the body keeps the score." There are many reasons that trauma and eating disorders co-occur. Eating disorders may be a way to cope the emotional dysregulation trauma creates. Eating disorders may also provide an admittedly false sense of control or act to purify the body. Another common dynamic in men and women whose traumas have been sexual in nature is that eating disorders can be used for protection, creating bodies that will be unappealing to potential intimate partners.

As with many of the psychological comorbidities we've discussed, trauma treatment is imperative to support those affected in developing happier, healthier lives.

Medical concerns

Most middle-aged adults are less physically resilient than younger people to the ravages of eating disorders. This often comes as an unwelcome surprise to some who have had eating disorders with minimal medical consequences. It is also one of the other differences between working with middle-aged adults and younger clients. Therapists should have a basic understanding of these complications and have trusted referral sources.

Eating disorders can come with a host of medical complications which are due to how symptoms disrupt body processes. Prolonged malnutrition, for example, can cause bradycardia (slow heart rate), hypotension (low blood pressure), and electrolyte imbalances. All place a strain on the heart (Bulik et al., 2007) and in severe cases, can lead to sudden cardiac arrest (Hsu, 2009). Purging can contribute to electrolyte disturbances, particularly hypokalemia (low potassium), which further increases the risk of life-threatening arrhythmias and cardiac complications (Baenas et al., 2024; Nitsch et al., 2021). Some of you may recall that Karen Carpenter died from heart failure due to cardiac arrhythmia. This was a direct consequence of her prolonged battle with anorexia.

In middle-aged adults, eating disorders frequently result in metabolic problems. Restrictive eating can cause malnutrition, leading to deficiencies in essential vitamins and minerals, including iron, calcium, and vitamin D. This increases the risk of osteoporosis, particularly in women (Pepe et al., 2020; Shufelt et al., 2017). People with anorexia nervosa often experience low bone mineral density due to the combination of nutritional deprivation and hormonal disruptions, which may persist even after weight restoration (Mehler & Brown, 2015). Some 60%–80% of women with anorexia nervosa also experience secondary amenorrhea, which can have long-term implications for bone health (Friedman et al., 2017). It can be disconcerting how bone density changes occur (especially in women who have already been identified as at risk. There was a period in which many of the clients I worked with were in boot casts due to fractures. Several of them were unable to stop exercising despite the boot, another indication of just how obsessive these disorders can become.

Other metabolic disturbances, such as hypoglycemia (low blood sugar), may also arise due to prolonged starvation (Mehler & Brown, 2015). Additionally, gastrointestinal issues are common in those with purging in their history. Chronic vomiting can also lead to esophageal tears, dental erosion, and gastroesophageal reflux disease (GERD) (Christensen, 2002; Conviser et al., 2014). Laxative abuse, often seen in bulimia nervosa, can cause electrolyte imbalances, constipation, and gastrointestinal dysmotility (Lackner & Ray, 2007).

Another metabolic issue, gastroparesis, is very common in midlife. Gastroparesis is a condition which involves delayed gastric emptying, which ultimately disrupts the stomach's ability to properly digest and move food into the small intestine. This leads to symptoms such as nausea, vomiting, bloating, and abdominal pain (Camilleri, 2007). The relationship between gastroparesis and eating disorders is complex, with eating disorder behaviors potentially contributing to the development or exacerbation of gastroparesis, while the symptoms of gastroparesis may reinforce disordered eating patterns. Sasha was one such client. Her stomach distention following meals exacerbated her body image concerns.

The endocrine system is another area of concern in middle-aged adults with eating disorders. Prolonged undernutrition can lead to hormonal imbalances. Such imbalances include low levels of estrogen in women, which can result in amenorrhea (absence of menstruation) and further increase the risk of osteoporosis (Katzman, 2003). Amenorrhea is also a direct cause of infertility for midlife women desiring to start or expand their families. Men with anorexia nervosa often experience low testosterone levels, leading to reduced libido, fatigue, and muscle wasting (Ehrmann et al., 2002). These hormonal disruptions are often persistent, complicating both treatment and recovery.

Social and functional impairment

The social and functional consequences of eating disorders can be particularly severe in middle-aged adults. They may experience challenges maintaining stable relationships and professional careers due to the time and energy spent managing the eating disorder. Sasha is a classic example of a very bright lady who has been unable to hold a job. She is not alone among SEED clients. She also has few friends and when she does run into those from college, they run out of conversation very quickly.

Research demonstrates that eating disorders often cause significant occupational impairment, with many affected individuals reporting difficulties in work performance due to both physical and psychological symptoms

(Wonderlich & Crosby, 2009). Furthermore, the presence of surrounding eating disorders may be more pronounced in this demographic, leading to social isolation (Rodriguez et al., 2020). This is one of the most devastating facets of eating disorders.

Significant shame and stigma

Midlife men and women may be reluctant to seek treatment due to shame and stigma. Stigma comes from the prevailing wisdom that eating disorders are "teenage problems." Shame can further perpetuate the eating disorders; it's hard for a person to tolerate such difficult feelings.

Shame can be defined as a complex emotional response consisting of several simultaneous emotions. These include feelings such as anger, sadness, disgust, and the belief that one is fundamentally "flawed" or "defective" (Gilbert, 2011). Feminist relational psychologist Judith Jordan further defines shame as a felt sense of unworthiness to be in connection, a deep sense of unlovability, with the ongoing awareness of how very much one wants to connect with others" (1989). Thus, shame creates distance from others, further reinforcing that one is shameful. A closely related concept is the idea of *body shame*, i.e., feelings of shame (i.e., hatred, anger) directed toward one's body (Troop & Redshaw, 2012).

Susan typifies Jordan's definition. Susan's deep shame was a result of her shy nature and her feelings of being different from her peers – there were no other people of color where she was raised. These factors were extremely difficult. The final piece of the puzzle involved the disclosure of a molestation by her uncle. Of all the clients to whom I've recommended a higher level of care, Susan was the last one who needed to be asked "how do you have an eating disorder at your age?" by a poorly trained clinician. This pinged her own beliefs of being somehow "alien" and contributed to her depression.

Therapeutically addressing and resolving shame can be challenging, whether in the presence or absence of a midlife eating disorder. The application in this chapter has some helpful suggestions to allow clinicians to explore shame.

For further reflection and application

1 Consider the many differences between midlife eating disorders and those that occur at younger ages. What have you seen among your own clients? What surprised you?
2 How have you seen shame manifest in your clients? Are there certain behaviors you see more often than others? Certain diagnoses?
3 As you learn more about the diagnosis of atypical anorexia, what reactions do you have? Have you worked with a client that seems to meet this criterion?

Clinician resource 3: exploring shame

The following resource can be provided to clients who enjoy journaling and self-reflection and is especially helpful for those that experience shame about their eating disorders or bodies. Clinicians may also use these prompts in session.

Note

1 Binge drinking was defined as four or more drinks on one occasion for females and five or more drinks on one occasion for males.

CLINICIAN RESOURCE 3: EXPLORING SHAME

This exercise allows you to explore shame and start the process of releasing it.

1   How do you define shame?
2   What does shame feel like in my body?
3   If my shame had a voice, what would it say?
4   Have you felt shame in other areas of your life? Describe this.
5   If applicable, how do I experience shame about my eating disorder?
6   How has shame impacted my relationships with family? Friends? Others?
7   If a friend was struggling in similar ways, what advice would I give?
8   Who or what in my life would help me cope with or challenge shame?
9   How has shame influenced your relationship with spirituality/the Divine?
10 What kind of support do I need to begin healing shame?

Chapter 4

Body image and eating disorders

Helping midlife clients to navigate body image is a common and surprisingly complex task. Body image is a person's mental or subjective image of one's own body – the picture we have in our minds of the size, shape, and form of our bodies and our feelings concerning these characteristics and body parts. Body image is fluid and changes from moment to moment. And most importantly, body image is separate from what a person *actually* looks like.

To understand midlife eating disorders, it's important to discuss the idea of body image and its various aspects. Why? Negative body image is one of the most robust and consistent predictors of dieting and eating disturbances (Kilpela et al., 2015; Stice, 2002). Body-image disturbance also predicts relapse following an otherwise successful treatment experience (Fairburn, 2008). This research highlights something many of us have seen; we can help clients to reduce or even stop symptoms such as binging or restricting, but that in and of itself does not change a person's body image. Even completely when a person's weight is restored or the person is symptom-free, the poor body image persists. Sometimes the best we can do is to normalize this.

Poor body-image disturbance can contribute to a range of issues, including depression, social isolation, anxiety, and low self-esteem (Merino et al., 2024). Negative body image affects people in profound ways.

This chapter will provide an overview of body image, including the socio-cultural and relational aspects of body image. We'll look at the ways each of us forms our unique body image and why despite similar pressures only some of us develop eating disorders.

Defining body image

Body image is a relatively simple concept – at least on the surface. Body image refers to an individual's perceptions, attitudes, and beliefs about one's own physical appearance (Cash, 2004). But that's where the simplicity stops. Body image reflects how people see themselves and how they feel and think about their bodies. Body image develops within the context of multiple external (society,

DOI: 10.4324/9781032615745-5

cultural standards) and internal (personality dynamics, unique experiences, traumas, etc.) factors. Already sounding complicated? It is.

Body image is a multidimensional concept that encompasses more than how we look or how others perceive us. Ken is a great example of this complexity. As a fitness coach, Ken was a walking advertisement for his own services: a classic "six-pack," tons of energy, and a winning smile. While Ken outwardly oozed confidence, his inner image contrasted sharply. When alone in the gym, Ken spent hours in front of the mirror flexing his muscles and scrutinizing his perfect body. But to him, it was hardly perfect. He typically found some part of himself lacking. In sessions, he criticized himself as "disgusting" and "old." This led to his working out relentlessly. Ken was especially sensitive to his hair loss, something that started when he was 19. His teenage years were torturous. Ken was the ubiquitous "fat kid" whose mom dragged him to Weight Watchers meetings. Now, Ken's insecurities ran deep, so deep in fact that he was profoundly lonely. He gently refused the attentions of the very willing women he coached. Instead, Ken focused on macros and calories, a joyless cycle he desperately wished to break.

Ken's story reflects many of the aspects of body image. Consider the following four:

1   *Perceptual body image* refers to how people *perceive* the size, shape, and appearance of their bodies. As with Ken, this mental picture may or may not align with a person's *actual* physical appearance. A distorted perceptual body image is common in people with eating disorders, who often perceive themselves as overweight, out of shape, etc. While they may be in larger bodies, their perceptions are frequently inaccurate. These misperceptions can lead to extreme dieting, excessive exercise, or restrictive eating.

2   *Affective body image* reflects the *emotional responses* people have toward their bodies, such as pride, shame, guilt, or contentment. When people feel satisfaction, pride, or neutrality, they have a positive affective body image occurs. Negative emotions like shame or disgust are typical of people like Ken who have poor body image. These emotions drive eating disorder behaviors. Feelings of inadequacy, shame, or disgust can lead to actions designed to "fix" perceived problems – a fix that never happens because the problem runs much deeper than anything losing weight can solve. Ken's focus on macros and the belief that he could feel better by changing his body is part and parcel with many people who compulsively exercise.

3   *Cognitive body image* involves the *thoughts and beliefs* people have about their bodies. These beliefs are shaped by external factors such as societal pressures, family influences, and media portrayals of body ideals, as well as personal experience. Individuals with eating disorders often have negative cognitive body image, where they obsess over "flaws" and engage in constant comparisons to societal standards, to friends, and even to their younger selves. It's a losing proposition, which only leads to false beliefs. "Thinner,"

"more toned," or "perfectly dressed" cannot equate with happiness or acceptance. As Ken grappled with leaving behind his image of the "fat kid" and recognized that his problems ran deeper than his appearance, he allowed himself more freedom to eat and to take rest days.

4 *Behavioral body image* refers to the *actions* individuals take in response to their body image, such as dieting, exercising, or undergoing cosmetic procedures. For Ken, negative body image was the driving force behind behaviors like restrictive eating and excessive exercise. What's ironic is that these behaviors contribute to body dissatisfaction, a concept we'll tackle shortly. Many of my middle-aged clients struggle with occasional behaviors, such as a new workout routine, while others engage in more extreme behaviors such as purging, starving, or laxative abuse.

Another idea to add to this already complex mix is the concept of *body-image dissatisfaction*, a negative attitude toward one's own physical appearance (Heider et al., 2018). Both Ken and Susan experience body image dissatisfaction. It's extremely common among people with eating disorders, with avoidant restrictive food intake disorder (ARFID) being the exception (more shortly). Body-image dissatisfaction occurs when there is a discrepancy between how people view their bodies (*actual* body image) and how they want their bodies to look (*ideal* body image) (McCabe & Ricciardelli, 2004; Heider et al., 2018). A key factor that contributes to body-image distress is the internalization of Western body ideals (Heider et al., 2018), something that all of us are exposed to regardless of our age.

Another relevant aspect of body image is the "whole vs. parts" theory. People with eating disorders often focus on one body part rather than viewing the body as a whole. This explains why people with eating disorders often have a distorted body image. The classic image of an emaciated young woman peering into the mirror and seeing someone with a vastly larger body is not really accurate. Instead, people are usually focused on a body part – their "huge butt," "flabby thighs," or "poofy belly." Their appraisal, however, is an absolute: "I'm too fat."

Think for a moment of Ken. In addition to his obsessive focus on the mirror, Ken had various *body checking* habits that reflect this "parts" idea. After meals, he would routinely scrutinize certain areas of his body (his stomach and hips) to see if he could pinch any excess skin. The fact that he never could did not dissuade him in any way.

What's interesting about the whole vs. parts theory is that most people who see their bodies as a whole have a more positive body image. It's one of the ways we can support them in challenging their negative body image.

Body image influences not only how we view ourselves but also how we relate to others. Maintaining satisfying relationships is important as people age (Bath & Deeg, 2005). Negative body image can create distance in relationships (Tiggemann & Lynch, 2001; Cash & Smolak, 2011). It can also affect intimate partners; couples who can engage in open, supportive dialogues about body image and aging are more likely to navigate challenges successfully, maintaining a healthier, closer relationship (Dittmar, 2009).

Negative body image can also affect friendships and desire to engage socially (Donnelly et al., 2016; Sabik, 2017). People with positive body image tend to experience healthier, more supportive friendships, as they are more likely to engage in open, nonjudgmental interactions (Tiggemann & Slater, 2014). In contrast, negative body image can lead to social isolation, increased self-consciousness, and less satisfying relationships (Grabe et al., 2008). Body image, then, can be both a protective and risk factor in relationships, depending on the context and how individuals navigate these issues.

Influences on body image

Our discussion so far has centered on defining body image and its role. We have not yet answered one question: what affects how we see ourselves?

Body image is influenced by many factors, including media, cultural norms, gender, and personal experiences (Grabe et al., 2008); personality traits, like perfectionism (Polivy et al., 2005); physical characteristics (Hurd, 2000); and traumas, such as sexual abuse (Kearney-Cooke, 2007). Trauma includes circumstances that limit a person's sense of safety, power, or control.

It's helpful to remember that these influences *can* support a positive body image, as well as a neutral or a more negative body image. It's the combination of factors in each person's history that matters.

Thus, body image is influenced by external factors – the context of *all* individuals within a given culture – and internal factors – those unique to each person. We'll tackle each of these in the upcoming sections. But first let's view this pictorially (Figure 4.1).

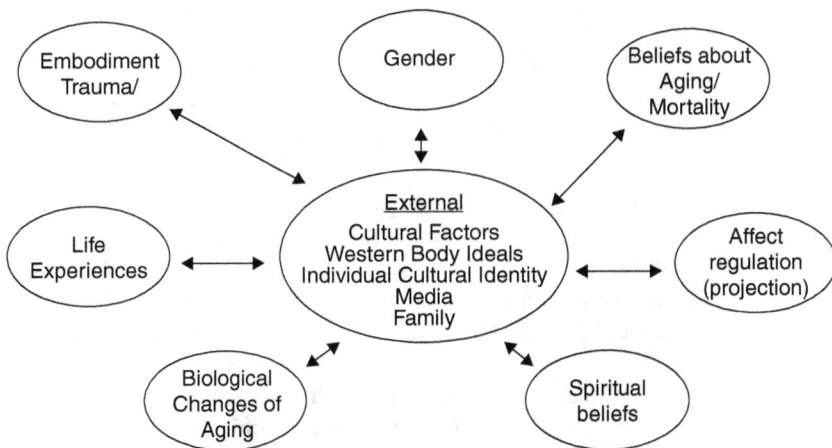

Figure 4.1 Midlife Body-Image Influences.

The external context: diet culture and sociocultural influences

As you consider the factors that influence body image, it's helpful to start with some reflection. Which of these factors stands out in your own history? Some likely do more than others. Now consider the inner circle, which has to do with cultural body ideals. What do you notice coming up for you? Perhaps it's a sense of not measuring up. Maybe it's a more neutral stance. Or, maybe, you've worked hard to move away from sociocultural standards.

For those who grow up in Westernized societies (e.g., the United States, Canada, the United Kingdom, Australia, and parts of Western Europe), an important consideration is the lens of *diet culture*. Diet culture is an overarching system of beliefs that equates thinness with worth, health, success, and social acceptance (Warren & Akoury, 2020; Keel & Forney, 2013).

Diet culture is something we are all exposed to, and it plays a central role in shaping body image and eating behaviors. Diet culture perpetuates a cult of thinness and supports restrictive eating practices, including judging certain foods as "good" or "bad." Diet culture advocates for intense exercise routines and espouses the ideal of a "perfect" body. These messages are reinforced by the advertising industry, the food industry, and even medical institutions. Think about some recent advertisements you've seen and how they depict people who are middle-aged or elderly. There's a notable lack of images of older people. When older people are shown, it's often as physically frail or cognitively impaired (Levy et al., 2014), a trend that intensified during the COVID-19 pandemic. These depictions perpetuate harmful stereotypes of aging.

Diet culture also influences the food industry, an industry that produces highly processed convenience foods – foods high in sugar and fat and low in nutrients – while also promoting "health" and the latest diet trends. If you've ever traveled internationally, perhaps you've noted that most groceries don't have the low-fat, low-flavor options we have. Our foods and their marketing are literally designed to make us fat (Chandon & Wansink, 2012), while the industry pushes low-fat, zero-calorie options. Not to mention the get-fit, get-thin messages the tabloids expose us to in the checkout line. Want to try Oprah's latest weight loss miracle? Here it is.

Some of these diet trends are so ubiquitous that our medical institutions promote weight loss as the primary solution to any perceived shortcomings – body-related or otherwise (Puhl & Latner, 2007). Have a cold? Lose your job? I've heard many a tale of people seeing their doctor for the flu or muscle aches – only to be lectured on their weight and walk out with a prescription for Zepbound.

Western culture values individualism and self-improvement. It's based on the belief that people can control their bodies and improve them by losing weight. Look at your social media feed. Instagram, Facebook, and YouTube encourage users to display their personal lives, including their bodies, in ways that highlight individuality and achievement (Tiggemann & Slater, 2014), with people publicly logging their exercise and weight loss. Influencers often sell "self-empowerment" through weight loss, fitness, and dieting. The self becomes a commodity, and achieving a certain body type (thin for women, muscular for men) is a form of social capital and identity. While we often think social media appeals only to the young, many middle-aged people avidly consumes these narratives. One emerging trend is the rise of graninfluencers – older content creators who post on social media outlets such as TikTok (Ng & Indran, 2023).

Given the difference between these body ideals and the actual body shape and size of most of the population – especially the middle-aged population – it is not surprising that many people view their bodies negatively (Tiggemann, 2004). This may be less the case if you happen to be part of a cultural or ethnic group that eschews the cult of thinness and values larger bodies.

A couple of examples may be helpful here. In Chapter 1, we met John, who was struggling with orthorexia. John's disordered eating was less connected to body image than many of the clients you'll meet in these pages. His close-knit group of gay friends could not fathom why John would want to lose so much weight. Many of his 70-something peers were runners and swimmers and worked out regularly. The preference was for fit bodies that his friends appreciated for their functionality – athletic but not overly muscular or overly thin bodies. These were pretty healthy standards. While this may not be an across-the-board preference, it was among John's peers. And this motivated John to seek support when his weight plummeted.

Like many social groups, LGBT clients have body-image norms of their own and are vulnerable to developing body-image and eating concerns. Many trans, gender-diverse, and queer men often have body-image concerns about muscularity, weight, size, body hair, height, voice, fat distribution, wrinkles, or aging. More "gendered" components of the body can be particularly challenging (Dalzell & Protos, 2020). John was fortunate to be exposed to some great role models.

A number of cultural groups bring protective factors to the mix – at least until they are inundated by Western ideals. A great example can be found among people of African-American ancestry. Maya Angelou's poem *Phenomenal Woman* typifies confidence over "skinny." Studies suggest that many African-Americans prefer larger bodies (Barroso et al., 2010; Kronenfeld et al., 2010) and are more satisfied with their bodies overall (Kronenfeld et al., 2010). More typically, body concerns are focused on other traits, including skin color, facial features, or hair texture (Roberts et al., 2006).

Despite these protective factors, many black Americans *do* struggle with eating disorders. Such body insecurities seem to increase with buy-in to Western ideals or with a lack of access to black culture. Susan, while biracial, had no exposure to black family or peers. Her beliefs about her body and its shortcomings were more consistent with diet culture. Susan spent hours each day scrolling social media and countless dollars on diet pills and fitness gadgets. This contrasts with Felicia, a black woman in her 40s.

While Felicia was raised in a predominately white area, her interactions with her wider family helped to support a healthy body image. "I remember one Christmas. One of my aunts could not stop saying how gorgeous and curvy I was," she says. "It felt great – I really felt seen. My mom was always so critical about how I looked." While Felicia briefly struggled to fit in with white peers, she was ultimately able to reject diet culture, embracing her "curvy" body. "I was really angry with my mom for a while – trying to make me fit in," she shared. "But now I realize she was scared for me. But I'm great just as I am." Felicia summarily rejected diet culture and feels good about herself and how she looks.

Diet culture fosters an unhealthy relationship with food and body size. It encourages people to view their bodies as projects to be fixed or controlled rather than as sources of vitality and self-expression. Food becomes something to limit rather than enjoy. Exercise becomes something punishing rather than fun. As people constantly strive to meet unattainable ideals, many develop disordered eating and hate the beautiful bodies they have.

Relational aspects of body image

Body image is deeply relational, shaped by both internal perceptions and social interactions. The doctoral program I attended had several professors who were very influenced by the work of the Stone Center's Jean Baker Miller and other second-wave feminist writers. I still love this approach and its relevance to working with eating disorders.

Miller's Relational Cultural Theory (RCT) emphasizes the role of relationships and their importance in the development of self-concept, including body image. Miller (1976) suggests that self-concept is not something that exists independently within an individual, but is co-constructed through relational experiences, particularly through mutual empathy, respect, and connection (Jordan & Hinds, 2016).

According to RCT, a person's sense of self "is created and sustained in connection with others. The self grows through both connection and disconnection, as the person finds themselves in relation to others" (Miller, 1976, p. 30). If a person's relationships are supportive and accepting, people are more likely to develop a positive body image. It's not limited to others accepting body differences; it's more of a sense of being "okay" in others' eyes. Conversely, disconnection in relationships, such as experiences of objectification, judgment, or unrealistic standards, can lead to negative body image (Miller, 1976; Jordan et al., 2011).

Kelly's story may shed some light on this idea. At 52, she's quick to point out the ways she no longer resembles the child beauty queen she once was. Kelly has stories galore about her pageant days, and many of these highlight experiences of objectification, criticism, and the strict diets she was forced to follow from the time she was 4 until the age of 12. Kelly's mother, a former model, was quick with correction and slow with praise. "There were many tears. I learned the importance of eating as little as possible, so I'd fit into my dresses," she says. "I never felt good enough or pretty enough or smart enough." Kelly's negative body image was rooted in the pageant environment and in the complicated relationship with her mother. She still feels that she is not enough to please her mother.

Body image, then, is not just an individual experience but a relational one. While Kelly's story is an extreme of sorts, our relationships play a role in how we see ourselves. The list of relationships that influence body image is long and includes family relationships, especially parental attitudes (van den Berg et al., 2007), peer relationships (Thompson & Stice, 2001), romantic relationships (Tylka & Wood-Barcalow, 2015), friendships (Vartanian & Dey, 2013), and professional relationships, including those of coworkers and healthcare providers (Puhl & Heuer, 2009). These relational dynamics are pivotal to how individuals view themselves. They are also key to transforming negative body perceptions.

When we consider the importance of relationships, one theme is the importance of the therapeutic relationship. RCT emphasizes the importance of the therapeutic alliance as a space for collaboration, mutual respect, and empowerment between the therapist and client. Interpersonal connections that provide space for vulnerability and authenticity can help individuals challenge external pressures and create more integrated and positive body images (Tylka & Wood-Barcalow, 2015). Additionally, therapists can model self-acceptance and body neutrality. By fostering a strong therapeutic alliance grounded in empathy and sharing, feminist relational therapists promote healing and personal growth (Jordan, 2016; Surrey, 1991).

Affect regulation and body image

Affect regulation (the ability to manage feelings and emotions) and self-regulation (the ability to manage and control emotional and behavioral responses) also shape how people experience their bodies and can be an underlying factor in disordered eating. We'll tackle this idea more fully in subsequent chapters, but this overview provides a summary.

Affect regulation is to maintain stability in the face of emotional distress. This means staying grounded when experiencing *any* emotion. This includes difficult emotions, such as anger or sadness, and more positive emotions, such as happiness. Having effective ways to regulate affect helps with stress management and coping, in navigating interpersonal relationships, and in maintaining mental well-being (Gross, 2002). In the context of eating disorders, emotional regulation refers to an individual's difficulty in managing and responding to emotional experiences in a flexible, adaptive way. Many of the clients I see struggle with modulating emotions, experiencing emotions very intensely, which can affect their well-being and self-perception (Gross, 2002).

Tod and colleagues (2016) looked at the role of emotional regulation in the development and maintenance of eating disorders. They found that emotional regulation was linked to body dissatisfaction and vulnerability to developing eating disorders. People with poor emotional regulation skills seemed to focus on their physical appearance or weight, a focus which may initially help them manage emotions, particularly stress or negative ones. Over time, this creates a feedback loop in which poor coping leads to more rigid eating behaviors. They may find themselves eating or restricting food to feel better about themselves physically, but the emotional soothing is short-lived. In fact, the eating disorder behaviors serve to increase body dissatisfaction.

The brief case below illustrates this connection.

Kevin, who is 45, has struggled with body dissatisfaction for most of his adult life. He often feels frustrated with his appearance and weight. Over the years, he noticed that these feelings are most intense during periods of high stress. When faced with work pressure, Kevin tends to emotionally eat to feel better. While he feels soothed by eating high-sugar, high-fat treats, this only exacerbates his dissatisfaction with his body.

Poor emotional regulation stems from a combination of genetic, environmental, and developmental factors. Some people may be predisposed to emotional dysregulation due to variations in their brain structures or neurochemical systems, such as the prefrontal cortex and amygdala, which are involved in processing and managing emotions (Schmahl & Vermetten, 2019). In addition, early childhood experiences, including inconsistent caregiving, neglect, or other traumas, contribute to maladaptive emotional responses and coping mechanisms. For example, children who grow up in environments with high levels of stress may struggle to learn effective emotional regulation skills, leading to difficulties in managing emotions in adulthood (Wooten et al., 2022). This makes sense given the strong connection between trauma and eating disorders. Many of you have probably noted that some of your clients can become very emotional very quickly – 0–60, so to speak.

Poor emotional regulation can also be influenced by social and cultural factors. People with poor support networks or who experience chronic stress may find it harder to remain emotionally balanced (Gross & Munoz, 1995). Their emotional responses become disproportionate or maladaptive.

Overview of gender and its role in body image

Gender also influences body image. The World Health Organization's website defines *gender* as "the characteristics of women, men, girls, and boys that are socially constructed. This includes norms, behaviors, and roles associated with being a woman, man, girl, or boy, as well as relationships with each other."

I'd like to broaden this definition to include the very important topic of gender diversity. *Gender diversity* refers to the inclusion of a wide range of gender identities beyond the traditional male and female binary. The gender-diverse spectrum includes people who are transgender, nonbinary, gender fluid, and many other identities (Dalzell & Protos, 2020).

We've already touched on gender and how it is connected to body image. This link involves distinct social, psychological, and cultural factors that influence men's and women's perceptions of their bodies. In large part, body image is influenced by differing expectations of males and females. Transgender, nonbinary, and gender-diverse people are also influenced by societal expectations and ideals.

Women

Think about the women you've seen depicted in magazines or who are highlighted on social media. What do they share? If you thought "they're all thin," you've noted what's known as the "thin ideal." And many are not just thin, they are *thin*. Women of all ages, including midlife, often buy into the ideal that you can never be thin enough.

For those of you old enough to remember (and others can look it up), think about British actress and model Twiggy. She is perhaps most famously known for her slim, boyish physique. While her extreme thinness garnered some criticisms, it also set the stage for societal body standards from the mid-1960s onward. As we think about middle-aged women, quite a few grew up in the Twiggy era, but few can ever be remotely as thin.

Research on the thin ideal dates to the 1980s and 1990s. Garner and Garfinkel (1980) were some of the first to explore how such societal emphasis on thinness contributes to eating disorders and promotes low self-esteem and body dissatisfaction. There is a large body of research that suggests that the internalization of the thin ideal is a robust predictor of eating pathology in women and, to some degree, in men (Schaefer et al., 2019; Warren & Akoury, 2020; Wilson et al., 2022).

Many middle-aged women feel these pressures to attain a thin body, often to their own detriment. Liza is a beautiful, curvy woman with plenty of male attention. "You'd think that at 50, I'd be able to stop dieting," she says with a laugh, "but chances are I'll be refusing my last meal because it's too fattening." While Liza has oodles of insight, she struggles with the thin ideal – a harsh taskmaster who demands she run on the treadmill after consuming anything. "I ran a mile the other day because I let myself eat a grape," she says. Liza struggles with the accompanying depression, anxiety, and, of course, eating disorder connected to this thin internalization.

Internalizing the thin ideal leads many like Liza to develop a distorted body image and the sense that their own bodies, very normal bodies, are "too big."

While it sounds almost factual, it's actually more of a judgment of value or worth, and many of the middle-aged women I treat feel inferior to people they know who are thinner. They often compare themselves with women who are years, if not decades, younger. They are also reminded of their own aging with new grays, wrinkles, and saggy breasts.

As women approach middle age, they experience many physical changes. Declining estrogen leads to a shift in body fat distribution, and more fat accumulates around the abdomen (Jensen, 2008). Women also experience a loss of lean muscle mass, which slows the metabolism, making it easier for fat to accumulate (Kuk et al., 2009). Middle-aged women often experience gradual weight gain, typically around 1–2 pounds per year, due to these physical changes (Kapoor et. al., 2017). Weight gain is more pronounced after menopause.

Of course, the body has much wisdom, and there is a good reason for many of these changes. As women age, body fat is important. It helps maintain hormone balance and supports estrogen production, which declines after menopause (Kuryłowicz, 2023). Body fat plays a role in bone health, metabolism, and cognitive function, all of which are crucial as women experience changes in their physiology with age (Cummings & Melton, 2002). Maintaining a healthy level of body fat can also help to buffer against the risk of fractures, depression, and metabolic disorders. Of course, despite these positive attributes, women often lament this weight gain and accumulated body fat due to the sociocultural emphasis on thinness. While some people maintain that this emphasis is shifting, I've seen little evidence of that among the women I work with.

One of the most harmful aspects of the thin ideal is that it undermines healthy body diversity. Only one very specific body type is seen as "good." This disregards the natural variety of body shapes and sizes among women, reinforcing harmful stereotypes and societal pressures. And the reality is that short of developing an eating disorder, most women simply can't attain this ideal body. I am one of them, coming from a genetic stock that births short women who are blessed with what people sometimes call good birthing hips. Ouch.

Body size is a highly genetic trait (Steinberg & Katz, 2009). When women learn to be more compassionate toward their bodies of all shapes, sizes, and ages, they can experience more freedom and feel better about themselves. This is one of the goals of the Health at Every Size (HAES) movement, which is a nondiet approach that provides a path toward body acceptance, self-esteem, and self-efficacy (Tylka & Wood-Barcalow, 2015). Working within a HAES-informed lens is imperative for clinicians who work with midlife adults.

Let's pause here to discuss another client. Sarah, a 45-year-old woman, has struggled with body-image issues throughout her life. Although Sarah has always had an average-sized body, she internalized the belief that thinness was synonymous with beauty and success, as reinforced by the media, her family, and peers. Some of Sarah's favorite memories involve her and her mother poring over the latest issue of *Vogue* and cutting out pictures of the models. She and her mom would post these on their refrigerator and use them as diet inspiration, trying one fad diet after another. These diets abounded in her youth: the Cabbage Soup Diet, Grapefruit Diet, and their fallback, Atkins.

As Sarah approached her 40s, she felt self-conscious about the natural changes her body experienced, such as small weight gain and the softening of her features. She often compared herself to younger, thinner women in magazines and on social media, believing that her worth was tied to her size. Such constant comparison fostered feelings of inadequacy and anxiety about her appearance. While she recognized that this has kept her from many of the aspirations she once had – to travel, to get a better job, and to find a life partner – she felt helpless about how to change the cycle. Her constant refrain was: "Just let me lose those 5 pounds."

Men

To understand societal ideals for men, one needs to look at the images portrayed in *Men's Health* and in fitness culture. These images feature men who are very muscular (yet thin), youthful, strong – difficult standards for those in their 40s or 50s (Barnes et al., 2020; McCabe & Ricciardelli, 2003). Societal demands to be thin yet muscular, combined with the physical changes and personal expectations related to aging, can lead to body dissatisfaction. Cumulatively, these pressures can contribute to a negative self-image, influencing overall well-being and mental health (Watters & Higgins, 2024).

As men enter middle age, they commonly experience a decline in muscle mass, a decrease in metabolism, an increase in body fat, and the classic "beer belly" – accumulated fat around the abdomen (Shakeri, & North, 2025). It takes longer for them to recover from physical activity, and they may injure themselves more easily. Men may also begin to gray, bald, or develop wrinkles, which can contribute to fears of losing their youthfulness and attractiveness (Bassett-Gunter et al., 2017; Mellor et al., 2019). These changes can impact perceptions of strength and vitality (Griffiths et al., 2018) and lead to heightened body dissatisfaction.

Men like my client David may respond by adopting extreme diets or engaging in excessive exercise. David ran 10 miles daily, despite the Northeast cold, snow, or his own injuries. His dietary intake was well below what would be appropriate; he skipped lunch daily and would meticulously count out the correct number of peanuts in a single serving. Sadly, this tall, lanky-framed former "fat kid" never felt thin or attractive enough.

While not the case for David, others I've worked with have combined extreme exercise with dangerous performance-enhancing drugs to attain these male ideals (Mellor et al., 2019). Some of these men develop a condition known as "muscle dysmorphia." While not a clinical diagnosis, it's one to certainly be aware of in all age groups. The belief for those with muscle dysmorphia is that one's body is too small or not muscular enough, despite often having a well-developed physique. It is considered a subtype of body dysmorphic disorder (BDD) and is sometimes referred to as "reverse anorexia." People who struggle with muscle dysmorphia weight lift excessively, diet strictly, and may use performance-enhancing substances, such as anabolic steroids, to increase muscle mass.

Both men and women may seek cosmetic surgery or other procedures to improve body image. Jim, who started balding at 30, was finally able to afford a hair transplant at 39. This cost him upward of $15,000 for results he was not fully happy with. Carl, a gay man in his 60s, would not be "caught dead without my toupee," made from human hair and costing him more than $4,000. Like Jim, he remained self-conscious despite this expenditure he could barely afford.

What about cosmetic surgeries? These may not necessarily improve body image either and can sometimes exacerbate dissatisfaction. A study by Sarwer et al. (2005) found that while some patients report initial satisfaction with their appearance after surgery, many experience little to no long-term improvement in body image, and some experience heightened dissatisfaction. Similarly, Cash and Smolak (2011) argue that individuals with pre-existing body-image concerns may find that surgery does not address the underlying psychological issues contributing to their dissatisfaction.

Educating men about healthy body standards, diversifying media representations of masculinity, and promoting body neutrality can reduce negative body-image concerns in men (Griffiths et al., 2015). Encouraging a more inclusive definition of masculinity and body image may also help to shift societal norms toward acceptance and well-being rather than unattainable ideals.

Transgender and gender-diverse (TGD)

Transgender and gender-diverse (TGD) people also struggle with body image. As an extremely heterogeneous umbrella group with many identities, it's difficult to draw generalizations about body image. The References section contains a reference to my first book that attempted to discuss TGD body image (Dalzell & Protos, 2020; Dalzell et al., 2022). Published in 2020, it's already woefully outdated.

TGD people are exposed to the same gendered ideals as the rest of us, and these influences are important to recognize. Some TGD people who struggle with *body dysphoria*, a feeling of discomfort or distress regarding physical traits that do not align with their gender identity (Dalzell et al., 2022). Body dysphoria can be particularly pronounced for those who have not transitioned or undergone gender-affirming surgeries or hormone replacement therapy (Budge et al., 2013), which can be the case for some middle-aged TGD people.

At 65, Robin (a TGD individual who uses she/her pronouns) is an example of some of these struggles. Robin is married with two children. Robin's son,

Kenny, has Down syndrome and still lives at home. Her conservative religious background and current circumstances create a situation where I am the only person who knows how badly she would like to be a man. Robin often expresses admiration for the younger generation. "They have such freedom," she says. "I often think about what my life would have been like had I been able to have some of the procedures they do. But at this stage, I couldn't do that to my family." Robin is a classic yo-yo dieter, and while she feels better in a broader, stockier body, she often gives in to her husband's criticisms, losing and regaining the same 15 pounds. "My husband always tells me how important it is to dress femininely and to be pretty. I hate it, but I can't think of leaving Kenny behind. I don't think I'll ever be entirely comfortable," she says.

For Robin, the pressure to conform to binary gender norms contributed to a host of mental health issues – anxiety, depression, and low self-esteem, all of which are all too common among TGD people (Meneguzzo et al., 2024). Robin felt pressure to be a good parent and partner as well as to maintain a feminine-appearing image despite her own discomfort. Hiding her identity contributed to the stress she felt and exacerbated her depression. People who can transition or align more fully with their gender identity also have to deal with external stigma, another factor that can lead to a more pronounced internalized dissatisfaction with their bodies (Rosenberg et al., 2014).

Trauma and embodiment in body image

Trauma plays a significant role in the development of eating disorders and negative body image. Chapter 3 touched on the connections between trauma and body image, a connection that we can see quite strongly in Carla's story. Her eating disorder began after a date rape in college. After a period of remission, Carla relapsed in her 40s, due to the demands of caretaking for her aging parents. As Carla began to understand just how traumatic and chaotic her childhood had been, she better understood the resentment she felt at taking care of her parents – and why she turned to food and alcohol to numb that resentment.

By midlife, many of the clients I see have experienced some form of trauma, either as children or as adults. What's often significant is that many middle-aged adults unintentionally minimize what they have gone through. This is so common that in my assessment, I often simply ask "what difficult life experiences have you had?" In fact, trauma is so common that I've set aside a chapter to discuss this more fully. Chapter 5 will look at the connections between acute and especially chronic traumas, embodiment, shame, and eating disorders.

For now, let's quickly preview the key themes connected to trauma and midlife eating disorders:

• Trauma can disrupt an individual's sense of self, affecting emotional regulation and normal coping. People who have experienced trauma struggle with self-esteem. These are all factors in the development of disordered eating behaviors (Brewerton, 2007).

- People who have experienced trauma(s) may use control over food and body size to regain a sense of power or safety in their lives (Cash & Smolak, 2011). This is another "a-ha!" point. Too often, clinicians frame eating disorder behaviors such as binging or restricting as "maladaptive." They are *adaptive responses* to maladaptive situations.
- Trauma can be projected on the body, and the body can be experienced as "bad." Conversely, other trauma survivors view their bodies as the currency that allows them some sense of power. There may be a distorted sense of self-worth tied to physical appearance (Johnson & Wardle, 2005).

It's important to take a thorough history, focusing on any difficult life experience that could be relevant in each person's history and experience of being in the body.

Biological changes and beliefs about these changes

While most therapists have limited medical training, some medical know-how is important in understanding eating disorders. Dr. Google can be a quick fact-check (if you stick with trusted sources), and finding collaborative physicians and dieticians is best practice (although often more difficult than it should be). Getting older is not for the faint of heart, and biology changes our bodies in challenging ways. Some of these ways are aesthetic, such as weight gain due to slower metabolism, decreased muscle mass, and hormonal fluctuations. As men and women experience these biological changes (menopause for women and andropause for men), they may notice impacts on body image, particularly in a society that emphasizes youthful appearance and thinness as ideals of beauty. Weight aside, there are other outward changes – our hair grays and thins, our skin wrinkles – that make us begin to look older to ourselves and others.

In addition to appearance-related changes, middle-aged adults may begin to develop chronic physical illnesses. Some of these may be related to diet or the consequences of longstanding eating disorder symptoms. We'll discuss this more fully in Chapter 6.

So, what separates those people who navigate age-related changes well from those who struggle? An important factor seems to be how people *perceive* these age-related changes (Bennett et al., 2024; Sörensen et al., 2021). Are they realistic about these changes? Are the changes controllable in any way? Are physical shifts seen as a normal part of aging? Or perceived as a personal failing? Some people with eating disorders, especially those who have spent years controlling their bodies, may experience even normal changes as betrayals. In response, they may ramp up (or turn to) restrictive dieting, excessive exercise, or unhealthy eating patterns as a means of counteracting these natural physical changes.

Body image and eating disorders 59

Life transitions

Life does change, and midlife is a time full of significant life transitions. Some of these include changes in family dynamics, career shifts, and losses. As you read this list, take a moment to consider if you have experienced changes like this, and how they made you feel. It's not easy.

Consider Sasha, who was facing her mother's potentially severe diagnosis. While Sasha's eating disorder began years earlier, the recent stress has started her on a classic eating disorder pattern: the binge/purge/restrict cycle. There are variations of this cycle with some clients binging then restricting – which leads to more binging. Others binge, then restrict to compensation – which again can lead to more binging. While there are many variations of this cycle, the key point is that it is a circular relationship, with one behavior influencing the other. It's important to educate clients about this cycle, including the very real physiological aspects of binging due to starvation (Figure 4.2).

No matter the specific symptom picture, life transitions can deeply influence body image and the development of eating disorders. As individuals face life changes, such as retirement, a geriatric pregnancy, or a child leaving for college, they may begin to focus on something they can control: their bodies. Heightened concerns about aging, physical appearance, and self-worth are common, and all potentially contribute to body dissatisfaction (Thomas et al., 2019).

Why do we see this focus on the physical? At heart, it's about identity shifts. Life transitions of any kind can lead to people reevaluating their identities. Sasha was the perennial kid, not the parent. It was a shift she was loath to make. Such life transitions can bring a sense of vulnerability or insecurity. Some people distract from these challenging feelings by focusing on their physical appearance. This works surprisingly well as a distraction and can also provide a false sense of control or self-worth (Griffiths et al., 2013). In midlife, women are particularly prone to developing disordered eating behaviors in response to stressors related to aging and identity shifts (Williams et al., 2024).

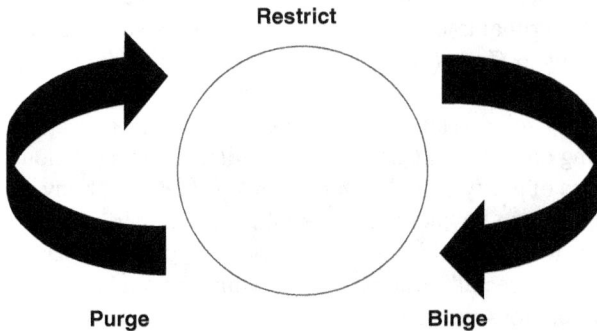

Restrict

Purge

Binge

Figure 4.2 The Restrict, Binge, Purge Cycle.

Understanding the emotional changes associated with midlife transitions is an integral part of the puzzle for clinicians working with this group – so critical that we'll expand more on this in Chapter 8.

Spiritual beliefs

You may be surprised to see spiritual beliefs listed as one of the factors in body image. For many people, spiritual beliefs play a significant role. So, what is spiritual? For this conversation, *spirituality* refers to a sense of connection to something greater than oneself. Spirituality can involve a search for meaning or purpose in life. Some people find meaning and purpose within their religious communities, while others may find it in Eastern spiritual perspectives. For some, spirituality may involve being in nature or in mindfulness. It's a broad definition that encompasses personal growth, inner peace, and the understanding of one's place in the universe (Pargament et al., 2021).

Spiritual beliefs can have a substantial influence on body-image perception and can be a mediating factor in eating disorders. Many people with eating disorders adapt core values related to self-worth to health and the physical self. Shifting these values can help tremendously.

Take a moment to consider your own religious or spiritual traditions. What did they teach you about your value? About taking care of yourself? About treating your physical self?

Judeo-Christian and Hindu beliefs emphasize the idea of "body as temple" – that the body is a sacred vessel that should be treated with respect, care, and as an expression Divine within. For example, *My Jewish Learning*, a website devoted to Jewish traditions, says Judaism teaches that "the body and soul are separate yet indivisible partners in human life." It goes on to emphasize that the body is a God-given tool for doing sacred, holy work in the world. In addition to the body being seen as an expression of divine creation, other spiritual traditions emphasize the interconnectedness of the body, mind, and spirit. This can foster a more compassionate and holistic approach to body image (Rosenfield, 2004).

So how did spiritual traditions become agents for shame and unhealthy practices? According to Cash (2004), this comes in when such approaches place their sole emphasis on ideals of purity or modesty. This can contribute to body dissatisfaction by reinforcing the need to deemphasize one's appearance rather than celebrating one's body (Cash, 2004). Similarly, some religious frameworks connect the idea of purity with the physical body, where the body may be viewed as something that can be "defiled" or is inherently impure. Some of my clients express that the use of certain symptoms, especially purging, is a means to purify the body. This is especially true when they come from a background of trauma or of extreme religious practices.

Thus, spiritual beliefs may either reinforce or challenge societal pressures surrounding appearance, either promoting acceptance or encouraging self-scrutiny.

Spiritual practices like meditation, prayer, or yoga can provide individuals with tools to cultivate self-compassion and mindfulness, fostering healthier attitudes toward the body (Cohn, 2017). We'll look more at this in Chapter 9.

Brief review of eating disorders

The prior chapter discussed the most common eating disorders, such as binge eating disorder (BED) and other specified feeding and eating disorder (OSFED). Here, we'll briefly focus on the criteria for each of the eating disorders, focusing on the characteristics and common body-image concerns associated with each.

Anorexia nervosa

Anorexia is a disorder in which people severely restrict their food intake, typically due to an intense fear of gaining weight. We often think of people who have anorexia as young, thin, female, and starving. We now know that food restriction can manifest differently for each person, such as a person who restricts certain food groups (such as fats and carbohydrates) rather than all foods. Some people with anorexia don't eat only carrots; yes, they may, but they may eat other things like cookies (maybe only one cookie, but again there are no hard-and-fast rules). We also know that body size may indicate anorexia – but in atypical presentations, the person may be in a larger body. It's important to look at the entire picture.

Anorexia, including first-time, recurrent, and chronic presentation, can be seen among middle-aged men and women. It can present less as a desire for a "perfect" body and more as an attempt to control aging or assert control over aspects of life that feel out of control. Most people with anorexia perceive themselves as overweight, even when they are dangerously underweight. This was the case for Sasha and many others I've known. Distorted body image is central to anorexia, as the individual's sense of their own size and shape is heavily influenced by the need to appear thinner. Anorexia, then, is not simply about food restriction but is intrinsically tied to an unhealthy preoccupation with body image, where control over food intake is central.

Among younger people with anorexia, there tends to be an idealization of the illness. While midlife adults are intensely fearful of gaining weight should they recover from anorexia, there may be slightly more insight into the problem. Anorexia is extremely dangerous, with the highest mortality rate of any psychiatric problem (Meczekalski et al., 2013). Suicide accounts for the second greatest proportion of deaths (Arcelus et al., 2011), a concern also seen in bulimia.

Bulimia nervosa

Bulimia involves binge eating followed by compensatory behaviors – behaviors intended to prevent weight gain. Purging through vomiting or laxative use is common, but other ways people purge include diuretic abuse/enemas or excessive exercise. While purging is one of the main aspects of bulimia, people with OSFED may also purge, as do some people with anorexia (anorexia purging type).

Like anorexia, bulimia can present in midlife or be a longstanding or recurrent issue. The lifetime prevalence of bulimia nervosa for adult women ranges from 1.7% to 2.0% and for men from 0.5% to 0.7%. These statistics represent all adults, not only middle-aged people (Keski-Rahkonen et al., 2007).

Binging and purging are often a means of coping with stress or body dissatisfaction. Men may experience bulimia as part of their attempt to achieve an idealized muscular body, often by severely restricting calories and engaging in excessive exercise, followed by periods of overeating. Such binging may be physiologically or psychologically driven.

Bulimia is closely linked to body image and an intense need to control shape and weight. People with bulimia often experience a strong internal conflict between the urge to eat large quantities of food and a fear of gaining weight. This conflict is compounded by feelings of shame, guilt, and a perceived lack of control during binge episodes. The compensatory behaviors that follow are attempts to counteract the binge and to maintain or lose weight, often driven by a fear of being seen as "fat" or "undesirable."

Of all the eating disorders, bulimia may be the one that causes people the most shame. It's common for people who struggle with bulimia to feel intense self-loathing following a binge. Shame can contribute to the development and maintenance of bulimia, as people with bulimia may conceal their behaviors out of fear of judgment, leading to a cycle of secrecy, self-criticism, and heightened emotional distress (Griffiths et al., 2015). Such shame undermines the person's self-worth, increasing the likelihood of disordered eating as a means of coping with negative emotions (Lange, 2020). This may be one of the reasons that bulimia is also highly linked with suicide (Perkins & Brausch, 2019). Bulimia is highly comorbid with alcohol use disorder (Lilenfeld & Kaye, 1996).

This complex interplay between bulimia and shame highlights the importance of addressing emotional and psychological factors in treatment.

This is a good time to briefly pause and introduce you to Karen, a 46-year-old lesbian woman with no children. Karen has alternately struggled with symptoms of bulimia and alcohol abuse. Karen has been alcohol-free for two years and is very involved in Alcoholics Anonymous (AA). Like many clients who have been in treatment for a long time, Karen has a good understanding of her illness. Karen cares a lot about how she looks and spends a significant portion of her salary on all manner of creams, Botox, and fillers.

Karen binges and purges daily, something that brings her shame. Recently her partner walked in on her when she was purging and told her in no uncertain terms that she was "disgusting." This has only made Karen crave food more, and she is desperate to stop the cycle.

Bulimia is dangerous in a different way than anorexia, with most medical complications linked to its symptoms. Recurrent episodes of binge eating followed by purging can lead to electrolyte imbalances, dehydration, and organ damage, affecting the heart, kidneys, and gastrointestinal system (Mayo Clinic, 2022). Chronic vomiting can cause dental erosion, esophageal tears, and an increased risk of arrhythmias due to low potassium levels (Treasure et al., 2010).

Equally dangerous is another form of bulimia that affects individuals with type 1 diabetes. *Diabulimia* is characterized by the intentional manipulation or omission of insulin in order to lose weight (Ip et al., 2023). Unchecked diabulimia can cause severe consequences, including hyperglycemia, diabetic ketoacidosis, cardiovascular disease, kidney failure, and neuropathy (Powers et al., 2020). Diabulimia is often underdiagnosed, as individuals may not openly discuss their behaviors due to stigma or fear of losing control over their diabetes management (Kınık et al., 2017). Early intervention and a multidisciplinary approach, including medical, psychological, and nutritional support, are critical (Huang et al., 2017). Data on the exact prevalence of diabulimia in midlife adults is limited, as most studies focus on younger populations.

Binge eating disorder (BED)

While the primary feature of BED is the binge episode, body-image concerns also play a role. People with BED often experience distress and shame about their binging and their physical appearance. Many people with BED perceive themselves as overweight, regardless of their actual weight (Grilo et al., 2019). This can exacerbate the cycle of overeating as a way to cope with emotional distress, anxiety, or negative self-perceptions.

Addressing body-image issues is an important aspect of treating BED. In fact, improving body image can reduce the frequency of binge eating episodes and improve overall mental health (Lewer et al., 2017).

Avoidant restrictive food intake disorder (ARFID)

ARFID is another eating disorder that people commonly associate with childhood, and indeed it often begins then. It can, however, persist into adulthood. People with ARFID are more than "picky eaters." ARFID is primarily driven by sensory sensitivities, fear of choking, vomiting, or other negative consequences associated with eating or from or a lack of interest in food. People with ARFID may experience strong aversions to certain textures, colors, or smells of food, or they may have an intense fear of choking or vomiting. As a result, their diet may become highly limited to a small range of foods (Kambanis et al., 2022). Many people with ARFID have diets that are so limited that they lead to significant nutritional deficiencies and extreme weight loss.

While ARFID doesn't always involve the same body-image distortions seen in disorders like anorexia nervosa, the restrictive eating habits that define ARFID can overlap with physical concerns, contributing to an unhealthy preoccupation with the body in several ways.

For adults with ARFID, food avoidance may stem from the fear of how eating certain foods could affect their body, especially in terms of weight gain or bloating. Even if weight control isn't the primary concern, anxiety about bodily changes can be overwhelming. Thirty-five-year-old Hannah's AFRID co-occurred with gastro-paresis, creating severe bloating and discomfort after meals. Hannah was extremely focused on the bloating and sensations of fullness. She developed a fear of eating and a need to control her food intake to maintain a sense of bodily autonomy. Dovey and colleagues (2008) were some of the first to point out this connection. Over time, such fears can become linked to body image, where any change in the body is magnified, fostering a preoccupation with body shape. For Hannah, these fears of weight gain looked a lot like those seen in people with anorexia.

This may be because ARFID is often accompanied by an increased aware-ness of internal bodily sensations (Hawkins & Dovey, 2009). While that may sound positive, people with ARFID may become hyperaware of sensations like fullness, nausea, or discomfort after eating, and this heightened awareness can lead to an overemphasis on the body's responses to food. Such hypervigilance can fuel food avoidance behaviors and contribute to preoccupation with bodily reactions (Greeson et al., 2019).

For further reflection and application

1   As you read through the various components of body image (perceptual, affective, cognitive, behavioral), what were your thoughts? Were there some that surprised you? As you consider your own body image, which seems most relevant?

2   In the context of your own clients, consider the contributors to midlife body image. Which ones have you seen more frequently? Are there some that you have not seen? Why is it important to consider all these factors?

3   Consider how body image plays a part in each eating disorder. In what ways do you currently work with body image?

4   Assess the presence or absence of spirituality in your life. What have your own spiritual traditions had to say about the physical self? How can you bring this into work with your clients?

Clinician resource 4: how am I influenced by diet culture?

A thank you to the National Eating Disorders Association and California State University for creating the Digital Footprint. The intention of the following activity is similar, although more geared toward middle-aged adults. This activity is used as homework to look at the ways in which body image is connected to the messages of diet culture. It also makes an excellent group activity.

CLINICIAN RESOURCE 4: HOW AM I INFLUENCED BY DIET CULTURE?

Step 1: explore your online presence

1 List the sites where you spend the most time:

- Write down the top five to ten websites/social media sites you visit most frequently. These may include:

  - Facebook, Instagram, Pinterest
  - Fitness trackers or health-related apps
  - Online shopping platforms

2 Track your visits:

- Over the next week, keep a log of the types of content you interact with:

  - How is your content related to body image?
  - Do you browse articles about dieting, weight loss, or appearance?
  - Are there any specific advertisements that focus on body appearance?

Step 2: analyze your digital content

1 What types of body-image messages do you see?

- Ask yourself:

  - Does your content reflect a body ideal (e.g., thinness, muscularity)?
  - Are the influencers or figures you follow largely promoting weight loss, workouts, cosmetic surgery, or antiaging treatments?

Step 3: introduce body-neutral and body-positive role models

1 Seek body-neutral role models:

- Explore online figures who emphasize body neutrality, body acceptance, or who celebrate aging and diverse body types. These might include:

  - Body-positive influencers: look for social media influencers or bloggers who challenge the narrow definitions of beauty, promoting self-love and confidence regardless of shape, size, or age.
  - Age-inclusive figures: find role models who embrace aging with grace and self-acceptance, such as individuals who challenge agist standards.

2 **Curate your feed:**

- Follow at least three role models who emphasize body neutrality or positivity.
- Unfollow or mute accounts that tend to make you feel critical of your body.

Suggestions for body-positive role models:

- **@i_weigh (Jameela Jamil)** – advocate for body neutrality; she walks the talk
- **@thebodyisnotanapology (Sonya Renee Taylor)** – promotes body liberation, self-love, and inclusivity
- **@lizzo (Lizzo)**– singer and advocate; promotes confidence for larger bodies
- **@zachmiko (Zach Miko)** – plus-size male model; promotes self-love
- **@tylerford (Tyler Ford)** – nonbinary, body-positive advocate who uses their platform to discuss gender, body image, and the challenges of navigating both

Step 4: reflect

1 Reflection prompts:

- Did you notice patterns that contribute to negative body image?

After curating your digital spaces to be more body-positive, how do you feel about your body now?

Chapter 5

Trauma, embodiment, and shame in midlife

If trauma, embodiment, and shame don't seem to be congruent ideas, think again. Or perhaps you've already picked up on these themes from our briefer looks at these topics. In Chapter 1, we met several clients with eating disorders. Central to many of their stories are histories of traumatic life events: sexual assaults, food insecurity, losses and impending losses, parents struggling with alcoholism (attachment trauma), and family rejection (which for many LGBTQ clients is also a form of identity trauma because they can experience the rejection as nonacceptance of their queer identity). Situations like these and many more are common in the histories of people with eating disorders. This is especially true when you look at midlife, a point at which most of my clients have experienced one or more significant traumas.

This chapter will expand upon themes in prior chapters, including defining trauma and the many types of traumas people experience, explaining the interconnections between trauma and embodiment, and discussing the impact of trauma – including shame – on people and how this connects to eating disorders. We'll expand upon several client cases to provide a thorough grounding, setting the stage for our discussion of treatment issues.

Defining trauma

In Chapter 3, we defined trauma as an individual's experience of an event in which a person's ability to integrate emotional experience is overwhelmed, or the individual experiences a threat to life or bodily integrity. This is a broad definition that reflects just how common trauma is in the lives of many people, particularly those with eating disorders.

Trauma, then, involves an intense emotional and biological response to an event that the person experiences as threatening or aversive (Dalenberg et al., 2017). Trauma can be classified into different types, such as acute trauma (e.g., a single event like an accident or assault) and chronic trauma (e.g., ongoing abuse or neglect) (van der Kolk, 2014). The impact of trauma is often felt in the body,

DOI: 10.4324/9781032615745-6

as individuals may carry the emotional and physiological scars of these experiences long after the event has passed.

Psychological and physical manifestations

Especially following acute trauma(s), individuals can develop symptoms of post-traumatic stress disorder (PTSD) and its accompanying reexperiencing (e.g., flashbacks, nightmares, body memories) and avoidance behaviors (avoiding reminders of the trauma). While PTSD is more common with recent or acute stressors, it can be a manifestation of ongoing or chronic traumas.

It's helpful to pause here and discuss the idea of body memories. While this is another trauma reexperiencing symptom, like a flashback, it's one we discuss less often. Body memories are body-based flashbacks. The body retains a memory of the trauma(s) and stores this experience physically.. I've seen it to be strongly associated with sexual abuse. Sasha, for example, described that a year or two after her sexual assault, she felt ready to start dating again. As she was getting ready, "I suddenly felt like I was back in my dorm room. I could feel my date's hands all over me and the sensation of being held down," she said, fighting tears. "It felt so real that I even had a dark bruise on my wrists just like when this happened. It was terrifying." Learning that body memories are a true trauma symptom was very helpful to her.

Other manifestations of trauma include chronic pain and conditions like fibromyalgia and chronic fatigue syndrome. Traumatic, overwhelming, or unprocessed events can lead to physical symptoms like muscle tightness, shallow breathing, which result in chronic pain, and/or digestive disturbances. These conditions also come with a host of psychological effects. Chronic pain, for example, is related to depression and social isolation. This is an example of the difficulty in separating body and mind; the physical affects the psychological.

Such bodily responses are the result of the nervous system's inability to fully discharge the energy created by the traumatic event (Blakslee, 2020). More on this shortly.

Chronic trauma refers to the experience of repeated or prolonged exposure to traumatic events. Some examples I've seen in clients with eating disorders include childhood abuse (physical, sexual, emotional), neglect, longstanding domestic violence, and witnessing parental violence. Besides the chronicity of such events, another commonality is that these traumas are relational in nature – that is, they occur within the context of important relationships and attachments.

Chronic traumatic stressors can have a significant effect on mental health. One of the most common manifestations of chronic trauma is depression – persistent feelings of sadness, hopelessness, and a loss of interest in previously enjoyable activities. People with depression can also experience emotional numbing and a sense of worthlessness (Tull et al., 2012). Eating disorder symptoms may for people to feel better about themselves such as by losing weight or bulking up or may provide a sense of aliveness (such as the high that accompanies a sugar rush).

Chronic trauma can also contribute to anxiety disorders, leading to heightened levels of fear, worry, and nervousness. This anxiety may manifest as generalized anxiety, panic attacks, or hypervigilance, often rooted in the repeated threat of danger or harm (Kupfer, 2015). People with anxiety often struggle with feeling grounded, and eating disorders may be a way to achieve this feeling. Eating disorders may provide a sense of safety. A person who has been sexually abused, for example, may binge eat to achieve a large body that is unappealing to potential abusers.

Addictive behaviors are also highly comorbid with trauma and midlife eating disorders. These may be substance-related disorders, such as the misuse of alcohol or cocaine, or non-substance-related behaviors, such as gambling or those related to sex, shopping, or exercise. Some people characterize eating disorders through an addiction lens, pointing to their ability to help people cope with chronic stress, as substances may be used to self-medicate or numb the emotional pain resulting from traumatic experiences (Khantzian, 1997).

Other indicators of chronic trauma include anger, overreaction to normal events, fatigue, sleep problems, misreading others' intentions or facial expressions, and feelings of being unsafe despite evidence to the contrary. Chronic traumatic stress is clearly detrimental.

Relational trauma

Relational trauma refers to the emotional, psychological, or physical harm that occurs in the context of interpersonal relationships, particularly those with primary caregivers or close attachment figures (Liotti & Gilbert, 2011; Herman, 1992). Most chronic traumas are also examples of relational trauma. Some examples of chronic/relational trauma include childhood abuse, neglect, abandonment and parental illness, or addiction. Other examples of relational trauma include family rejection, such as that which John, from Chapter 1, experienced.

Relational trauma affects one's sense of self and trust in others. As you think about your own clients that have experienced relational trauma, take a moment to consider their trauma story. Were they abused by primary caregivers? Neglected by caregivers? Abandoned? Stepping into a parentified role because a parent was ill or struggled with addiction? Their trauma story may tell you a lot about what they learned about attachment figures. For example, they may have learned that they can't trust others, or that they are "not enough" for parents to get well. They may not feel safe or secure in relationships. Relational traumas can severely affect a person's sense of self-worth, safety, and ability to trust others.

Judith Herman (1992), whose theories are well known in the trauma world, suggests that trauma survivors experience a breakdown in the ability to form secure attachments, as their relationships are often characterized by fear, betrayal, or neglect. This relational aspect highlights how trauma isn't just an isolated event but is embedded in the dynamics of abusive or controlling relationships, influencing the survivor's ability to trust, connect, and heal.

Many survivors of childhood traumas go on to be retraumatized by our mental health care systems, which often view these wounds as "personality disorders" – rather than manifestations of chronic relational trauma. There is a distinction here; a personality disorder implies that there is something wrong with the individual. In contrast, looking at someone's relational pattern as a manifestation of past trauma implies that the trauma itself did harm. People who have a history of chronic relational trauma often fear abandonment, demonstrate patterns of unstable, intense relationships, feel chronically empty, and have difficulty modulating emotions.

Herman (1992) emphasizes that an important aspect of recovery requires rebuilding relationships, particularly with others who are safe, validating, and empathetic. This can include the therapist as well as trusted others.

Defining embodiment

Embodiment refers to the lived experience of the body – how people perceive, inhabit, and interact with their physical forms. It is the way people experience their body not only as a biological entity but also as a source of identity, agency, and emotion (Young, 2005). A positive sense of embodiment supports well-being, agency, and connection, whereas disruptions to embodiment – often through trauma or illness – can result in disconnection, discomfort, and distress. When individuals feel at peace with their bodies, they are more likely to experience resilience, even in the face of stress, trauma, and adversity.

Beyond these "heady" definitions of embodiment, I'll add a simple one that applies to many people with trauma and eating disorders: embodiment as a sense of being at home in the body. Feeling at home in your body involves a profound sense of comfort, ease, and acceptance. It's a feeling of being grounded, present, and in sync with oneself. Being at home in the body also means being nonjudgmental about one's physical self. It's not about having a perfect body, but about embracing it as it is.

Embodiment comes with self-acceptance and the ability to honor the body's needs. These needs can involve nourishment, rest, or movement. It can also mean enjoying the sensation of being inside one's own skin, relaxed and at peace.

Trauma disrupts an individual's sense of embodiment. Trauma creates a profound disconnect from the body. For many individuals struggling with eating disorders, their bodies become sites of tension and conflict. These factors contribute to maladaptive coping mechanisms, including eating disorders, addictive behaviors, or the co-occurring disorders. If the trauma is sexual trauma or another body-related trauma, such as childhood illness or disease or physical abuse, this disconnection from the body is often exacerbated. The body may be viewed as a source of shame or danger (Herman, 1997).

Trauma can also severely affect an individual's sense of self-worth and body image, increasing vulnerability to eating disorders (Cohen & Blanton, 2015). Individuals with histories of trauma may also engage in eating disorder behaviors as a means of coping with or avoiding painful memories, emotions, or sensations associated with the trauma. For example, restrictive eating may serve to exert control over a body that feels unsafe or uncontrollable (Brewerton, 2007). Alternatively, binge eating may be used as a form of emotional numbing or self-soothing (Schwitzer et al., 2001). Restrictive eating or purging may be a way to regain a sense of control over one's body, to purify the body, or to dissociate from physical sensations altogether. This disembodiment, in turn, exacerbates the cycle of trauma, eating disorder behaviors, and emotional distress.

Many of these factors were present for Holly, an intelligent, attractive woman in her mid-30s, who was molested by her paternal uncle as a young child.

Holly's abuse went on until she was a teen. When she did attempt to tell her parents what was happening, they accused her of "making up stories." They only believed her when her father saw a sexually explicit photo of Holly in his brother's wallet. Holly was humiliated that her father saw these photos. While her parents cut off contact with her uncle, for Holly it was too little, too late.

As an adult, Holly has a difficult time recognizing her worth – let alone her physical appeal. While she's extremely perfectionistic about her appearance, she's also often baffled by the attention she often receives from men for her beauty. For Holly, the perfectionism is a mask; for many men, it is an invitation. Perfect Holly has always eaten sparingly and carefully, but this restrictive pattern has ramped up since a coworker has made his amorous attentions known. "I feel disgusted by the way he looks at me," she says, "I'm enormous – and dirty. Purging is the only thing that makes me feel clean, but even that doesn't last long." As Holly has eaten less and less, she's noticed urges to binge eat. This has scared her so much that she's finally willing to try to address the eating disorder and the childhood sexual abuse.

From the discussion so far, you can see that for people who struggle with eating disorders and have a history of trauma, the body becomes a source of conflict. Such individuals may develop a distorted sense of their body size, shape, or function, or may project feelings of shame and disgust on their body. Holly and many others often adopt extreme behaviors aimed at controlling their weight, such as restrictive eating or purging (Cash & Smolak, 2011). Some may make themselves less attractive through overeating. Understanding the function of eating disorder symptoms often helps uncover the story of trauma, particularly key words such as "dirty," "filthy," or behaviors like the need to "cleanse" or "purify."

Disembodiment contributes to the persistence and severity of eating disorders. This is especially true at midlife, when trauma has persisted for so long.

Psychologically, the body becomes a battleground for power, control, and identity, with the body perceived as something to be manipulated rather than experienced or nurtured. It is a prison rather than a home.

Years ago, I worked in a group therapy program for eating disorders, where I facilitated an activity where group members drew their bodies as a literal home. Group members came up with some frankly disturbing homes. These were homes with barbed wire fences or floating in space, homes missing roofs or doors, and homes that were misshapen or disproportionate. Even the colors (blacks and grays) evoked strongly negative feelings. It wasn't about artistic quality – it was about trauma. Later, I'll share a similar activity you can try or can use with clients.

Christine Caldwell (2018) is another author to discuss embodiment. She calls being fully embodied "bodyfulness." In a bodyful state, there is an acceptance and appreciation of one's bodily nature, a nonjudgmental engagement with body processes, and an ethical orientation to take the right actions physically. People with eating disorders hold an antithetical stance, judging their body's needs, processes, and appearance. Paths to bodyfulness include conscious breathing, gentle movement, emotional connection, and various somatic practices. Most importantly, bodyfulness is not just about techniques but about creating a dynamic and informed relationship with one's body.

Trauma affects the mind *and* body. It's helpful to understand this intersection, especially when working with midlife clients whose eating disorders often begin with the heartbreaking traumas they have experienced.

The somatics of trauma

If embodiment is our lived experience of the body, trauma is the disruption of embodiment. Somatic psychologists, including Bessel van der Kolk (2014), Peter Levine (2015), and Ogden et al. (2006), are leaders in the field and have studied the effects of trauma on the body. Trauma alters the body. Trauma rewires brain regions involved in stress response and memory processing. This includes the amygdala, hippocampus, and prefrontal cortex (van der Kolk, 2014). This helps to explain the often-spotty memories of trauma survivors, as these brain regions play a critical role in how we form, store, and recall memories. Other potential effects include an inability to properly process emotions associated with memories (which could affect the intensity or vividness of emotional memories), difficulties with executive processing (planning and completing tasks), poor Impulse control, and problems with attention and focus.

Now let's consider these changes within the context of long-term trauma. Many people with eating disorders and trauma live in a state of chronic stress. This is the autonomic nervous system in action. During traumatic events, the sympathetic nervous system (responsible for the fight or flight response) can become activated and remain stuck in an overactive state, while the parasympathetic system (which calms the body down) may be underactive. This imbalance can lead to symptoms like anxiety, hypervigilance, dissociation, and chronic tension. It can feel like being on 24/7 high alert – a constant scanning for threat and assessment of "is this dangerous?" while bracing for that likelihood. This response, while protective, is exhausting.

It's important for clinicians to recognize that such shutdown/freeze response occurs *concurrently* with high arousal. Let's briefly discuss Cameron, who struggled with both anorexia and panic disorder. His early years were extremely traumatic. Cameron grew up with an affluent workaholic father and a stay-at-home mother. While others knew him as an only child, he had an older half-brother who was diagnosed with schizophrenia. From an early age, Cameron knew this, and knew that his mother had been so overwhelmed by his brother's illness that she'd left her prior family and married Cameron's father. "If it wasn't for him being so sick I'd never have been born," Cameron sadly shared.

As a child, Cameron had severe separation anxiety and constant fears that his mother would abandon him. He became a quiet high achiever, terrified of missteps. His perfectionism extended to his food intake and his body. Cameron felt "grounded" by his constant hunger and strict exercise routine. Cameron wound up marrying a woman who physically resembled his mother to an almost eerie extent. This is where the similarities ended; she was highly empathic, connected, and loved Cameron deeply. She was also frustrated by Cameron's irrational jealousy of any time she spent with others. Arguments often ended with her in tears and him seemingly completely shut down. This shutdown was a form of freeze.

It wasn't that Cameron wasn't aware of his emotions; it was that he was split off from them. To cope with overwhelming emotions, survivors of trauma may dissociate from their bodily sensations, creating a disconnect between their mind and body. This can lead to numbness, detachment, and an inability to fully process emotions. About the only emotional state Cameron strongly connected to was anxiety, which became the status quo. Fear, anger, and sadness were absent, and his hunger further distanced him from it.

In one session, Cameron discussed his fears of abandonment. I noted how outwardly calm he appeared. Cameron was stunned. He then proceeded to share that he was extremely anxious. He was so frozen that I interpreted it as "calm," like the way his wife interpreted this freeze state as "detached." This was amid significant emotional turmoil. While he was anything *but* shut down, there were no physical cues that others could see.

This really drives home how trauma can become trapped in the nervous system. Freeze responses, as well as fight/flight responses, while protective in moments of trauma, often outlive their usefulness and can lead to long-term issues (Levine, 2010) such as chronic tension, anxiety, and even chronic pain (Ogden & Fisher, 2015). Cameron often complained of back and neck issues. Trauma survivors can also have difficulty moving *between* states of arousal (e.g., fight or flight) and states of true calm (e.g., rest and digest) (Blakslee, 2020). This ability is essential for trauma processing.

Teaching people how to *pendulate* – to move between states of discomfort or distress and more comfortable bodily states – allows the nervous system to regulate and gradually release trauma (Levine, 1997). We support this through the process of titration. *Titration* involves experiencing small, manageable amounts of the trauma at a time, rather than overwhelming the system with the full intensity of the traumatic memory or sensation all at once. This helps prevent re-traumatization and supports a gradual healing process.

While I've tried to simplify some complex processes, I would encourage you to consult the authors cited here for a deeper dive. Simple or no, there are some important takeaways as we consider the connections between trauma, embodiment, and eating disorders:

- Include body-based/somatic practices in your work with anyone with eating disorders. While not everyone discloses trauma, you are likely seeing some manifestation of trauma.
- Do not assume people can "cope" or "regulate." They likely cannot, and the idea of giving up the regulatory effects of restricting, binging, or purging can be terrifying.
- Trauma healing should be gentle and gradual.
- Trauma and eating disorder treatment involves increasing body awareness as a way to reconnect to the physical self. Disconnection is often a manifestation of trauma.
- Healing trauma requires more than just talking about it. Trauma is healed *through* the body. Because trauma is physically stored in the body, therapeutic interventions need to involve the body as well. Techniques such as breathwork, gentle movement, touch when appropriate, and grounding exercises help clients re-establish a sense of embodiment and reconnect with their physical sensations (Blakslee, 2020; Caldwell, 2018).
- Trauma work includes embodiment work – the ability to feel grounded, connected, and in tune with one's body. Supporting people's ability to integrate trauma reestablishes a sense of coherence between their mind and body (Ogden et al., 2006).

Shame

Shame is the most powerful, master emotion because it's the fear that we're not good enough, and when deeply rooted in trauma, it can feel like a constant belief that we are fundamentally flawed, not just because of something we did, but because of who we are.

(Brown, 2021, p. 147)

Allow this powerful quote by psychologist Brené Brown (2021) to reverberate for just a moment. Do any of your clients come to mind? Many of mine do. This is especially true of middle-aged clients who often come with the powerfully destructive combination of an eating disorder, a history of trauma, and chronic shame. You'll meet many of these clients in the pages to come.

Brown's (2021) shame research emphasizes that shame, especially when intertwined with trauma, isn't just about feeling bad for something one has done; it can become an internalized belief that one is inherently flawed, unworthy, or "a failure." Similarly, Kurtz (1990) describes shame as reflective of "not just any lack or failure, but of the deficiency of the self as self, as human being. Shame testifies not to wrong-doing but to flawed be-ing" (p.17).

These beliefs are incredibly powerful and often fly in the face of any evidence to the contrary. Chronic shame colors all aspects of a person's life. Trapped in a never-ending cycle of inadequacy, people who hold deep shame often turn to food, alcohol, self-harm, or addictive behaviors to assuage these painful feelings. These behaviors then fuel the shame, creating a shame spiral.

As you consider these words, you may be beginning to fully consider the psychological impact of shame (and why it is that eating disorders so often feel like the answer). Shame affects not only the psychological (intense self-consciousness, sadness, humiliation) but also the physical and psychological realms. As I considered which of my clients would be illustrative as a composite here, many came to mind, but a couple stood out due to the depth of this experience for them.

To best understand Maureen, we start not with her own story but with her mother's. Maureen's mother Charlotte grew up in an impoverished family with little parental energy for supervision. Not surprisingly, Charlotte found herself pregnant at 15, the father being a young man with similar roots and a bad temper. No one wanted Charlotte to be tied to him, and the family quickly arranged for her marriage to a much older man. While this allowed Charlotte to escape some of the humiliation of her situation, it also bred resentment, and she often regaled the young and sensitive Maureen with "what could have beens" and nicknames such as "bastard child."

If this wasn't bad enough, it seemed like her stepfather's gesture in marrying her mother was less about altruism and more about his attraction to young girls. Charlotte was nearing the end of her appeal, and at 15, young Maureen was soon the stand-in. The sexual abuse began in earnest when Maureen was only five and Charlotte was pregnant with Maureen's half-brother. Maureen's childhood comprised abuse heaped upon abuse, with assaults by her uncles and stepfather, who made her feel responsible for their actions. She felt trapped and unable to tell anyone about the abuse due to the family's position within their Christian community.

The only respite available to Maureen appeared to be a local pastor who ran a local youth program. The pastor also manipulated this impressionable young woman, and while he did not physically assault her, he would often ask voyeuristic and inappropriate questions. Maureen's "respite" became a trauma of its own, one that extended to the present day. When I met Maureen, she was working as the director of the Christian preschool the pastor owned. Maureen's daily binging and purging became the thing that provided the only true, although temporary, relief for her. She described the binge as the necessary step to ensure the purge – something that "cleansed" her.

Most of us would agree that Maureen's story is truly horrific. While some people like Cameron conceal their traumas under a mask of stoicism, Maureen practically oozed trauma. Tangney and Dearing (2002) identified a physical response they call the "shame response." The shame response is characterized by slumped posture, lowered head, and averted eyes. This physical reaction looks like hiding from the world, and such withdrawal is common. Maureen often felt judged by others (a dynamic further perpetrated by her boss, the pastor) and considered herself "stupid" and a "failure," her doctorate notwithstanding. Maureen would also describe her shame as a physical weight she carried, one that even a larger body could not hold.

Other physical manifestations of shame

In addition to this physical "shame response," I have often noticed that in midlife men and women, chronic shame comes with other physiological consequences. We've already discussed the body's natural stress response, involving the activation of the sympathetic nervous system, which contributes to a heightened heart rate, sweating, and shallow breathing. People like Maureen may feel physically sick or fatigued as the emotional weight of shame takes a toll on the body.

Chronic shame can also lead to long-term physical effects, such as increased risk for cardiovascular issues, gastrointestinal problems, and weakened immune function, as stress hormones like cortisol are released continuously (Bradshaw, 1988). Shame, then, affects one's physical health and mental well-being.

Other psychological manifestations of shame

"Worthless," "inadequate," "fundamentally flawed," "exposed," "humiliated." When people sit on the couch and describe their innermost feelings, words like these often point to the psychological nature of shame. Shame is deeply tied to a person's self-concept, and this may come across as self-deprecating or being overly selfless, especially in cases like Maureen's, in which the vultures were constantly primed to swoop in and take advantage of her kind nature. At this extreme, selflessness led to Maureen neglecting her personal needs, being unable to stand up for herself, and being unable to set boundaries with others. This played out in many of her relationships.

In other clients, shame can lead to self-criticism and perfectionism. Holly is a great example of that. And as most of us know, perfectionism is often linked to eating disorders (Frost et al., 1990), especially anorexia and bulimia. In anorexia, perfectionism often manifests in the desire to achieve an "ideal" body weight and shape; in bulimia, perfectionism may be linked to feelings of failure or to their lack of control over eating (Shafran et al., 2004). Perfectionists like Holly also tend to engage in rigid thinking patterns, which may reinforce disordered eating behaviors. This includes all-or-nothing thinking about weight, body image, and food intake (Bardone-Cone et al., 2007).

Gilbert's (2003/2011) work underscores the impact of shame on mental health. Shame can exacerbate emotional struggles like depression, anxiety, eating disorders, and addictive behaviors. In its most destructive form, chronic shame leads to worsening depression, even suicidal ideation. People who experience pervasive, ongoing feelings of inadequacy or self-loathing can become very entrenched in these feelings. It's a heartbreaking cycle. Many people with chronic shame cannot see what truly wonderful people they are. Maureen certainly fit that bill.

Spirituality and shame

Ram Dass, who has been a spiritual inspiration to many, shares this story on his website:

> Like in India when I went there last time, two years ago, one of my lovely old friends up in a village in the mountains, said to me 'Ram Dass, you're looking so old.' He said 'You're so grey.' Now, at first my reaction to that was my Western cultural reaction of 'Oh god — that's terrible', but then when I quieted down, I heard the tone with which he was saying it. He was saying it with great respect and delight. Like I had now become one of the elders in the society and he was saying 'Wow, you've done it, you've grown old, how great.' Embracing aging is a journey that everyone must take.

While the story is striking on many levels, one of the most important is the shift in perspective from a traditional Western mindset to that of India where Hinduism is a strong influence. In Hinduism, the body is considered a temporary vessel for the soul. Imagine if everyone could embrace such a philosophy.

While Western spirituality and Judeo-Christian beliefs share some of these beliefs, they are often presented concurrently with messages that reinforce sin and personal imperfection. People raised with these beliefs may feel deeply ashamed of their actions and identities. Layer this with trauma, especially sexual trauma, and shame is often the outcome.

This was the case for Jane, who is now in her late 30s. As a teen, Jane was actively involved in her church youth program as a leader who made a vow of chastity and wore a purity ring. She was not only shocked but also flattered when the church pastor, an older married man, made sexual advances. This situation continued until her parents discovered explicit letters and contacted the authorities. They did not blame Jane for what happened, but she blamed herself.

Jane has held on to this shame for many years, seeing herself as "damaged" and "a whore" and "sinner." "He was someone everyone admired," she said. "I felt like it was all my fault, and that I was leading *him* astray." This is from a young woman who was not only a decade younger than her pastor but who appeared far younger, both physically and emotionally. Jane's shame, while initially fueled by her childhood abuse, now extends to many areas of her life, including shame at her alcohol use and bulimia.

Over the years, Jane has disconnected from any community or practice that has a spiritual focus. Several people Jane knows are active in Alcoholics Anonymous (AA), but Jane gives them, and the program, wide berth. While she realizes that AA would be helpful in supporting her recovery, she is afraid that others will reject her once they realize how "damaged" she is.

One of the most challenging aspects of shame is its connection to what many authors call "self-condemnation" (Woodyatt et al., 2017). Self-condemnation involves harshly judging or criticizing oneself, often in a way that is negative or unforgiving. Self-condemnation leads to guilt, shame, and low self-esteem. In some cases, it can be a destructive pattern where a person becomes trapped in a cycle of self-blame with no room for self-compassion or understanding. Jane's strongly held belief in her own "badness" fits that scope. The flip side, forgiveness – especially self-forgiveness – is a construct common to both religiousness and spirituality.

Shame creates disconnection from one's sense of self, others, *and* a higher power. People may grapple with feeling unworthy of divine love, forgiveness, or acceptance. The feelings of being "damned" or "irredeemable" or "lost" are common spiritual manifestations of shame, which can foster a sense of isolation or alienation from one's faith or spiritual supports (Brown, 2006).

People with internalized religious or cultural narratives around sin and moral failure experience heightened shame when they feel they have failed to live up to their moral or ethical standards in some way. This includes examples like Jane, who perceived her pastor's sexual advances and her response as a moral failure. Her bulimia and alcohol further convince her of this.

Mortimer (2019) conducted qualitative research on eating disorder relapse, focusing on two factors: diagnostic crossover, moral failing, and shame. Specifically, Mortimer studied the experiences of people whose eating disorders had shifted from anorexia to bulimia – a common dynamic at midlife. The research is fascinating. People who had previously controlled weight through restricting and now through binging and purging experienced this shift as a shameful moral failing. This was true to such an extent that it affected the individual's identity.

Core beliefs around moral failure can also cause people to question their worthiness of grace or spiritual fulfillment. Furthermore, shame may prevent individuals from seeking spiritual connection or participating in religious rituals, exacerbating feelings of disconnection, and further deepening the sense of spiritual emptiness. Reclaiming one's own sense of spirituality can be very helpful and provide a foundation and community they have otherwise been lacking.

Empirical evidence suggests that many dimensions of forgiveness are associated with better addiction recovery outcomes, and that self-forgiveness may be the most important dimension (Webb, 2021; Webb & Boye, 2024). Thus, connection to spiritual and faith communities that encourage self-forgiveness and self-compassion can be very healing. Many of my clients embrace such approaches and benefit from them. Tara Brach and Sharon Salzberg offer some wonderful free online resources about loving kindness. Kristin Neff has some great resources as well, including a "compassionate body scan."

Resilience and reclaiming embodiment

Resilience is the capacity to recover from or adapt to adversity, trauma, or stress. It is not simply about "bouncing back" from hardship but involves growth and transformation in response to challenges (Masten, 2001). Similarly, Tedeschi and Calhoun (2004) describe *post-traumatic growth* (PTG) – positive psychological change that people may experience following a trauma.

From this perspective, the person is an active agent in their healing process, with body and mind capable of change and recovery. This growth can take many forms. This includes discovering new possibilities and opportunities, realization of one's inner strength, improved relationships, appreciation of life, and spiritual growth (Tedeschi & Calhoun, 2004).

In the context of eating disorders, it involves reclaiming a sense of connection to the body – learning to trust and care for the body once more, despite its past trauma. A resilience-based approach acknowledges that healing from shame and trauma is not linear, but it is possible. We will return to this idea more fully in Chapter 9, but a few examples may be helpful here.

Through practices like somatic experiencing, mindfulness, and eye movement desensitization and reprocessing (EMDR), people can rebuild healthier relationships with their bodies. Schwartz and Knipe (2017) advocates for the importance of somatic approaches in trauma recovery, emphasizing the need for clients to gradually re-engage with their bodies in ways that feel safe and empowering. For example, practices like yoga, mindfulness, and body-based therapies allow individuals to reconnect with their physical sensations, enabling them to process trauma in the body and rebuild trust in themselves. Mindfulness-based interventions are also promising. Mindfulness encourages people to be present with their bodies without judgment, creating space for self-compassion and acceptance.

Mindfulness practices, such as mindful eating and body scanning, also allow connection with the sensations of hunger and fullness (Kristeller & Wolever, 2011), which is an important aspect in treating eating disorders. These practices also promote emotional regulation.

Relationship and shame: the importance of connection

A resilience-based approach also emphasizes the importance of social connection and relational support. We have seen that trauma, by its nature, isolates individuals and fosters feelings of shame and alienation. It's important to cultivate supportive, validating, and healing relationships in order to build resilience.

According to the Stone Center's Relational Cultural Theory (Jordan & Hinds, 2016), the process of developing resilience is inherently relational; it acts as an antidote to trauma. In the context of eating disorders, support from loved ones, group therapy, or peer communities can provide the validation and connection necessary for healing. It's important to build connective communities where people at midlife feel valued and encouraged.

When people feel accepted and valued for who they *are*, rather than their appearance, it contributes to a healthier body image. Supportive relationships can foster a sense of belonging and safety, which are crucial for individuals recovering from both trauma and eating disorders.

For further reflection and application

1 As you read this chapter, what aspects of the material helped you to best understand the interconnections between trauma and eating disorders? Did a particular client come to mind as you read this?
2 How can you adopt a more trauma-informed approach in your current practice? What practices or suggestions resonate the most?
3 Investigate resources for supportive groups, especially those that cater to people at midlife. Some places to investigate include the National Eating Disorders Association (NEDA) and Anorexia and Related Disorders (ANAD).

Clinician resource 5: body as a home (art activity)

This resource is an adaptation of the art activity described in this chapter. It invites clients to explore the concept of embodiment by imagining their body as a home. It encourages participants to reflect on how the physical body functions as a place of residence for thoughts, emotions, and experiences. You can also adapt it as a guided meditation.

Clinician resource 6: trauma healing practices

This resource can serve as a handout for clients to quickly review some common techniques for trauma healing and resourcing (a precursor to trauma processing). It includes somatic practices, journaling, breathwork, nature connection, and grounding. These practices also support embodiment.

CLINICIAN RESOURCE 5: BODY AS A HOME (ART ACTIVITY)

Materials needed:

- Paper (preferably large)
- Drawing tools (pencils, colored pencils, markers, crayons)

Instructions:

1 **Preparation:**
   Begin by thinking about how it feels to inhabit your body. Imagine your body as a home where all parts of you live. This place holds your mind, heart, and soul.

2 **Drawing your body as a house**
   Start by drawing your body as a house.

   - **Head:** consider how your thoughts and vision shape your world. Is your head the roof, an attic, a skylight, or something else?
   - **Torso:** where do your emotions, actions, or energy feel most concentrated? This torso could be the living room, the kitchen, or the heart of the home.
   - **Arms and hands:** do they represent how you connect to the world, give love, or protect yourself? Or do they represent something else?
   - **Legs and feet:** how do your legs help you take action/move forward in the world?

3 **Personalizing your home**
   As you draw, include symbols or images that reflect parts of your identity.

   - What colors would your home have?
   - What meaningful objects would you include?
   - Would you place anything sacred in your body-home?

4 **Reflect/process as a group**
   Once you've completed your drawing, take a moment to reflect.

   Consider:

   - How does your body feel as a "home"? Is it a place you enjoy residing in, or does it feel uncomfortable? If so, what can you do to change this?
   - What parts of your "body-home" need attention or care?
   - What elements in your life contribute to well-being and safety in your body-home?
   - How can you nurture your body-home so it feels more peaceful, loved, supported?

CLINICIAN RESOURCE 6: TRAUMA HEALING PRACTICES

1 **Yoga and gentle stretching.** Somatic practices like gentle yoga and stretching calm the vagus nerve, resulting in feelings of balanced relaxation. Practices like restorative yoga or stretching, which focus on breath awareness and slow movements, are especially helpful.
2 **Journaling for emotional expression.** Journaling allows expression of thoughts and emotions and offers insights into emotional patterns. Any form of journaling can be helpful. Examples include free writing or expressive journaling, gratitude journaling, and bullet journaling.
3 **Breathwork.** Breathwork helps regulate the nervous system, calm the body's stress response, and promote emotional release. It can reduce feelings of anxiety or panic and bring individuals back to the present moment. It can be as simple as taking a deep breath in and out.
4 **Spending time in nature.** Time in nature promotes grounding and relaxation. It offers a peaceful environment that can reduce stress and provide emotional and mental clarity. Being in nature often helps people feel more present and connected to the world around them. This is also a great chance to practice mindful breathing.
5 **Grounding.** Grounding techniques help individuals stay present and connected to their body, especially when feeling overwhelmed by trauma-related memories or flashbacks. It helps to reduce dissociation and re-establish a sense of safety. There are many great examples of grounding. One common one is the "5-4-3-2-1" grounding technique: identify five things you can see, four things you can touch, three things you can hear, two things you can smell, and one thing you can taste. Another way to ground is "earthing" – standing barefoot on the ground and focusing on the sensation and the connection to nature.

Chapter 6

A changing relationship with the body

Aging, illness, and body disconnection

In our chapter on body image, I encouraged you to look at your social media feed and notice the messages you consume daily. Perhaps you focused on ads for the latest diet and exercise programs. If you are over 40 and identify as a woman on social media, you may also have noticed something new: pricey potions that combat wrinkles and photos of "old/young" women – gray hair but gorgeous and young-looking. One exhorts: "Ever felt like a gray old hag while your friend looks like they found the fountain of youth?" Those are [gasp] some mighty high stakes. Who wouldn't shell out $100 or more on the latest fountain of youth?

If women's feeds are filled with exhortations to look youthful, men's feeds are geared toward virility and performance. Looking at the emails that have slipped past my husband's firewall, I see every manner of performance-enhancing teas, balms, and pills – even a "Vietnamese Passion Brew." His feed is full of those same men with a full head of gray who look like they've stepped out of *Men's Health.*

While the messaging is different, these messages very effectively feed our collective insecurities. Don't get me wrong. I applaud people's efforts to look and feel their best. But when it comes at the expense of self-esteem and self-respect, it's a problem.

Many women at midlife and beyond continue to experience pressure to meet Western society's female beauty standards of youthfulness and thinness. Maintaining a youthful appearance is often associated with attractiveness and social advantage for women. While men experience fewer of the messages aimed at youthfulness, their lens is equally challenging: they are expected to be muscular and virile, which is not the norm for many men at midlife.

In Chapter 4, we defined body image as people's perceptions, thoughts, and feelings about their physical appearance. While that is a broad definition, we often think of body image as focusing only on weight, shape, and body size. In fact, body image is much broader. It encompasses many aspects of physical appearance and accomplishment: hair (or lack thereof), skin, face, body shape, posture, and weight. And within these categories, we can break down each into subcomponents. I've found this very important in understanding individual body image.

DOI: 10.4324/9781032615745-7

Personal experiences, societal ideals, and cultural influences all shape body image. Body image is also *not* static. It can shift based on personal experiences (illness and divorce, for example). Identity affiliation is also an important facet of body image. Sam's quote captures the experience of one transman. But it is not the experience of every transman.

This chapter will discuss the expected biological changes of aging, with an emphasis on how these changes affect people psychologically. Western culture is agist and does not value the physical changes we all go through; these are the antitheses of Western beauty ideals. We will also look at how illness can change one's relationship with the body. Such illnesses include difficult diagnoses, such as cancer and autoimmune disorders, which affect about 5% of the world's population. While these conditions can occur at earlier ages, onset and peak can often occur during midlife (Amador-Patarroyo et al., 2012). Finally, we'll look at how all of these factors are connected to the development of eating disorders.

The thin-young ideal

I invite you to think back now to Figure 4.1, which provides a model of midlife body image. In this schema, external factors (such as Western body ideals) provide the backdrop for which people of all ages develop their beliefs about body image. The outer circles comprise the individual factors unique to each person, such as traumatic experiences, gender norms they adapt, individual biological changes, and beliefs about aging.

Please take a moment to reflect on the latter two factors – biological changes and beliefs about aging. Think about yourself and at whatever age you are today. And now, allow whatever is present with just this direction to come to mind. Perhaps what comes is an image of yourself at a younger age, free of wrinkles or signs of aging. Perhaps it's a montage of images of yourself at many ages, all equally precious. Perhaps it's a memory of impatience with someone older who is holding up the supermarket line. Whatever comes to mind is fine. Just note what comes up without trying to change it.

What does this brief exercise show you about body image?

When I first did this exercise, I thought of a client whose resilience through a difficult diagnosis I really admired. Physically, I'd describe her as older and slender, looking younger than her years, and fashionably dressed to impress at any yoga studio. We resemble each other in stature, but little else. This is the image in my psyche. I encourage you to try this out yourself and with your clients. It can lead to some great conversations.

Exercises like this can open dialogues about many aspects of body image. Out of the many things that can come up in these exercises, why is that memory or image coming up at this time? Is it something more transitory, concerning a present-day issue?

This is also a great way to talk about the so-called *thin-young ideal*. Stop, and again think of a cultural icon of at least 40. Perhaps what came to mind are actors such as Cameron Diaz, Kerry Washington, and Brad Pitt. They typify the thin-young ideal, a societal perspective that emphasizes thin bodies and venerates youth. As with other body-image ideals, these beliefs may be so deeply held that people are unaware of their own biases in that regard.

The literature has included various perspectives on the thin-young ideal. For example, in the 1990s, Fredrickson and Roberts proposed a theory of women's body image that they called "Objectification Theory." They framed body image within the realm of sexual desirability. "The common thread running through all … is the experience of being treated *like a body* (or a collection of body parts) valued predominately for its use" (Fredrickson & Roberts, 1997, p. 1). This sexualized view includes the ideas that males evaluate women through their gaze and that this objectification results in women treating themselves as objects to be looked at and evaluated.

Other authors have similarly looked at this idea of sexual desirability and have included traits such as physical attractiveness and youth. In his paper, Bruss (1989) studied how physical attractiveness was a key factor influencing sexual desirability and mate preference across different cultures. Pawlowski and colleagues (2000), Fink and Penton-Voak (2002), and Singh (1993) looked at various factors, such as men's preference for younger women because of their greater fertility and reproductive potential, and also body shape, touching on a pivotal influence on sexual desirability.

Youth as an indicator of attractiveness and positive body image begins early. Gendron and Lydecker (2016) conducted a cross-sectional study that examined college students' perspectives on body image, aging anxiety, agism, and gender. Results from this study demonstrated associations among objectified body image (surveillance, shame, and control), body-image avoidance, aging anxiety (fear of older people, psychological concerns, physical appearance, and fear of losses), agism, and gender. In another fascinating study, Rittenour and Cohen (2016) used age progression to assess body image-related anxiety. The group exposed to age progression experienced more anxiety and negative emotions. They also tended to deny that the age-progressed photos resembled them. These are two very interesting looks at agism and veneration of the thin-young ideal.

Gendered views

One aspect of midlife body-image concerns societal views that reflect a gender bias. Older women often discuss a dual standard in which aging in men is seen as "natural," and aging in women is seen as a sign of ugliness or decline. Thus, society places judgments on normal changes, such as gray hair, wrinkles, and weight gain, even as women are encouraged to maintain a "youthful appearance" and not "surrender" to signs of aging (Liran-Alper & Kama, 2007). Women feel a constant pressure to achieve these standards, lest they become irrelevant.

The beauty industry has capitalized on these fears, and in many circles, procedures like Botox, plastic surgeries, and other cosmetic procedures have become the norm rather than the exception. Aharoni Lir and Ayalon (2024) point out that "Under the media's influence, women spend increasingly more time managing and regulating their bodies (p. 258)."

Janie is one example. At 45, she felt as if she was at the pinnacle of her career. As a knowledgeable and dynamic pharma rep, Janie was often called on to train newer and younger reps. She enjoyed this role until she noticed how quickly doors opened for the younger, fitter versions of herself. What started to "smooth out" her wrinkles soon morphed into multiple cosmetic procedures, including a liposuction. She soon noticed that she felt okay about herself only when she was seeking the next improvement. "I wish I'd never even started on this roller coaster," she now reflects. "If only women could be fully accepted, wrinkles, grays, and all."

The research affirms Janie's view. One interesting study comes to us from Aharoni Lir and Ayalon (2024). They conducted a qualitative study that focused on the perceptions women have of aging-related appearance changes, as well as how they cope with such changes. The researchers held focus groups with 19 women aged 54–76. At these focus groups, women were shown clips of films starring older characters and were asked to share their impressions. Several themes emerged. These are described below and seem to reflect the diversity of women at midlife and the differing and sometimes contradictory stances they hold.

- *The perception of aging as a loss, accompanied by grief.* Much of the grief contained in this theme has to do with one's appearance being "ruined."
- *Women's perceptions of the gendered aspects of the appearance culture.* Within this theme, there is an "acceptance" tinged with anger and sadness.
- *Beauty care as a choice that contributes to positive control and self-esteem.* Women in this focus group viewed things like putting on makeup as a choice that they could make to feel better about themselves.
- *The need to produce visibility in a society in which older women become invisible.* One participant described aging women as "transparent old women," referencing a sense of invisibility in a society that venerates youth.
- *Age as a release from social disciplining.* For some women in the group, aging allowed them to move away from the norms of the youth-ideal and allowed them to stop engaging in behaviors intended to conceal aging.

Women's relationships with aging, then, are complex and full of nuance. For those who continue to buy into the need to remain youthful, it's helpful to understand the ways aging-related physiological changes shift the body away from the thin-young ideal. These shifts are connected to thinness and weight, as well as the way that the aging body performs. Let's expand our definition of body image to look at this in more detail.

An expanded definition of body image

In Chapter 4, we saw that body image is multifaceted. We looked at the perceptual, affective, and cognitive aspects of body image. Within those definitions, we noted that body image connects to both our actual and idealized appearance, within the context of societal norms that value thinness. We've now expanded this definition to include youth as a facet of body image. This facet seems to play a synergistic role with thinness, leading to body dissatisfaction and a need to control the body's natural changes. These include changes in weight, overall appearance, and the way the body functions or performs.

Now let's zoom out and connect these with the biological changes associated with normal aging.

Weight involves how a person perceives their actual body weight and how this affects self-esteem. During midlife, women often experience a weight gain of approximately 1.5 pounds annually (Immatters, 2023). This weight gain is influenced by hormonal shifts, changes in physical activity, and decreased muscle mass. Similarly, midlife men tend to gain an average of 1–2 pounds per year (Flegal et al., 2012). While this aging-related creep is gradual, it does have psychological consequences, especially in people who have been more conscious of weight.

Men and women are affected in slightly different ways (Fikkan & Rothblum, 2012). In Western culture, women may feel more pressure to maintain a youthful and slim appearance. Slimmer bodies are associated with social and sexual desirability, attractiveness, and increased opportunities in such areas as employment and relationships (Peat et al., 2008; Puhl & Brownell, 2006). The latter study (Puhl & Brownell, 2006), for example, looked at the social stigma faced by larger-bodied individuals and how weight-based discrimination affected their opportunities in various areas of life, including employment and social interactions. It highlighted the advantages thinner individuals tend to have in social and professional environments.

In midlife, these factors may be felt keenly. My client Cara, for example, would often lament that the "young, thin, cute" sales reps in her company found easy access to opportunities to interact with clients. While she was more seasoned, she often felt passed over for workplace promotions. I've heard similar laments for those women entering the often-deflating world of online dating, where those who look their ages or who are less objectively "attractive" are less likely to receive "swipes" (Toma & Hancock, 2016). Those women who are in larger bodies may be more likely to be fetishized in the dating world, something many women are not seeking (Khandpur, 2015).

While aging men are less targeted by societal beauty standards related to youthfulness, they do experience pressure to maintain a muscular physique (McDonald & Thompson, 2016), a goal that may not be realistic as they age. Such societal expectations can contribute to body dissatisfaction and lead to disordered eating, particularly among men who have struggled with body image in the past (Barnes et al., 2020). We'll explore this more in the following section.

Appearance includes aspects like hair, skin, and overall physical features. Appearance-related concerns are common among people at midlife, where the motivation may be to reduce the visible effects of aging. Box 6.1 highlights the many facets of appearance-related concerns. Appearance-related concerns may also be pivotal in transgender people, whose eating disorders can be less about weight and more about achieving a certain physical appearance. In addition to being a factor in the development of eating disorders, such concerns at times are so magnified that they indicate the presence of a more distinct diagnosis, *body dysmorphic disorder* (BDD), which we'll discuss shortly. Because of the many types of appearance-related concerns, Box 6.1 contains many references that can be used for a deeper dive.

Box 6.1   Appearance and body image (and references for further information)

Hair

- *Volume/thickness:* age-related balding and hair loss can affect body image, whether this is connected to "normal" hair thinning/loss or a medical condition such as alopecia (Aukerman & Jafferany, 2023; Peera et al., 2024) or cancer (Gibson et al., 2021). Aging men may be particularly sensitive about hair loss or balding (Aukerman & Jafferany, 2023). Hair is also a "gendered" feature with implications for middle-aged transgender clients who may feel significant appearance-related pressure (Dalzell & Protos, 2020).
- *Texture:* whether hair is straight, wavy, curly, or coily can affect body image. This may be of particular concern for African-American clients. Societal preferences for straight hair are highly rooted in racism (Harris, 2019) but can negatively affect clients whose natural hair is curly or "kinky."
- *Condition:* healthy, shiny hair is often idealized, and factors like dryness, dandruff, or hair loss can affect how someone views their appearance (Nayak et al., 2017; Dimitrov & Kroumpouzos, 2023).

Skin

- *Complexion:* skin tone (light, medium, dark) can be a source of pride or concern. Many cultures have idealized certain complexions tied to race and ethnicity. These perceptions are especially important among African-American clients (Awad et al., 2015) who may be socialized to prefer lighter skin tones.

- *Texture/clarity:* smooth or rough skin, including concerns like acne, scars, or wrinkles, can affect how someone views their skin. Clear skin is often equated with beauty and health, leading some to feel self-conscious about blemishes, pimples, or other skin imperfections (Nayak et al., 2017; Dimitrov & Kroumpouzos, 2023).
- *Wrinkles/lines:* wrinkles, fine lines, or loss of elasticity can alter a person's body image, especially in Western societies that value youthfulness.
- *Body skin:* this includes the appearance of skin on the body – how it feels, whether it has visible signs of cellulite, stretch marks, or other skin changes. This can be one of the challenges associated with pregnancy (Linde et al., 2024).

Face

- *Facial structure:* the shape of the face (oval, round, square, etc.) and features like the nose, jawline, cheekbones, and chin can influence body image (Sicari et al., 2023). A common concern involves protruding cheeks, which can create the illusion of "chubbiness."
- *Eyes:* the size, shape, and color of the eyes, including eyelash length, may contribute to how one perceives their facial beauty (Nguyen et al., 2009; Papadopulos et al., 2019). Eye shape can be especially relevant among people of Asian descent (Nguyen et al., 2009), and various cosmetic procedures are becoming more common. This includes eye-opening surgery, also known as blepharoplasty, which is popular among Asian people.
- *Smile:* teeth (white), lips, and the overall smile are often scrutinized in body image (Sicari et al., 2023).

Body shape

- *Proportions:* the relative size of different parts of the body, such as the waist, hips, shoulders, and bust, can influence body image.
- *Muscle tone/fat distribution:* how muscle and fat are distributed across the body can contribute to a sense of physical attractiveness or dissatisfaction. This is a key aspect for people who are experiencing age-related changes in body fat distribution (Raggio et al., 2020; JafariNasabian et al., 2017).
- *Height:* taller or shorter body frames can either empower or cause feelings of inadequacy, depending on individual or cultural preferences (Song et al., 2023).

Body hair

- *Presence or absence:* hair growth on the body (legs, arms, chest, etc.) is a point of focus in many cultures, with some ideals favoring smooth, hairless skin while others embrace body hair. This can be a significant body-image factor in transgender people (Dalzell & Protos, 2020).

Posture

- *How you carry yourself:* good posture can make a huge difference in how we perceive our body. Standing tall can create the illusion of confidence, whereas slouching may negatively impact self-image.

Other features

- *Hands and feet:* in some cases, hands and feet can be a focus of body image. People may pay attention to nail grooming, the appearance of veins, or overall size and shape.
- *Neck and throat:* the visibility of the neck, throat, and collarbones can be a significant factor for body image. Some may focus on wrinkles, sagging, or other signs of aging in this area. There may also be an idealization of protruding collarbones as a sign of thinness.

Body dysmorphic disorder

BDD involves an intensely obsessive preoccupation with perceived flaws or defects in physical appearance, which may be minor or nonexistent. The perceived flaw can be just about anything. My client Ella was preoccupied with a facial blemish so tiny that I could barely see it, but she was convinced that other people could and that it made her appear "monstrous." Like many body-image disorders, it's sad to see the extent to which people go to hide these minor "flaws" and the amount of pain they cause. Ella would spend countless hours putting on makeup and would often refuse to leave the house because she felt so negatively about herself. Other people I've worked with have focused on the size or shape of their nose, their skin, or any of a myriad of imperfections that make them feel somehow less-than.

Like Ella, people with BDD often engage in repetitive behaviors like mirror checking, excessive grooming, skin picking, camouflaging, or seeking frequent reassurance from others about their appearance. These behaviors are driven by distress and may interfere with daily life. The disorder can lead to significant emotional distress, depression, anxiety, and social isolation (APA, 2013; Phillips, 2004).

As you stop for a moment to consider Ella's story, you've probably noticed some similarities and differences between BDD and eating disorders. While both involve problems with body image and distorted perceptions, BDD is more focused on specific perceived imperfections (such as a nose or skin), while eating disorders are typically centered on overall body shape and weight. People struggling with either of these disorders may engage in body-checking behaviors such as mirror-checking or excessive grooming. They may also be perfectionistic, about both body image and other aspects of life. Finally, there is an overall sense of compulsivity in both BDD and eating disorders. While there are similarities between these concerns, it's usually not difficult to differentiate between them.

There is one presentation of BDD that can be more challenging to distinguish from eating disorders. This is when BDD is associated with body symmetry. This specific form of BDD involves an intense preoccupation with how symmetrical the body or specific features are, even if the asymmetry is not noticeable to others or is minimal. People who struggle with this kind of BDD feel that any perceived lack of symmetry in their face, body, or other features makes them unattractive, flawed, or abnormal.

I met 38-year-old Samantha in an inpatient eating disorder program. This extremely attractive woman was exercising intensely and restricting her food intake to such an extent that she'd fainted at work, scaring her co-workers and resulting in her concerned supervisor urging her to seek help. From the start, it was obvious that while control was one aspect of Samantha's presentation, she was not focused on weight loss or a belief that she was fat. At times, she even commented negatively about how thin her face had become but felt that it was a "necessary tradeoff." As we delved more deeply into the sources of Samantha's distress, she was able to share how anxious she felt about the perceived asymmetry in her body.

It turned out that Samantha was convinced that her posture was uneven, making her stomach look "lopsided." The excessive exercise was focused on achieving more balanced proportions. She also believed that by restricting her food intake, she could maintain a leaner, more symmetrical body. Samantha was ultimately able to shift these beliefs using a combination of medication and therapy.

Performance includes how the body moves, its strength, and its overall functionality. It's not only about how physically strong a person is, as what we are terming "performance" applies to many different body systems – muscles, bones, and joints. These, in turn, affect strength, agility, endurance, and balance. We'll be looking more closely at these changes throughout this chapter.

Body-image concerns related to performance are common among midlife men and women. The biological aging process influences body image and affects a person's self-perception, self-efficacy, and sense of control. Box 6.2 provides a summary of some of the normal biological changes related to aging.

Box 6.2   Physical performance and body image

This table summarizes factors related to performance in aging, focusing on both physical capabilities and how they contribute to body image:

Factor	Description
Hormonal changes	*Decrease in testosterone (men) and estrogen (women).* These hormonal changes drive decreases in bone and muscle mass, slow metabolism, and produce weight gain and contribute to cardiovascular changes. It can also affect sexual desire and functioning in men and women.
Muscle mass	*Decrease in muscle mass with age (sarcopenia).* This becomes more marked at older ages and can contribute to mobility issues (Larsson et al., 2019).
Cardiovascular health	*Decline in heart function and lung capacity with age.* This often starts at midlife, where people may notice shortness of breath during exertion, as well as fatigue and sensitivity to infection (Sharma & Goodwin, 2006).
Bone density	*Decline in bone density due to aging leading to increased risk of injury.* This is especially critical in terms of nutritional health and needs. Osteoporosis can lead to compression fractures and breaks, especially of the hips and spine. A history of eating disorders increases the risk of osteoporosis (Robinson et al., 2017).
Flexibility	*Loss of flexibility due to changes in joints, muscles, and connective tissues.* This can affect the range of motion, increase the risk of injury, impair balance, and increase the risk of falls.
Joint health	*Increased stiffness or pain in joints.* This is commonly associated with arthritis, particularly osteoarthritis, which occurs when the cartilage that cushions joints breaks down over time due to natural aging processes. This leads to pain and stiffness, especially after periods of inactivity.
Endurance	*Decreased stamina and ability to sustain prolonged physical activity.* As people age, their stamina and ability to sustain prolonged physical activity naturally decline due to physiological changes, like muscle loss (sarcopenia), reduced aerobic capacity, decreased joint mobility, and changes in the cardiovascular system (Milanović et al., 2013).

(Continued)

Factor	Description
Balance and coordination	*Decline in motor coordination and balance with age.* Reduced muscle mass and strength in the legs and core muscles affect balance and stability. A breakdown of the vestibular system can lead to dizziness.
Lowered immune function	The immune system declines with normal aging. This can result in increased susceptibility to illness.
Physical activity levels	Regular appropriate exercise maintains strength, flexibility, and mobility.
Self-efficacy	Confidence in one's ability to perform physical tasks. This is the primary effect of performance-related changes.

Men and women each experience a decline in physical performance during midlife, but the nature of this change differs. For women, the decrease in physical performance is linked to the onset of menopause, which can lead to joint pain, reduced flexibility, and slower metabolism (Maki & Resnick, 2000). These biological changes lead to a decline in physical performance and the potential for weight gain. Additionally, women may begin to shift from strong and confident to "weak and compromised." In men, the decline in physical performance is more gradual due to a slower reduction in testosterone, which affects strength and endurance. The changes men experience are often less emphasized in society compared to the physical changes women experience (Lachman et al., 2015). That does not mean that men do not struggle, however.

Margot is a good example of how common biological changes related to aging can lead to body-image and/or eating concerns. Margaret often begins her story with the loss of her husband, which occurred more than a decade ago when she was 40 and he was just 50.

"My husband and I would go to the gym together. We'd bike and lift weights and were rarely still," she says. "I initially resisted going back to the gym because of all the reminders of him there. Now I'm trying to be more active, but I just can't do these things the way I used to. I feel old with a capital O." To Margot, "old" equates with "weak and compromised" and "out of control." It has drastically affected her confidence. Margot is quick to say, "I can't" when friends have suggested active activities, things like whitewater rafting. "This would have been a sure yes when I was a little younger," she says.

To compensate, Margot eats restrictively. She's terrified of gaining weight. "I just don't need the food. I'd be a blimp if I ate more," she says. This has created a vicious cycle, reinforcing her sense of physical frailty and low self-confidence.

"I hardly recognize myself," Margot says. The irony is that an overly thin body is not Margot's ideal; she craves the toned, powerful body she once had.

As you've likely noted, performance-related body-image concerns are also often tied to self-efficacy. Margot's "I can't" is a classic indicator that she does not feel fully efficacious. While aging brings physical limitations, it's how people view these limitations that affects them emotionally (Cash & Smolak, 2011).

As people age, they experience changes in physical abilities, such as strength, flexibility, endurance, and coordination. Do they see such changes as normal? Manageable? Overwhelming? Or something they need to control?

Control is not intrinsically problematic. For example, if someone notes a decrease in muscle mass and engages in gentle weight-bearing exercise, there's no problem. Light weights, yoga, and Pilates are a few examples. Better yet if the exercise is joyful. This was *not* the case for Charlie.

Charlie, a man in his late 60s, is a "former fat kid." His eating struggles started early and have continued throughout his adult life. He often sounds like an advertisement for Weight Watchers with phrases like "I'm just one bite away from being that fat kid again," and "Nothing tastes as good as thin feels." In reality, Charlie's tall, lean frame nearly borders on emaciated. As he's aged, this has become more marked. But Charlie sees himself differently than do concerned family and friends.

Charlie runs at least 5 miles a day, no matter the weather or the effects on his body. "I'm like the mailman – nothing stops me," he says. With smartwatch in hand, he arduously monitors, graphs, and evaluates his blood pressure, recovery rates, and any data he can find. "My body performs even better than when I was younger," he says.

Recently, Charlie sustained a stress fracture but just kept on running. He was surprised at the doctor's reaction and indignant that his body would show any signs of weakness.

Menopause/andropause

Of the biological changes associated with midlife, menopause in women, and andropause in men, is one of the most challenging to navigate. While these phases are distinct in terms of gender, they share similarities in their physical, emotional, and psychological impacts. While we've briefly touched on this topic, let's expand upon it by meeting Jill, a 52-year-old woman who began struggling with an eating disorder after entering menopause.

"Pregnancy, and now this?" Jill laments. "How much more can women take?" Jill's joking manner belied the pain of what she calls "menopause hell." Jill experienced common symptoms like hot flashes, night sweats, and mood swings – her previously strong libido dropped. "I just don't feel sexy," she says. "Whether it's the night sweats or the weight gain, I'm not interested." Jill and her husband are "trying to figure things out," and are hopeful that they will find ways to connect again.

As Jill discusses the trials and tribulations of menopause, control – or lack thereof – is a common theme. "First the symptoms, then the sex, and now scale," she says. "No matter what I did, the weight just keeps piling on." Despite sticking to her usual diet and exercise routine, Jill has gained about 15 pounds, mostly around her abdomen. "I've always been in control of my body, and now I feel like it's betraying me." These factors triggered a sharp decline in her self-esteem. "I just can't hide it anymore," she says. "And I feel awful about myself."

Jill started severely restricting her food intake, cutting out entire food groups, and exercising excessively. Yet, her weight continued to fluctuate, leading to helplessness and frustration. She recently began to binge eat at night. "I can't stop myself when the cravings hit. It's like I'm out of control," she says in a tearful voice. These binges were followed by feelings of shame and self-disgust. "I'm at my breaking point. I think I'm finally ready to deal with this," Jill says. "I just don't know if I can ever accept my body for what it is."

Menopause

Jill's story highlights some of the challenges of menopause. Menopause is a natural physiological transition that marks the end of a woman's reproductive years and is characterized by the permanent cessation of menstrual periods. This typically occurs between ages 45 and 55, though the age of onset and duration vary from person to person (Bacon, 2017). Menopause influences women's physical and mental health, one impact being eating disorders (Baker et al., 2019). In addition to hot flashes and night sweats, women also experience sleep issues, vaginal dryness, and weight gain, as well as possible emotional changes such as mood swings, depression, irritability, and a reduction in self-esteem (Avis et al., 1997).

Andropause

Andropause describes age-related changes in male health, particularly the decline in testosterone levels. It is sometimes referred to as "male menopause" due to the symptoms and hormonal changes that occur as men age. It differs from female menopause, however, in that it involves not a sharp drop in hormone levels but a gradual decline. Typically, andropause occurs between the ages of 40 and 60, although it can happen earlier or later. The condition is linked to testosterone-level decreases – a natural part of aging, but this decline can vary widely among men.

Symptoms of andropause may include fatigue, depression, irritability, decreased libido, sexual dysfunction, sleep disturbance, and increased body fat. Not all men will experience all of these symptoms, and some may experience them to varying degrees. The decline in testosterone can also affect other aspects of health, including bone density, mood, and cardiovascular health.

Jim, a college professor, began experiencing symptoms of andropause at about 50. These included fatigue, reduced libido, mood swings, and occasional irritability. Jim found it difficult to accept the changes occurring in his body. His sense of self-worth, which had long been tied to his professional success and physical appearance, began to erode. He found himself feeling anxious about aging, specifically about his loss of vitality and muscle mass.

Jim's concern about his body led him to become increasingly fixated on his appearance. Jim found that the obsessive calorie counting provided a distraction from his other anxieties as well as the illusion that he could control his aging body. The obsessive counting soon gave way to skipping meals, which Jim was convinced would counteract the weight gain he feared. The eating disorder, which seemed to have evolved as a way for Jim to lessen his anxiety and to regain some control over his changing body, began to take a toll on his mental health. Like Jill, Jim began the process of therapy unsure if he could tolerate being without the reassurance of having a way to "control what is happening to me."

Menopause, andropause, and weight gain

One of the most prominent physical changes associated with both menopause and andropause is weight gain (or fears of weight gain). During menopause, women often report an increase in abdominal fat, slowing metabolism, and a decrease in muscle mass (Lovejoy & Sainsbury, 2008). Similarly, men in andropause also experience an increase in abdominal fat and a reduction in muscle mass as testosterone levels decline (Muller & Roos, 2015).

This weight gain, particularly around the midsection, often affects body image. Women may feel less attractive and less feminine, while men may experience a decline in their masculinity and virility. We saw these factors at play with Jill and Jim.

Studies examining the interplay between menopause/andropause, weight gain, and body image are lacking; one recent study is of note. Medeiros de Morais and colleagues (2024) looked at body-image dissatisfaction and weight gain in a group of women in menopausal transition. About 80% of the women in the study classified themselves as dissatisfied with being overweight, and about 80% of the sample would be considered clinically "obese" or "overweight" by medical standards. Furthermore, these women also tended to overestimate their body size.

While more research is needed, it seems likely that the perception of one's body during midlife can be a significant emotional challenge, as many people are not prepared for the physical changes that occur. While body image lays the foundation, it is in the very individual struggle each person experiences that can lead to or exacerbate eating disorders.

Wrinkles/skin elasticity

Nothing says "aging" more than those fine – or not so fine – lines we all get as we age. For many people, these visible signs of aging affect confidence, self-esteem, and body image. These changes often begin to become more noticeable at midlife and are another area our clients navigate at this already complex time.

As people age, the production of collagen and elastin decreases, leading to a gradual reduction in the skin's elasticity. This loss of firmness and resilience makes the skin more prone to sagging, thinning, and the development of wrinkles, especially in areas where the skin is subjected to repetitive movement, such as around the eyes, mouth, and forehead. There are many factors that contribute to the skin's aging process, such as loss of moisture and fat. Genetics also plays a role, as do factors such as smoking, diet, stress, and excessive sun.

With a focus on youth, smooth skin and foreheads have become another beauty trend that the aesthetics industry has fully embraced with products such as Botox (Gart & Gutowski, 2016; Hong, 2023). Botulinum injections (Botox) are the most common nonsurgical procedure for both men and women across all age groups. The International Society of Aesthetic Plastic Surgeons (ISAPS, 2023) estimates that about 9 million people throughout the world had Botox injections in 2022, a 26.1% increase from the year prior. Women seek cosmetic procedures more often than males (Abelsson & Willman, 2021), although men are seeking cosmetic procedures more often.

While there remains a difference in the volume of procedures between men and women, this is an area to be monitored continuously. The industry predicts continued growth in the cosmetic market for men and for people of color (Schlessinger et al., 2017).

Do these procedures result in increased self-esteem? The jury is out, with studies showing a mixed picture (Jones et al., 2002). While some procedures seem to increase self-esteem and decrease depression, these changes may be short-lived (Botox, for instance, typically lasts only four to six months). Other studies have found continued depression and anxiety after the surgical or nonsurgical intervention (Bascarane et al., 2021). These studies remind us of the importance of taking a body-mind approach and providing support to anyone struggling with self-esteem and/or body image – even when the obvious physical source of such distress is being addressed.

Physical illness

The midlife years are a time when there can be a sudden shift in health status, whether due to a concern related to the physical changes we've just discussed or to a new or worsening disease. At this time, when physical functioning begins to decline, people may also begin to grapple with chronic illnesses (Lachman et al., 2014). Such conditions include high blood pressure, cancer, arthritis, type 2 diabetes, and various autoimmune disorders. The latter can be especially prevalent in women due to an age-related weakening of the immune system combined with hormonal fluctuations connected to menopause. These physical health conditions can contribute to eating disorders/disordered eating. Jamie is a good example of this interconnection.

At 45, Jamie seemed to "have it all," a great job, solid family relationships, and excellent physical health. Jamie had struggled with bulimia at various times in her life, although symptoms had waned in recent years. "I was happier than ever. I'd remarried the man of my dreams and was feeling confident," she says. At first, it was little things. "I was more tired and got cold really easily," she continues. "Then it was the weight gain. I was not connecting with my husband in the bedroom, and I wasn't sure if it was that or something else." Her primary care physician was somewhat dismissive, telling Jamie that these were all signs of perimenopause.

"It just got worse," she says. "My skin was so dry it looked like a peeling sunburn. But the worse was my concentration. I didn't recognize myself." People around Jamie began to think that her illness was psychosomatic. Her husband, who had been supportive, pulled away. "He was MIA. And here I was thinking I must be dying." What made this scenario even worse was that Jamie's own mother had died young, and she was convinced that her kids would soon be motherless.

Jamie went from a top performer at her job to being put on notice that she was at risk of losing it. As the stress skyrocketed, the bulimia returned with a vengeance. Jamie's days became so focused on binging and purging that she ultimately did lose her job, which she now believes was the best thing that ever happened to her.

Jamie was ultimately diagnosed with Hashimoto's disease, an autoimmune disease whose onset is often at midlife. Jamie's bulimia seems to have been an enactment of the chaos of living with this undiagnosed autoimmune condition.

While a full discussion of midlife onset health conditions is not possible, we'll focus on a few in this section – those that seem to be most highly comorbid with body-image and eating disorders.

Cancer

The relationship between cancer and eating disorders is intricate and involves both the psychological toll of a cancer diagnosis and the physical changes brought about by treatment. Some common dynamics include the use of eating disorder symptoms and behaviors to gain a sense of control (Matthews et al., 2019) or as a way of coping with difficult emotions (Krause et al., 2018). Eating disorders can also serve to self-soothe or emotionally regulate (Hossein et al., 2015).

Clients going through cancer treatment need specialized emotional support that addresses the overlap between body-image issues, emotional distress, and eating disorders.

Cancer can occur at any age, but the risk increases with age. Cancer Research UK (n.d.) states that cancer risk increases as we age, with most cases found in people over the age of 50. The most common cancers are breast, lung, colon, rectum, and prostate cancers. A cancer diagnosis is often a life-altering experience, and it can evoke a range of intense emotions that have profound psychological and physical impacts.

When faced with a cancer diagnosis, some common feelings include shock, disbelief, and fear of mortality. While Jamie did not have cancer, "dying young" was a strong fear, as was the sense of disbelief that she could look and feel so badly so suddenly.

Cancer patients often experience significant distress due to the perceived threat to their life and the uncertainty surrounding the treatment process (Mazzocco et al., 2019). Depression and anxiety are common. These emotions are not only a response to the illness itself but are also compounded by the long-term treatments required, which often include chemotherapy, radiation, and surgery (Zhang et al., 2021). Furthermore, cancer patients often report a sense of loss in relation to their former selves, their physical appearance, and their previous sense of normalcy. These changes can exacerbate preexisting body-image issues and contribute to the development or worsening of eating disorders.

The changes in physical appearance brought on by cancer treatments – such as weight loss or gain, hair loss, scarring, and altered facial features – can significantly affect self-esteem and body image. Two major things arise: first, cancer and other debilitating illnesses bring a "new normal" and, second, can result in survivors questioning "Who am I now?" People going through cancer treatments may feel a loss of control or autonomy.

Changes in physical appearance connected to cancer treatments are also incredibly difficult. Some of the common physical changes include weight loss or gain, hair loss, scarring, and altered facial features. All can significantly affect self-esteem and body image and contribute to the development or worsening of eating disorders. Other cancers, including those that affect body parts connected to sexuality, are also difficult. These include gynecological cancer, breast cancer, penile cancer, and testicular cancer. While those may be especially difficult due to perceptions about a loss of sexual desirability/virility, all cancers may be challenging.

Gibson and colleagues' (2021) recent publication looked at the experience of survivors of head and neck cancers, which are among the cancers with the most profound physical changes. The researchers focused on the lack of preparation within medical systems as well as survivors' adaptation to altered appearance. Other researchers have looked at body image and its connection to other types of cancers and cancer-related changes, such as lymphedema and mastectomy (see Kołodziejczyk & Pawłowski, 2019; Morales-Sánchez et al., 2021).

Another interesting study looked at "psychological resilience" as an aid to a more positive body image. Izydorczyk and colleagues (2018) explored the relationship between psychological resilience and body image in women who have undergone mastectomy for breast cancer. The researchers looked at whether resilience could act as a protective factor for maintaining a positive body image after the surgery. The findings suggest that higher levels of psychological resilience, which they operationalized as optimism and capacity to mobilize oneself, openness to new experiences and humor, consistency and determination, coping with negative emotions, and failure tolerance, were associated with better body-image outcomes. The more resilient individuals are better able to cope with the physical and emotional changes after a mastectomy. This highlights the importance of fostering resilience in supporting women's psychological well-being during their cancer recovery, something that is lacking in our current medically focused treatment environment.

Let's pause here to look at how psychological resilience plays a role in fostering more positive body image and self-concept. Ava is a 39-year-old single woman who was diagnosed with Stage 1 breast cancer following a routine mammogram. With a strong family history and a positive BRCA test, Ava opted to go through a mastectomy and reconstruction. "I won't lie," she says. "The decision was tough, and my mom and sister both tried to talk me out of it."

While she knew it would be a long road, she preferred mastectomy to other options. Ava's resilience – as seen through her sense of humor, curiosity, and investment in the process and ability to cope with minor setbacks – was evident. She continued to attend therapy sessions throughout her treatment, even electing for a phone session the day after her surgery.

In fact, Ava was so resilient that her treatment team questioned whether she was being genuine (she was!) She became aware of that as she was joking with the team about using her own body fat for breast augmentation during reconstruction. "I knew those love handles would come in handy," she joked. Ava was excited to celebrate five years post-treatment last month.

Type 2 diabetes

Type 2 diabetes is a chronic medical condition characterized by the body's inability to effectively use insulin. Unlike type 1 diabetes, where the body produces little to no insulin, individuals with type 2 diabetes can initially produce insulin, but their cells become resistant to it over time. As a result, blood sugar levels remain high, which can lead to various complications if not properly managed (Powers et al., 2020).

The onset of type 2 diabetes is gradual and often occurs in middle adulthood, typically around 45 years old, although it can occur earlier depending on individual risk factors. Key risk factors for developing type 2 diabetes include genetic predisposition, a sedentary lifestyle, poor dietary habits, and larger body sizes. The condition is more common in individuals with a family history of diabetes, and it is often associated with other metabolic conditions, such as hypertension and high cholesterol.

There is a strong connection between type 2 diabetes and body size. Excess abdominal fat is considered one of the most significant risk factors for the development of insulin resistance. The connection between body weight and type 2 diabetes also plays a role in body image. Carroll et al. (1999) studied a large sample of people with type 2 diabetes, assessing the correlation between body dissatisfaction and perceived blood glucose control. Participants, especially females, had a higher level of body dissatisfaction, which was associated with a discrepancy between current and desired body perceptions. The presence of binging behavior significantly lowered their self-esteem. Kokoszka et al. (2022) found similar results in their study of 100 adult clients. The authors of both studies conclude that the societal emphasis on thinness coupled with stigma associated with body size can create challenges for people with type 2 diabetes, making it hard to adopt healthy lifestyle changes.

Autoimmune illnesses

Midlife is also a time when autoimmune illnesses may arise for the first time. Between the ages of 40 and 60, the immune system response decreases, and this previously helpful system can begin to damage the body rather than protect it. These result in the so-called "autoimmune diseases of middle adulthood," including rheumatoid arthritis, lupus, myasthenia gravis, multiple sclerosis, Hashimoto's thyroiditis, and Sjögren's syndrome (Cooper & Stroehla, 2023). Autoimmune diseases strike women about four times as frequently as men, which has been explained by a myriad of factors ranging from hormones to evolution differences.

This section will highlight just a few of these illnesses to provide a sense of how they affect people physically and emotionally.

Jamie, whom we met earlier in this chapter, provides an example of some of the difficulties associated with autoimmune illnesses. These diseases often manifest with symptoms such as chronic pain, fatigue, joint inflammation, and skin rashes, which can profoundly affect a person's physical appearance and emotional well-being. Despite how debilitating these symptoms can feel, primary care physicians and specialists often view them as "vague" or "inconclusive." As with Jamie, diagnosis often takes a winding path, and many people with these illnesses are misdiagnosed, their concerns are minimized, or they are met with skepticism. Many women are told that the symptoms are perimenopause or menopause.

I have seen the difficulties experienced by clients who have been met with similar confusion or denial. Deborah, in her early 40s, is another veritable powerhouse, whose energy levels prior to the onset of ankylosing spondylitis were enviable. Her symptoms were, in many ways, even more vague than those of Jamie: severe back pain and stiffness, severely limiting her mobility. Deborah tried several routes to help herself, including chiropractic care, with limited success. Her primary physician was less than helpful, blaming the symptoms on her weight. This left her even more despondent. This trend of long intervals between an initial diagnosis and treatment plan is very common.

Xiang and colleagues looked at the average time for diagnosis of autoimmune rheumatic diseases (such as rheumatoid arthritis, lupus, Sjögren's syndrome, and axial spondyloarthritis). They found long time periods between accurate diagnosis (up to 38.7 months for Deborah's condition). That's more than three years of suffering until any treatment at all. During this time frame, Deborah's efforts to lose weight and follow a gluten-free diet resulted in her relapse into binging behavior. This only worsened the picture.

Autoimmune illnesses can have a profound effect on a person's sense of independence and autonomy, as well as body image. Deborah needed to significantly limit many of her activities. Jamie's story is similar. She also had a difficult time finding a medication that helped lower her thyroid numbers without causing severe racing of her heart. This, her skin dryness and flaking and notable hair loss left her feeling trapped, overwhelmed, and extremely self-conscious about the physical changes.

While each of these diseases can be managed, it's important to take a proactive approach and not allow the effects on body image, self-esteem, and other life areas to be dismissed or minimized. The connection between autoimmune illnesses, body image, and eating disorders is a field that merits further study (Gonzalez et al., 2018; McCormack et al., 2025; Lauriat & Samson, 2014).

A changing relationship with the body (body-in-relationship)

A subtheme throughout this chapter and book has been that at all life stages, including midlife, clients experience a changing relationship with the body. When you think about relationships, what are the elements of a healthy relationship? An unhealthy relationship? As you consider this question, how do these traits apply to the body?

When viewed against the backdrop of biological changes and societal preferences toward youth, this changing relationship may need some navigating, as most complex relationships do. In Chapter 9, we will expand upon these ideas, but for now, here are some areas to consider as clients navigate body changes:

- How and what are clients communicating to their bodies? Is this communication positive or negative? Are there judgments? Are clients listening to what their bodies are communicating to them in return?

- As clients navigate body changes and difficulties, how are they handling discord? Is there a gentle and direct approach that furthers, rather than shuts down, communication? How are key supports navigating conflict?
- Are clients showing up and focusing on their own needs consistently? This idea can be applied to *any* bodily need but is especially important when the body needs rest or nourishment.
- Are clients practicing body compassion and gratitude? Even in cases where there are dramatic shifts in abilities or performance, gratitude and compassion can shift focus in a positive direction.

For further reflection and application

1   As you read through this chapter, did any specific clients come to mind? Are these clients actively working on body image or receiving support for an eating disorder? If the answer is no, did this chapter provide areas to consider further?
2   Think about some of the stories your clients have shared regarding their experiences within the medical system. What do those stories reflect? How might you partner with medical providers to address gaps in knowledge?
3   List five body-related things you are grateful for (see the following resource which uses a small-group format to support gratitude for the body.) It's helpful to try strategies such as this yourself prior to asking clients to do so.

Clinician resource 7: body gratitude

This resource is designed to be a small-group experience. Here's an activity designed to help people experiencing age-related body changes embrace and befriend their new bodies. The goal is to foster self-acceptance, build body positivity, and encourage a healthier relationship with aging.

CLINICIAN RESOURCE 7: BODY GRATITUDE

Materials:

- Comfortable seating (chairs, cushions, or yoga mats)
- A journal, pen, and notebook for each participant

Instructions:

1 **Introduction:**

   - Begin with a short introduction about the importance of acknowledging and accepting the changes our bodies experience over time. This can be done in a prior psychoeducational session or as part of this group.
   - Share that aging invites opportunities for a deeper connection with oneself.

2 **Body scan:**

   - Lead a gentle body scan meditation, encouraging participants to focus on each part of their body without judgment. If you need an example, consider Kristin Neff's "Compassionate Body Scan."
   - Prompt participants to notice any thoughts, images, sensations, or areas of tension. Acknowledge these feelings with kindness, noticing but not trying to change anything.
   - Provide an ending prompt supporting participants in thanking the body for all it has done and continues to do – whether it's the heart beating, the legs supporting them, etc.

3 **Gratitude journaling:**

   - After the meditation, ask participants to take a few minutes to write down the following:

     - Three things they appreciate about their body as it is right now (this could include functionality, resilience, appearance, etc.).
     - One thing they're learning to love or accept about themselves as they age.
     - A specific memory where their body served them well (e.g., running a race, childbirth).

   - Encourage group members to be honest and kind with themselves and in support of other group members.

4 **Sharing in pairs or small group:**

   - After journaling, invite participants to share one of their reflections with a partner or in a small group.

Chapter 7

Affect regulation and its role in midlife eating disorders

While midlife eating disorders can be maintained by any of the factors depicted in Figure 1, a central theme for most adults involves difficulty with emotional/affect regulation. *Affect modulation* (also called *emotional regulation*) refers to a person's ability to manage and respond to emotions without becoming overwhelmed (dysregulated) or needing to numb these emotions. Addictions, eating disorders, and self-harm behaviors are remarkably effective ways of tamping down difficult emotions. Clients like those quoted above discover that eating disorder symptoms, such as restricting, binging, or purging, can provide almost instant relief when they are struggling emotionally.

While at first this may sound appealing, emotional numbing constricts a person's ability to feel any emotions. Over time, symptoms become entrenched, making it harder to process and deal with emotions in a healthy way. For people who also have a history of trauma (that's many clients struggling with midlife eating disorders), emotional numbing is a kind of defense mechanism that protects the person from feelings that are too intense to handle in the moment. However, while it might provide temporary relief, it can prevent them from healing and moving forward. When people habitually feel numb, it can be harder to connect with others, which can lead to a sense of isolation or loneliness. If these are not enough motivation to begin to develop healthier ways to cope and modulate, numbness also affects people's ability to feel joy (and isn't that an essential need?). They may feel emotionally "unwell" or lack a sense of purpose.

While most therapists could agree that such activities as self-soothing, distress tolerance, and radical acceptance are important skills for all of us, feeling emotions can be a hard sell for clients. Sometimes the only "sell" is that eating disorder symptoms have made a person's life unmanageable, or such symptoms are no longer effective at numbing.

Let's take a moment now for a brief self-assessment. How do you manage your own emotions? Which emotions feel the hardest? The easiest? Now think back to your own family of origin. What did you observe about managing and expressing emotions? Was emotional expression welcomed? Discouraged? Now

DOI: 10.4324/9781032615745-8

ask your clients those same questions. You'll likely hear the origin story for clients who have more difficulty tolerating emotions. Alternatively, you may uncover some myths about emotional expression.

A common theme in many of the stories I hear involves people being discouraged from expressing difficult emotions. This can be especially true for male clients. Emotionally hard times often come with the injunction to "pull yourself up by the bootstrap." Another common story is that role models demonstrated extreme stoicism in the face of extraordinary life events – including those which may have been very painful, such as personal losses. Or there may have been a parent whose emotions were so big that there was no room for others to have feelings. Another common theme involves a parent or parents who numbed their emotions with substances like alcohol or food. This list goes on: it's rare to encounter a person with a midlife eating disorder who can feel a strong emotion or emotions and "ride the wave" of the emotion. It's equally rare to find such clients who use healthy ways to soothe or modulate.

As we have seen, a history of trauma can also affect a person's ability to emotionally modulate. Psychologist Dan Siegel coined the term "window of tolerance" to indicate the optimal level of arousal within which people can effectively process and integrate emotional experiences. Repeated traumatic experiences can narrow a person's window, which decreases their ability to tolerate emotional intensity. This can also mean that the person is more easily triggered by reminders of their trauma. Within these more narrow or constricted windows, people can become "hyperaroused" and experience high levels of anxiety, anger, or other difficult emotions, or they may become "hypoaroused," which is a state of shutdown, numbing, or depression. If you are new to Siegel's work, it may be helpful to familiarize yourself with it.

Marsha Linehan (2015) is another pioneer in the field of emotional regulation. Her approach, Dialectical Behavior Therapy (DBT), contains a section on emotional regulation. Written for the therapist to support the client, this can be a helpful way to familiarize clients with many of the skills that they may need. According to Linehan, the goals of emotional modulation are to help people understand and name emotions (helpful, given the alexithymia often seen in people with eating disorders), decrease the frequency of unwanted emotions, and decrease emotional vulnerability and suffering. Another point that Linehan makes in support of learning to feel emotions is that emotions allow for reciprocal relationships by communicating to others (such as through facial expressions) and communication with oneself (such as "gut feelings").

A closely related idea involves distress tolerance (Linehan, 2015). The idea of "riding the wave" of an emotion is an analogy for distress tolerance. Consider the metaphor of surfers, who calmly welcome a wave (the bigger the better), skillfully navigate the crest, and enjoy this peak only to calmly float it out until they reach the shore.

Emotional modulation and distress tolerance can be helpful as can out-and-out distraction. With encouragement (and patience), clients will find what works for them.

This chapter will discuss the important role of emotional modulation in the development and maintenance of midlife eating disorders.

What is a "maladaptive coping strategy"?

As we have seen from the clients we met in these pages, midlife eating disorders are diverse. A factor that connects many midlife eating disorders involves the use of eating disorder symptoms to cope with or manage emotions. What makes eating disorder behaviors "maladaptive" is that they constrict emotions and prevent healthy emotional expression. This negatively affects a person's physical and emotional health.

As you considered the prompt "how do you manage emotions," how did you respond? I spend time with loved ones (including my cats), read, or journal. These may be ways to take stock of what is making me feel a certain way or may allow me to be more mindful of my own experience. Perhaps you mentioned similar coping skills or named things such as going to the gym or taking a mindful walk. Many people have an array of strategies. And while these strategies can reduce emotional intensity, they rarely erase emotions entirely. So even after the intensity of the emotion decreases, there is often a residual emotional load. This is another idea that may take some getting used to for clients.

When you compare reading, petting a cat, or taking a walk with something like binge eating or purging, you can see the contrast and why eating disorders are considered maladaptive coping mechanisms. I have also heard some clinicians refer to eating disorder symptoms as "ineffective behaviors," but I don't see that as completely honest. They can be very effective, albeit harmful.

Positive coping strategies include an array of behaviors, including those that provide temporary distraction from a challenging emotional state, and distress-tolerance skills, which may include strategies to reduce the intensity of emotions or stepping back from emotions and taking stock. Positive coping strategies also include self-soothing, strategies that involve engaging in pleasant, comforting, calming activities focused on the five senses. Examples of self-soothing include looking at beautiful scenery, listening to soft music, smelling a scented candle, tasting some tea, or putting lotion on one's body. We'll look more fully at positive coping strategies in other parts of this book.

Another aspect of emotional modulation is the idea of flexibility regarding choosing emotional-modulation strategies (Dougherty et al., 2020). Dougherty looked at emotional regulation flexibility and disordered eating and found that the lower flexibility was associated with more compensatory behaviors. Thus, the more entrenched the person's eating disorder symptoms are, the less likely they are to seek healthier alternatives (such as self-soothing) and the more likely they are to use strategies to compensate for calorie intake.

What can make it challenging to understand the role that midlife eating disorders play regarding emotional modulation is how complex a person's emotional life can be – especially with the overlay of trauma.

Marybeth is a good example of the complexities of midlife eating disorders as emotional-modulation strategies. At 38, Marybeth has been struggling with the first onset of an eating disorder.

"I've always been particular about how I look," she shares. "But I never thought that I'd have an eating disorder." This was Marybeth's opening statement during her intake session and demonstrated some of the myths she held. Her eating disorder was not about vanity but deeply connected to managing the emotions she'd suppressed about her childhood trauma.

"I had a pretty challenging adolescence," Marybeth says. "By the time I was a high school senior, I was drinking more than most of the guys I dated. And the sex – you don't even want to know about that." As her behaviors escalated, her parents' patience waned. Marybeth was sent to a therapeutic program for troubled teens. "It was the best and worst thing that ever happened to me," she shared. "It helped me to remember what happened to me, but I also saw and heard things I should never have known."

Marybeth recalled several incidents of molestation by her parish priest when she was 8. As her story emerged, her parents became increasingly distant. While they continued to pay for her treatment, they made it clear that they did not believe her. Marybeth literally shut down her own feelings to salvage the relationship with her mother and father. "This awful man hurt me so badly. And my parents would not tolerate one negative word about him or their beloved church," she explained. "Every time they called or on their rare visits, I pasted on a smile. I pretended to be okay."

Now a parent herself, Marybeth struggles. "I am always on edge – tense." A friend helped her identify the fear about her daughter's safety. "It was just so uncomfortable to be that tense. I think that the binging helped initially," she says. "The purging – well, I don't want to gain weight, so what else can I do?" Marybeth acknowledges that the binging no longer brings much relief, but she can't imagine giving it up. "Now I know it's so many emotions. The fear that something bad could happen to my daughter. The anger at my parents. And the out-and-out rage I feel at the priest. He changed my whole life. I am terrified that he's still hurting some other little girl."

Marybeth's story demonstrates the intricacies clinicians find in tracing the tangled roots of midlife eating disorders. Marybeth's symptoms helped her to manage the many emotions she'd been forced to repress. While the binge eating initially provided a respite, it was not an "adaptive" way to manage emotions. The binge eating was soon joined by purging. Purging can also provide a sense of "relief" and "numbing."

In a prior book, my coauthor and I (Dalzell & Protos, 2020) explained that eating disorders can be used to gain power/control, to dissociate from painful emotions, to express pain, as a way to numb or modulate emotions, and as a means of self-harm. Many people with a history of eating disorders – especially trauma survivors like Marybeth – struggle with alexithymia, a term that means "without words for emotions." Alexithymia is a type of avoidance response in which people are forced to shut down their own emotions. Marybeth's need to appear "okay" to her parents was a form of emotional shutdown. As an adult, she often struggled to understand what she was feeling. While Marybeth could not understand her emotional world, she was able to *feel* the emotions on a somatic level. It was a state of hypervigilance and high alert – fears about her daughter's safety and bodily reminders of her own undigested emotions. Until she untangled this complexity, Marybeth was puzzled by her own binge eating.

People like Marybeth who have complex and unnamed emotions also often struggle with internal interoception – an understanding of *what* they are feeling in their bodies. Interoception is a complex neurobiological process that we will summarize later in this chapter. Marybeth was acutely aware of, and uncomfortable with, the tension she felt in her body. She did not realize, however, that this tension indicated how she was *feeling*. Such difficulties with interoceptive awareness can extend to other body cues such as fatigue, hunger, and fullness.

Research on eating disorders and emotional modulation

The idea that eating disorders are a disorder of emotional modulation is not new. What is less well captured in the research, however, is the complexity of people's situations. Marybeth is the rule in my practice, *not* the exception. It's important, then, to fully consider the many factors that play a role in midlife eating disorders. Marybeth found sobriety helpful, but that treatment did not include either trauma work or support for emotional modulation. Thus, we need to take a fuller scope.

Despite the limitations of existing research, a quick review of the literature is helpful for gleaning information for helping clients to emotionally modulate. In the trauma world, it is part of trauma resourcing.

Resourcing refers to the process of developing and strengthening clients' abilities to cope with and manage distressing emotions and memories. These "resources" can include personal strengths, positive memories, and coping mechanisms that can be used to maintain emotional stability when processing traumatic experiences. The goal is to ensure that clients feel safe and grounded, especially when confronting difficult memories, and that they have psychological tools to regulate emotions during the therapy process (Shapiro, 2017). Taking this a step further, it also helps clients not to turn to the eating disorder as a way of soothing, regulating, or grounding.

Research indicates that difficulties in differentiating, describing, and regulating emotions play an important role in eating disorders (e.g., Aldao et al., 2010; Haynos et al., 2018). Leppanen et al. (2022) conducted a meta-analysis to explore associations between maladaptive emotional regulation strategies and eating psychopathology. They found that ruminations and nonacceptance of emotions were most closely associated with specific eating psychopathology. The authors suggest that successful treatment must consider interventions that target emotion regulation, specifically rumination and difficulties accepting emotions.

Functions of eating disorders

If you ask ten people to describe the ways their eating disorders help them to function, you will likely get ten different – but connected – answers. The list that follows shows the many ways that eating disorders can be ways to cope. When people experience stressful situations, they simultaneously experience emotions. The four most common emotions are anger, happiness, sadness, and fear. The other emotions are an outgrowth of these four.

If you think back, for a moment, to the prompt asking which emotion (or emotions) are most challenging, anger, happiness, sadness, and/or fear may have been among your responses. Even happiness, which is arguably the most positive of these emotions, may be challenging. My client Bob grew up in a household in which he and his unruly siblings were *not* allowed direct access to food. There were locks on cabinets, the refrigerator, and anywhere food was stored. As a 40-year-old adult, Bob struggles with binging, which he has traced back to the need to "celebrate" any success (major or minor) – and "any," literally, means anything that could vaguely be a success. He celebrates when his team wins, he has a good night at work, his wife compliments him – the list goes on. While we both know that he could benefit from some deeper trauma work, he's also poignantly aware that he needs to find other ways to express happiness. Binging has created its own host of problems.

A way to "celebrate" is one way eating disorders provide a function for emotional modulation. Some other functions include:

- Numbing/distraction/sedation
- Comfort/nurturance
- Providing a sense of power and control in the face of strong emotions
- A way to dissociate from strong feelings/dissociate from the body
- Expressing pain
- Helping discharge anger
- Releasing tension built up from hypervigilance

Some of these things may surprise you at first. But if you think of the many clients you have worked with, you will likely understand most of these. Let's take a closer look at each.

Numbing emotions/sedation. Many addictive behaviors, including eating disorders, can be a way to numb emotions (Wildes et al., 2010). These emotions can be connected to past trauma (they usually are) or present-day situations. "If I can stuff myself enough, I can sleep at night," a client with trauma-related nightmares reported. Another client used her purging behavior to "numb" rather than sit with difficult emotions. Distraction is also closely related. In difficult moments, eating may offer a temporary distraction or a way to numb uncomfortable feelings.

Using food to numb emotions is a coping mechanism that many people rely on, often without fully realizing it. "Emotional eating" occurs when food is used as a way to deal with uncomfortable feelings such as sadness, stress, loneliness, anxiety, or anger. While eating may provide temporary relief, it doesn't address the underlying emotional issues, and over time, it can become a pattern that's difficult to break.

Comfort/nurturance. Food and eating can feel very nurturing. Our earliest experiences of comfort often occurred with the breast or bottle. Food can be a source of emotional solace, especially in times of stress, sadness, or anxiety. "Comfort foods" may evoke positive memories or associations from childhood, family gatherings, or special occasions. These foods might be rich in flavor, familiar, and often associated with warmth and care. There may be a sense of nostalgia or instant gratification.

One example that comes to mind is Robin, who struggled with her eating disorder lifelong, but first asked for help in her late 40s. She described binging on "cheap chocolate." This would be something she would not desire at other time. As we discussed this, she recognized that when her family emigrated to the United States, they could not afford luxuries, so "cheap" chocolate is what provided comfort in childhood, and when she needed to soothe herself, this was her go-to food. Additionally, foods like chocolate or comfort foods (pizza, chips, etc.) can create a quick "rush" that makes you feel better in the moment.

Power and control. Many people struggling with eating disorders do feel powerless in the face of difficult emotions. Let's consider Marybeth once again. As she shared more of her trauma story, it became apparent that when she was sexually assaulted by her priest, she felt terrified and helpless. When she experienced any closely connected emotion as an adult (including vulnerability), she returned to the eating disorder. In her case, this is when she would restrict her food intake – only to later binge eat.

When a client expresses that an eating disorder is a way to assert power or control, it's helpful to peel back the layers. Why do they need to feel more powerful? Is there an emotional connection here? Like Marybeth, it may be that when they relinquish this rigid control, strong emotions surface.

Dissociation. Eating disorders, particularly those on the binge eating spectrum, are remarkably effective at allowing people to dissociate and to escape from emotional pain. Randy binged to avoid feelings connected to his early trauma. Keith was bullied at work, and binging was the *only* thing that would distract him.

Dissociation often involves a sense of detachment from one's body. For some, overeating/binge eating is a way to re-establish a connection with the body. It can be a method of grounding oneself in the physical world and feeling something tangible, especially if the person feels disconnected from their body or experiences body numbness.

Expressing pain and discharging anger. With the strong connection between alexithymia and trauma, it is not surprising that eating disorders may be a way to express pain. Eating disorders often create changes in the body, and they can be a way to visually show others that we are experiencing pain. Rosey, who just turned 30, is an example. Rosey is a transgender female, and family members refused to use her name and pronouns, which created sadness and anger. Rosey's visible weight loss helped her parents and other family members to recognize her pain. Restricting her food intake was a way to discharge anger.

Release tension. This function refers to the use of eating disorders to release somatic tension. Such tension may result from emotional suppression or hypervigilance. If you think back to Marybeth's situation, this idea comes across in her story.

Interoception

Interoception refers to the perception of bodily sensations and signals from within the body – providing a moment-by-moment mapping of the body's internal landscape (Khalsa et al., 2018). Interoceptive awareness is the ability to recognize, interpret, and respond to these internal bodily cues, such as hunger, thirst, and fatigue. Hilde Bruch (1978) was the first person to identify a disturbance of body cues in anorexia. Today, we recognize the validity of that facet of many eating disorders (it is not limited to anorexia). Many studies demonstrate the strong connection between interoceptive awareness and emotional modulation (Frank et al., 2019; Khalsa et al., 2022), especially in people with midlife eating disorders.

Interoception is a complex biological process that includes several facets. Sensing, interpreting, and integrating information about the body is related to different elements such as interoceptive attention, detection, discrimination, accuracy, insight, sensibility, and self-report (Khalsa et al., 2022). Thus, while a person may attend to an internal state, such as tension, racing heart, there may be a lack of insight into what that state is communicating. Alternatively, there may be a tendency to overfocus on such a state, such as in clients who struggle with anxiety and may notice even minor bodily changes or interpret these changes through a negative or pessimistic lens. People who have eating disorders may struggle with any facet of interoception. Some common things I see are a failure to attend to where they are feeling certain emotions or sensations in the body, what the body is communicating on a sensory level (e.g., "I am tired"), or how intensely they are feeling something (an over- or underevaluation of hunger or fullness). There may also be a misuse of food to address physiological cues, such as eating sugar to wake up if a person experiences fatigue.

Khalsa and colleagues (2022) link difficulties with interoception to several mental health concerns, including eating disorders, panic disorder, substance use disorder, generalized anxiety disorder, and post-traumatic stress disorder (PTSD). Due to the comorbid nature of these concerns, it's helpful to be aware of the many ways interoceptive difficulties manifest and to ask clients specific questions about their internal states, experiences of body cues, and emotional connection.

Interoceptive awareness and emotional modulation. The connection between interoceptive awareness and emotional regulation has been highlighted in various studies. Emotions are often accompanied by physiological responses, such as changes in heart rate, breathing, and muscle tension. People with a high level of interoceptive awareness are better able to identify and manage their emotional experiences (Füstös et al., 2013). When people can more accurately assess their emotional states, they can respond appropriately, whether it is through self-regulation, empathy, or effective decision-making.

For example, imagine you are in a meeting and you begin to notice that your heart is racing and your breathing is more shallow. What emotion are you feeling? Interoceptive awareness enables you to recognize these sensations as signs of anxiety. This may signal "I should try to use some coping or self-soothing strategies, such as deep breathing or relaxation exercises." In contrast, individuals with low interoceptive awareness may be less likely to identify these physiological signs and may struggle with managing their emotions, leading to heightened emotional distress (Domschke et al., 2010).

Some common somatic cues are listed in Table 7.1.

Table 7.1 Interoceptive and Emotional Awareness

Physical sensations	
Hunger	Empty feeling in stomach, growling or rumbling noises
	Light-headedness or weakness
	Irritability or low energy
	Craving specific types of food
Fullness	Stomach begins to feel some pressure and tightness
	Food may not be as tasty
	Better mood or focus
	Fewer thoughts about food, cravings have been satisfied
	May have more energy, may feel a little bit of sleepiness

(Continued)

Table 7.1 (Continued)

Physical sensations	
Thirst	Dry mouth or throat
	Fatigue or headache
	Dark yellow urine or infrequent urination
	Craving for water or fluids
Sleepiness/fatigue	Drowsiness or yawning
	Difficulty keeping eyes open or focusing
	Slower reactions or thoughts
	Heaviness in limbs

Emotional sensations	
Anxiety	Racing heart, shallow breathing
	Butterflies in stomach or nausea
	Tightness in chest or throat
	Restlessness or feeling on edge
	Sweating or shaking
Anger	Increased heart rate or blood pressure
	Clenched fists or jaw
	Hot sensation in face or body
	Tension in shoulders or neck
	Feeling flushed or "pumped up"
Sadness	Heavy or tight chest
	Tears or lump in throat
	Low energy or motivation
	Slumped posture or feeling small
	Decreased appetite
	Oversleeping
Happiness	Warm, light, or fluttery feeling in chest
	Smiling or laughing spontaneously
	Increased energy or excitement
	Calm or peaceful feeling
	Euphoria or contentment
Fear	Rapid heart rate or palpitations
	Dry mouth or difficulty swallowing
	Shallow or rapid breathing
	"Cold sweat" or chills
	Butterflies in stomach or dizziness
Relaxation/ calmness	Slow, steady breathing
	Reduced muscle tension or softening of body posture
	Warmth in chest or face
	Deep, comfortable sighs or yawns
Guilt	Heavy or sinking sensation in the chest or stomach
	Tension or unease in the body
	Uneven breathing or difficulty making eye contact
	Restlessness or nervous fidgeting

As you scanned this table, were there any surprises? If you ask many midlife clients "What does hunger feel like?" or "What does fear feel like?" or any question connected to physical or emotional sensations, they may have difficulty responding. Providing them with guidelines like the one above is often helpful. Conversely, some clients recognize cues to experiences such as hunger only when it has reached a more intense level. There are also hunger and fullness scales you can offer such clients, but I find it simplest to ask, "were you a little hungry," "moderately hungry," or "extremely hungry?"

Emma is a good example of a client who'd spent so much time ignoring her hunger cues that she rarely recognized them until the hunger was intense. With a long history of food restriction and compulsive exercise, Emma did not follow the common course we often see at midlife – binging – but instead doubled down on the exercise. She spent hours each day exercising. Like many people with interoceptive difficulties, Emma also struggled with emotional awareness.

At 44, Emma is not new to her eating disorder. "Even though this started in my 20s, I think I am finally ready to make a change," she says. "I am just so tired of this being my whole world." Emma's eating disorder began shortly after graduating from college and leaving her parents' house. "It was the perfect storm," she says. "I could eat, or not, whenever I wanted." At times in her life, Emma has had periods of partial remission but has been struggling more since she turned 40. "There's just something about 40 that sounds so old," she shares. "I feel like people take me less seriously rather than more."

Emma's history and current symptoms include food restriction and compulsive exercise. She also has trouble with connecting with her body and its cues. "I never feel hungry," she says. "I usually wait until I feel dizzy to eat anything."

Emma's emotional state is also closely tied to her eating. She experiences significant anxiety about food and body image, and her anxiety frequently manifests as physical tension and stomach discomfort. However, Emma has difficulty recognizing these bodily sensations as emotional signals. Instead, she interprets them solely as reasons to engage in restrictive eating or exercise. The lack of interoceptive awareness complicates her ability to regulate her emotions effectively, as she is unable to identify the root causes of her distress or use her body signals to indicate the need to soothe using more positive strategies.

Supporting clients in emotional modulation and interoception

Teaching emotional modulation and interoceptive awareness involves fostering a deeper connection with emotions and body sensations. This section provides a brief overview of some approaches that enhance interoceptive awareness. These include self-monitoring, mindfulness, and emotional-regulation techniques.

Self-monitoring (Snyder, 1974) is the ability to observe one's inner and outer states and to adjust based on situational cues. This term is often used in response to social cues, but here we are using it more broadly to include observing and tracking one's thoughts, feelings, behaviors, and body sensations. Some techniques for self-monitoring include emotional/somatic recognition (identifying specific emotions), journaling, and self-reflection. Such increased self-awareness allows for understanding of patterns and triggers, leading to improvements in emotional regulation.

Mindfulness practices are another effective method to support emotional modulation. Mindfulness practices improve awareness of emotions and promote acceptance of difficult feelings. Mindfulness cultivates a nonjudgmental awareness of internal experiences, including emotions, thoughts, and physical sensations. Mindfulness exercises, such as body scans, encourage individuals to focus on different areas of their body, paying attention to any emotions, sensations, or discomforts without judgment. In addition to reduced reactivity, mindful activities such as reappraising situations, shifting perspectives, and engaging in more adaptive coping mechanisms can lead to greater cognitive flexibility.

While we often think of mindfulness as connected to meditation and more internal experiences, somatic exercises also fall into this category. Activities such as yoga or tai chi can promote body awareness by encouraging individuals to focus on their breath and movements, fostering an enhanced connection to internal bodily states (Kabat-Zinn, 1990). These practices not only improve interoceptive awareness but also contribute to better emotional regulation by promoting relaxation and reducing stress.

Other useful techniques can be found in emotion-focused therapy (Greenberg, 2002) and sensorimotor psychotherapy (Ogden & Fisher, 2015). These approaches emphasize body awareness to regulate emotions and process trauma. By helping people become more attuned to their bodies, therapists can assist in improving emotional modulation and overall psychological well-being.

For further reflection and application

1 What emotions are hardest for you, the therapist, to tolerate? Which emotions are you most aware of? What helps you to cope? This may be helpful for you to assess, as well as your clients.
2 Do you practice self-monitoring? Mindfulness? If so, what have you noticed about these techniques? These are often helpful as a tool for therapists as well as clients.
3 As you consider the clients you work with, which functions of eating disorders seem to apply most broadly? Were there any on the list that you found unfamiliar or surprising?

Clinician resource 8: emotions in motion

Here's a simple therapy activity designed to help with emotional tolerance and/or modulation. It combines mindfulness, emotional awareness, and self-regulation techniques and is applicable to a variety of settings. It can be used in an individual or group context.

CLINICIAN RESOURCE 8: EMOTIONS IN MOTION

Grounding and relaxation

- Have clients begin by finding a comfortable space to sit or stand. Ask the client to close his or her eyes and breathe deeply, inhaling slowly for four counts, hold for four counts, and exhaling for six counts. Repeat this breathing pattern for one to two minutes until the client is relaxed and grounded.

Identifying emotions

- Ask the client to think about any strong emotions that have surfaced recently or may be occurring right now. You may wish to have a feelings wheel or list handy for clients who experience more difficulty connecting to emotions.
- As clients run through the emotions they have noted, ask them to observe where in their body they feel the emotion and how that emotion shows up (e.g., tight chest, clenched fists, warm cheeks, a feeling of openness or expansion).

Body movement and expression

- Ask the client to choose one emotion to focus on, then begin to move the body in response to the emotion. The movement should start out gently and then become clearer, even exaggerated as the emotion intensifies. An example of moving in response to the emotion is that if they are feeling anger, they could make movements like stomping their feet, clenching their jaws, or shaking their fists. Some clients may need to envision the story connected to the emotion or the person. For clients with more difficulty, you can choose a more positive or neutral emotion, such as joy or enthusiasm.
- Spend three to four minutes moving with each emotion they identify. After each emotion, pause and check in with how the body feels. Try to refrain from verbal processing in the moment, as it can take a person out of the experience.
- Ask clients to notice when the emotion begins to peak and recede. If the emotion remains and feels uncomfortable, try the breath pattern 4, 4, 6 to release the emotion.

Processing and mindful reflection

- Process the emotions that arose during the activity, exploring why certain movements or emotions came up and how the client can apply emotional

modulation techniques in real life. Some questions that are helpful to ask the client to consider:

- Why am I feeling this emotion right now?
- How intense is the emotion (1–10 scale)?
- How did my body feel during the movement?
- How did I feel after expressing the emotion physically?
- Have any emotions shifted or changed throughout the activity?
- What do I need to do now? How do I follow up (e.g., specific forms of coping, soothing, or emotional modulation)?

- If further exploration is indicated, clients may continue this process for homework.

Chapter 8

Transitions and midlife eating disorders

Midlife is a period of transition, marked by psychological, relational, and physical changes to a person's life and within the family life cycle. We don't always consider the role of changes such as empty nest, changes in family structure, losses, and caretaking – and their contribution to midlife eating disorders. In adolescence and young adulthood, for example, the theme of transition is common; for many young men and women, eating disorders follow life changes such as transitioning from high school to college. Just as adolescence is a time of shifting identity, pressures, and changes in environment and support systems, so is middle adulthood. The compounding nature of these changes can overwhelm existing coping mechanisms, making individuals more vulnerable to eating disorders as a form of emotional regulation or self-control. Eating disorders can also be a way to distract from emotional pain, to create a sense of "routine," and to help people express difficult emotions.

Midlife transitions are unique in that they often represent an accumulation of multiple shifts occurring in a condensed timeframe. Sasha, whom you met in Chapter 1, was experiencing both simultaneous potential loss of her job and her mother's health concerns. Carla had similar factors: a workplace in which she felt devalued, passed over in favor of younger coworkers, and a mother whose dementia came with new and emotionally complicated caregiving responsibilities. Susan, who had recently seen two children off to college, was facing a shift in her role as a mother and wife. John was struggling with the loss of his mother-in-law and his husband's wish to relocate. As you can see, it's often more than one change, and the changes do not have to be wholly negative. Whether a positive, neutral, or negative change (often a literal or figurative loss), change can be challenging.

This chapter will focus on the many transitions of midlife. We will take a detailed look at several typical transitions, including:

- Empty nest leading to changing roles
- Changes in marital/partnership relationships
- Significant losses/deaths

DOI: 10.4324/9781032615745-9

- Other changes in relationships, such as becoming a caretaker
- Career stresses and changes

While these changes are universal, people experiencing them often feel sadness, loss, or other strong emotions when they occur. These transitions may also conflict with a person's other priorities or demands. Employer may provide time off to workers who must manage their aging parents' health concerns, and work colleagues often express impatience or messages that suggest a lack of commitment to one's career. Such time off may be unpaid. It may be challenging to navigate competing concerns, adding stress to already stressful life events.

Beyond lack of social support, men and women with eating disorders also experience feelings of disengagement and loneliness. There has been some research into the relationship between loneliness and emotional dysregulation as connected to binge eating in bulimia and binge eating disorder (Southward et al., 2014). The role of loneliness can be circular; it can be a causal factor and a sequela of disordered eating. The eating disorder can *become* one's primary relationship.

This chapter will illuminate these themes through case illustrations. Susan, whom we met in Chapter 1, is a good example of eating-disorder onset after her children moved out. When this occurred, her husband distanced himself, coping through longer working hours and leaving Susan alone at dinnertime. Susan's social supports were minimal, and her primary relationship became the one she developed with an eating disorder.

In this chapter, we will also meet Troy, a 70-year-old man. Troy has always had a challenging relationship with food. As a younger person, he was larger than his peers, which changed when he got older and grew taller. Troy has always had relational difficulty and believes he may have an undiagnosed autism spectrum disorder. His current marriage is his second; he was married in his 20s and 30s but divorced for many years afterward. He has minimal contact with his adult children. During his divorce, he struggled with alcohol abuse but is now sober. Troy has recently retired from a demanding but satisfying job, though this has been a significant loss. He and his wife hope to travel in their free time.

Later, we will learn about Troy's responses to his wife's development of dementia, a very difficult life transition during which he coped by engaging in compulsive cardio exercise and weightlifting. His and other stories in this chapter illustrate how transitions can contribute to the onset or exacerbation of midlife eating disorders.

Midlife challenges, roles, and opportunities

A central theme throughout this book has been the changing landscape of research and theory of midlife development. Those of us lucky enough to have reached this or a later developmental stage may have seen firsthand that many misconceptions exist about the nature of midlife and the developmental mile-stones and challenges faced by middle-aged adults. Margie Lachman (2015) and colleagues have rallied around this developmental timeframe, encouraging exploration as a means of debunking false narratives and increasing resilience. Lachman and Infurna et al. (2020) view midlife as a developmental period that encompasses a unique constellation of roles and life transitions that are distinct from those of earlier and later life phases. This is a pivotal period focused on balancing gains and losses, linking earlier and later life periods, and bridging generations (Infurna et al., 2020).

A defining feature of midlife includes balancing multiple roles while expe-riencing life transitions. While each person is unique, by midlife, people will have typically become adept at balancing multiple roles. These roles include family roles (spouse/partner), career- or work-related roles, friendships, caregiv-ing (for children, parents), and roles within community, political, or religious organizations (Infurna et al., 2020). During this time, they may also experience life transitions related to marriage and marital decisions (divorce, widowhood, remarriage), parenthood (or not), multiple careers, launching children into adult-hood, and retirement planning. These are some of the more common transitions associated with middle age.

One of the interesting features of middle adulthood includes middle-aged adults' central role in bridging generations (Infurna et al., 2020), acting as the "glue" of sorts for older and younger generations. Middle-aged adults often translate ideas, values, and experiences between generations, helping older gen-erations understand shifts in identity, language, or cultural norms. They may find themselves the organizers of things like family get-togethers, phone calls, or group chats. Middle-aged adults may pass down wisdom or teach life skills. The most well-known aspect of bridging generations involves providing emotional and practical support. They are part of the so-called "sandwich generation" in which they may be charged with taking care of both their aging parents and their own children. This is perhaps one of the biggest challenges of midlife and is often an aspect of midlife eating disorders. We'll look at this in depth later in this chapter.

In looking at midlife, it is sometimes hard to separate challenges and opportu-nities. Midlife comes with a mix of reflection, transition, and at times turbulence. Some challenges are universal, while others depend on personality, culture, or life circumstances. During this developmental phase, people are often at the pin-nacle of their careers and at the peak of their earning potential. They may also have a greater ability to engage in family leadership, community, volunteerism, and spiritual practice. There may be an opportunity (however difficult) to look at one's identity and assess or reassess meaning and direction. Such reevaluations can also occur because of an empty nest. As children grow and leave home, there is often a need to reconnect with a partner or rediscover parts of oneself. Some people end up confronting longstanding relationship dissatisfaction, leading to either repair or endings. At midlife, we may also see a growing intolerance for inauthenticity – whether in work, relationships, or self-expression.

While any of these factors can contribute to eating disorders, depression, or psychological distress at midlife, many people also thrive at this time. Maria, a recently retired high school teacher and mother of three, is one example. Her youngest child has just started college. This is the "first time in three decades that the nest has truly been empty," she says.

With her children grown and her career behind her, Maria now finds herself with the freedom and time to explore aspects of life that were previously placed on hold. "It's a mixed bag," she says. "I am not sure what this next chapter brings, but all in all, I'm excited to find out." Maria has started engaging in activities that hold deep personal meaning. She has joined a local meditation group, is journaling daily, and is taking courses in comparative religion and philosophy. She describes a growing desire to understand her place in the world beyond her roles as mother and teacher.

"I am feeling more grounded and alive than I have in years," she says. She views this phase of her life not as an ending but as a beginning – an opportunity for personal and spiritual growth now that her primary caretaking responsibilities have shifted.

Understanding loss as a broad construct

In contrast to Maria, some people – especially those with eating disorders – point to loss in their lives. *Loss* is a multifaceted construct that encompasses both tangible and intangible experiences. Tangible losses include concrete events, such as the death of a partner, job loss, or physical health decline. Intangible losses, however, involve abstract but deeply impactful experiences, such as the loss of identity, purpose, or a sense of control (Boss, 2006).

Loss disrupts a person's sense of continuity, identity, and security. It can also challenge assumptions about oneself and the world. When people experience loss, particularly in midlife when multiple losses may converge (e.g., career changes, relationship shifts, physical aging), it can trigger a crisis of meaning and evoke grief, anxiety, or helplessness (Neimeyer, 2001).

Losses often require the individual to reconstruct their identity and worldview, a demanding task that can lead to emotional instability. Unresolved or unacknowledged loss can result in various psychological and behavioral sequelae, including depression and anxiety, substance use disorders, and disordered eating and/or eating disorders.

Let's now apply these concepts to some of the developmental transitions we've already looked at. Family and role changes, such as empty nest and changing parental roles, can be challenging for some like Susan. For Susan, the loss of day-to-day parenting responsibilities led to a shift in her identity and a sense of purposelessness. "I was no longer a mom," she says. "I didn't know exactly who I was. But dieting and exercise allowed me a sense of purpose." Carla's complex history is more recently punctuated by the loss of her personal freedom as caregiving becomes a central role in her life, as well as the loss of career stability; competing with younger colleagues has left her feeling under-valued and pushed aside at work. "Skipping lunch" has led Carla into a cycle of binging and weight gain.

Other losses include the loss of emotional intimacy or connection that some partners experience, the disability or loss of a partner or spouse, changes in health or self-identity, or existential losses such as unrealized dreams or life goals. Table 8.1 describes some of the common losses associated with midlife eating disorders and corresponding opportunities.

Table 8.1 Transitions (Losses and Opportunities) Associated with Midlife

Transition	Losses	Opportunities
Family changes		
Empty nest and changing parental roles **Caregiver to aging parents/"sandwich" generation**	Shift in parenting responsibilities can lead to identity changes and may create emotional distance or search for new meaning Shifting dynamics as the parent-child or relationship shifts; loss of freedom and increased stress	*Rediscover own identity and passion; cultivate deeper relationships with children/partner; practice self-care* *Deepen bonds with parents and partner; develop resilience, empathy, and purpose through caregiving; increased ability to multitask or assess priorities*
Disability or death of a spouse/ partner **Changes in partnership relationships** **Marital/partnership distance** **Infidelity**	Loss of companionship and shared life plans; adjustment to life as a single person or caregiver Decrease in intimacy or connection as partners grow in different directions; may reveal incompatibilities Betrayal of trust, grief, dissolution of the relationship	*Cultivate a support network and engage with community; rediscover parts of self through solo growth* *Personal growth, independence; potentially rekindle the relationship in a healthier form* *Clarify boundaries; open the door to healthier, more authentic relationships*

(Continued)

Table 8.1 (Continued)

Transition	Losses	Opportunities
Grief/loss of loved ones		
Death of family members or friends **Loss of community or social circles**	Awareness of mortal self and others; grief and complex grief Relocation or death can reduce social interaction and result in loneliness	*Deepen appreciation for life and relationships; create new ways to honor and remember loved ones* *Build new communities aligned with current values and lifestyle*
Career and financial		
Retirement (voluntary or involuntary) **Layoffs, job instability, or career changes** **Competing with younger colleagues**	Shifts in identity; less routine and purpose; potential financial concerns Increased vulnerability, fewer opportunities for older workers Feelings of being outdated, undervalued; struggle to keep up with evolving technology or work culture	*Freedom to pursue dreams and hobbies, volunteer work, travel* *Reinvent career paths aligned with values or passions; explore entrepreneurship or flexible work* *Embrace mentorship and leadership roles; focus on collaboration rather than competition*
Existential or emotional loss		
Unrealized dreams or life goals	Reflecting on what hasn't been achieved can bring regret or disappointment; a sense of "time running out" or mourning the "road not taken"	*Make peace with the past and focus on the present; redefine dreams to align with current values*

One commonality of the role changes shown above is the relational nature of the challenges. This is a repeated theme in this book. Midlife presents a unique convergence of challenges that are deeply relational in nature. We have seen that growth and healing occur through meaningful connections, and midlife often disrupts or redefines key relationships, whether through the empty nest, caregiving roles, or partnership changes. Using Jordan's (2016) Relational Cultural Therapy (RCT) as a lens allows us to look at the challenges and opportunities of shifting relationships.

For example, becoming a caregiver to aging parents while adjusting to an "empty nest" forces individuals to renegotiate their roles in longstanding relationships. These shifts can challenge one's sense of identity, but a relational lens invites us to view these changes as opportunities to deepen mutual empathy, foster authenticity, and cultivate growth in connection – with children, partners, and themselves.

Loss – whether of loved ones, social circles, or roles in the workforce – also marks midlife and can foster feelings of disconnection, grief, or inadequacy. RCT reframes these moments as junctures for building or rebuilding relational resilience. The pain of infidelity or marital distance, for example, may not only expose disconnection but also open pathways to re-engage in more authentic, emotionally attuned relationships. This was the case for Susan, whose stuckness in seeing the relationship with her eating disorder as her only important relationship was initially hard to shake. She slowly began to trust her treatment team and interact with her daughters in a more reciprocal way. They stepped up to support her in ways that her husband could not, and while we were initially concerned that this would be too much pressure on her children, they matured in unexpected ways. Being involved in Susan's therapy bolstered her children's confidence, and they and Susan all became closer. Ultimately, Susan was able to resume more of a parental role. While she and her husband have not been able to heal their distance, Susan has been able to reframe it and is currently focusing on creating an attuned relationship with herself.

Likewise, career disruptions or health changes challenge personal and social identity. These can also be met with unexpected support networks that affirm worth beyond productivity. Several of my clients who have faced layoffs or career changes have used the resources provided by their current places of employment to reassess their own career goals, and they have connected with men and women going through similar transitions.

It is connection – not isolation – that provides a path to rediscovery, healing, and meaning. This will be more fully illustrated in the next section and as I share more of Troy's story.

Family role changes

Family role changes are among the most common midlife transitions. These include empty nest, assuming caregiving roles (for own parents or partners), or changes in marital/partnership arrangements due to growing apart, infidelity, or other reasons.

Let's return now to Troy, who recently retired with the goal of traveling and spending time with his wife. Troy initially sought out therapy as he contemplated retirement and made the decision to move on from a lucrative but demanding position. He'd been retired only about a month when he noticed signs of his wife's memory issues. "I just didn't notice anything when I was working," he said. "But the more I noticed, the more obvious it was." Initially, Troy responded to his wife's cognitive decline with impatience, attempting to show her that her thinking was "illogical." When he was able to understand that she had no control over the memory issues, he was able to shift to a more neutral and compassionate approach, and he even had a brief period when he felt closer to her and as if he was helping.

As his wife's condition ultimately progressed, her personality became angrier and more combative. "I think if she'd let me continue to help her or was nicer, I could have handled it better," he said. The final straw came when his wife left their home in the middle of the night, and when the police brought her home, she angrily told them that he was "holding her prisoner." Shortly after, Troy made the difficult decision to admit her to a memory care facility.

At first, her absence was a relief. Then the reality began to sink in. "It was all over," he said. "All of our dreams for travel, connection. Gone." Troy started a new hobby – running – short distances at first, and then more. "I just wanted to be healthier," he said. Next came the prepackaged low-fat, high-protein meals. Troy's weight plummeted, and he had less energy. Troy finally sought help after he nearly passed out on a run.

As Troy began to share more of his struggles in therapy, we were able to reassess what he wanted his life to look like. "I spent my professional life making money," he shared. "Now I'd really like to give back." Troy volunteered at a local food pantry and felt good about helping his community and the connections with other volunteers. "I feel like I am accepted for *me* for the first time in my life," he shared. "Not for the expertise I bring to a career or employer."

As Troy adjusted to this "new normal," his exercise decreased, and he was able to add back many of the foods he'd been missing.

Troy's story illustrates the difficulty of family role changes, as well as the ways that aligning with current values and new connections can be helpful in supporting change. As we have already seen, this developmental stage is one in which health concerns often arise or intensify. When this occurs, there is often a need to re-evaluate priorities and focus. While Troy and his wife were managing a very difficult and unanticipated circumstance, situations like this do occur frequently.

Let's turn now to some common midlife family changes and look at how eating disorders may step in to fill a need or provide comfort.

Empty nest

"Empty nest" is a phase experienced by middle-aged parents when their children reach adulthood and begin to live independently, away from their family homes. This period may start when children leave home for college, marriage, or jobs. From Chapter 3, you may recall Lara, whose child left home for college. Similarly, Susan had empty nest times two, with both daughters leaving for college.

More than any in this book, her story illustrates how challenging this transition can be. These struggles are so common that the symptoms of depression, loss, and loneliness that many people experience when children leave home have been called *empty nest syndrome.* Some of the signs of empty nest syndrome include loss of purpose and motivation, loss of control, irritability, loneliness, and constant worries about children (Khatir et al., 2024). Some authors speak about the empty nest as an expected stage in the family life cycle, associated with loneliness, depressive symptoms, and sociability (Kristensen et al., 2021; Murugan et al., 2022).

Murugan and colleagues (2022) looked at a group of empty nesters to assess whether they were experiencing psychological concerns. They found 61% of the participants they surveyed were lonely, 17% reported to have depression, and 52% experienced low to minimal social support. Loneliness and depression were found to be correlated. This study is representative of other recent studies cited here. While there have not been formal studies that have found connections between empty nest and eating disorders, this is a strong anecdotal connection.

Some of the factors that seem to mediate whether parents struggle with empty nest include whether parents have a strong sense of personal identity outside the parenting role (those who have had the primary responsibility for caretaking may struggle more), the strength of bonds with partners, friends, and support systems, those who feel excited about their newly found sense of freedom, and the ability to create new routines and responsibilities. In contrast to these healthy dynamics, she had neither a strong connection with her partner nor a sense of purpose beyond parenting, until the eating disorder filled that purpose.

Eating disorders can sometimes emerge or intensify during the empty nest as a way of coping with difficult emotions or filling psychological voids. They can serve certain psychological or emotional functions at this time, several of which can be seen in Susan's story. Eating disorders – especially anorexia – can be used to reassert control over at least one part of life (food, body, routines) when other parts feel uncertain. "If I can't control the girls being gone, at least I can control what I eat," Susan would often say. For Susan, being a parent was her core identity. When that role shifts, people may seek a new focus – sometimes turning to body image, health, or weight in a way that becomes obsessive. Susan would often make comments like, "If I'm not needed as a mom anymore, maybe I can be really good at being thin." As she became thinner and thinner, the intensity with which she held on to her eating disorder intensified.

The absence of daily caregiving can lead to feelings of emptiness, loneliness, or grief. Food restriction or bingeing may function as a distraction, a form of self-soothing, or even an unconscious way to *feel something* when numbness sets in. Conversely, many people struggle with the intense emotions that come with an empty nest – grief, guilt, regret, and fear of aging. Eating disorders often function as a numbing tool or a form of emotional regulation.

Eating disorders can also provide a sense of coping with a strained or nonexistent relationship. Once children leave, unresolved issues in a relationship may become more apparent. Disordered eating can serve to distract or to manage anxiety. Eating disorders can also be a less conscious way to bring a spouse or partner closer – such as an effort to become more appealing or to appeal to a partner's sense of loyalty as the need for more care becomes apparent. As in earlier ages, eating disorders can be a way to seek nurturance and support.

Caregiver to aging parents

In the United States, the number of those who provide caregiving for older adults (defined as those aged 50 or older) has increased by 7.6 million since 2015, with one in six Americans now providing care for an older adult (National Alliance for Caregiving and AARP, 2020). It's likely that many middle-aged people will need to assume some kind of caregiving role, whether supporting a parent in financial matters, providing support with activities of daily living, or practical support such as driving family members to doctors and appointments.

Caregiving can be challenging. While community resources such as adult day care and senior centers can lighten that load, they can be difficult to find. It is equally difficult to find trustworthy in-home caregivers or services. Another potential obstacle involves navigating healthcare systems and health-insurance hurdles.

If those challenges are not enough, caregiving takes a significant emotional toll. Both the older adult and the person providing care may struggle with the role reversal of the "child" becoming the caregiver. This may be especially challenging in relationships that have been distant or conflictual. Family disagreements are common, particularly in cases where there are multiple children, who may not see eye to eye about care decisions. In some cases, there is an inequity in which child or children share the caregiving burden, leading to resentment. Stress, burnout, and guilt are common emotions.

And what of the so-called *sandwich generation* – midlife adults tasked with caring for their own children alongside aging parents? As people have put off starting families until older ages, being "sandwiched" has become a more common scenario. Providing simultaneous care for children and older adults is not easy. This is especially true when older adults have more challenging diagnoses such as dementia.

Research shows that caregiving takes an emotional toll (Do et al., 2014; Hodgdon et al., 2023). Eating disorders can sometimes emerge or worsen as a coping mechanism to manage overwhelming emotions or regain a sense of control. For some people, it can also be a way to numb feelings. For some caregivers, eating disorders like binge eating can be a form of self-care, something that is pleasurable. Alternatively, eating disorders can be a way to punish oneself due to guilt around not "doing enough."

As with the empty nest, people who take on caregiving roles may feel they have lost touch with their own identity. An eating disorder can fill that void by providing structure or a sense of identity – something they feel is "theirs" amidst caregiving demands.

Finally, eating disorders can be a cry for help of sorts. Disordered eating can unconsciously serve as a way of expressing distress or indirectly asking for support. Ellen's story illustrates some of these dynamics.

Ellen is a woman in her early 40s. She has always been a stay-at-home mom. She and her husband, Bruce, have one child, Clark, who is 12. Clark has Down syndrome and severe food allergies. While Clark does a lot for himself, Ellen has always been protective of him and is cautious about what he eats. Ellen's husband travels frequently for work, and her mother, Mimi, has always been a source of support and connection for her and Clark. "Mom used to be like a superwoman – she could do anything," Ellen shared. "But now I see her slowing down. She no longer feels comfortable driving or doing many of the things she used to."

Ellen has grown sad and overwhelmed as a result of these changes and feels anxious much of the time. Mimi was recently diagnosed with macular degeneration, a progressive illness that will eventually take her sight. Ellen now feels like the tables have turned; her mother needs her now. But Mimi is too stubborn to accept help, which frustrates Ellen. "I feel angry, frustrated, and then bad that I feel this way," Ellen shared. "In many ways, I feel like I am grieving the parent I used to have."

Ellen's weight loss started slowly – skipping meals when she was too busy – but lately, it seems to have gotten worse. When Bruce returned from a recent work trip, he was shocked to notice just how much weight she'd lost. "It was like I was looking at a shadow of who she used to be," he shared. Bruce ultimately made the decision to take some time off from work to support Ellen and to help her and his mother-in-law make decisions about the next steps. With Bruce's support, Ellen was able to begin to regain some of her lost weight. The couple felt closer than they had in a long time.

Marital discord, infidelity

With all the transitions noted so far, it's probably not surprising that midlife can be a time when people reevaluate longstanding romantic partnerships. This can be, in part, due to a suddenly empty nest, or it may just signify two people growing in different directions. This individual, rather than joint, growth may reveal incompatibilities. If they cannot bridge this distance, a couple may ultimately make the decision to separate or divorce, or they may seek alternative sources of physical or emotional connection.

Infidelity can be particularly devastating. Betrayal often leads to self-blame, poor self-esteem, and hyperfocus on physical appearance – all of which are significant risk factors for eating disorders. Individuals may attempt to "fix" themselves physically, erroneously believing that if they were thinner or more attractive, their partner would have remained faithful. In such cases, disordered eating becomes both a punishment and a desperate attempt to regain control. Should infidelity lead to the end of the marriage, people may also experience many of the same identity shifts we've discussed previously in this chapter. This shift from husband/wife/partner to single life, people may feel at odds and seek a new focus – sometimes turning to body image, health, or weight in a way that becomes obsessive. An eating disorder might serve as a substitute purpose or project. "I felt such a sense of purpose when I was working," shared Tia. "I started feeling pretty crummy about myself when I retired. At some point, my focus shifted, and I thought, I can be really good at being thin." Food may also be a way to fill the void – literally and emotionally. Food becomes a substitute for connection, purpose, or routine.

Grief/loss of loved ones

Up to now, this chapter has focused on loss as a broad construct. Here, we'll focus on bereavement and its connection to midlife eating disorders. Grief is a natural and deeply personal response to loss, especially the death of someone we love. Attachment theorist John Bowlby says, "Loss of a loved one is one of the most intensely painful experiences any human being can suffer." Grief, especially the death of a partner or close family member, often brings a cascade of emotional and practical challenges. The experience of grief varies from person to person, shaped by the nature of the relationship, the circumstances of the loss, and individual coping mechanisms.

Grief does not always follow a linear path. It can ebb and flow, resurface years later, or express itself in unexpected ways. While grief is a normal part of life, certain losses – such as the death of a partner, parent, or other close family member – can feel particularly destabilizing and all-consuming. In some cases, grief presents in a way that stands out as a deviation from what is considered "normal," due to the length of the grieving process, the intensity of symptoms, or the impairment of social, occupational, or other important areas of functioning. This syndrome has been called many things, including *pathological grief*, *traumatic grief* (as it is often tied to sudden, shocking, or violent losses), and *complicated grief* (Nakajima, 2018). Symptoms of complicated grief include difficulty accepting the loss, emotional numbness, self-blame, or anger. There may also be difficulty moving on from the loss, extreme loneliness, difficulty trusting others, or considering life meaningless – which can lead to suicidal thoughts.

While all loss is challenging, losing a partner or a family member is one of the most profound forms of grief. It can disrupt every aspect of a person's life, identity, and emotional world. For many, the grieving process lies somewhere in between "normal" and complicated. Such grieving may include significant emotional intensity: the grief may come with waves of sadness, anger, guilt, confusion, or even numbness. Common psychological responses include intense sadness, guilt, anger, anxiety, loneliness, and disorientation (Stroebe et al., 2017). These emotions can feel overwhelming and hard to process.

When someone loses a spouse or parent, they may also lose a part of their identity – such as that of a husband, wife, daughter, or caregiver. This can leave a person feeling unanchored or purposeless. The absence of a loved one can create a deep sense of emptiness and make people question "who am I?" Identity or role loss is especially prevalent in cases where caregiving or emotional interdependence defined the relationship (Neimeyer, 2012), such as an aging couple caring for one another.

It can also lead to social withdrawal or feeling misunderstood by others who have not experienced a similar loss. There may be a disruption of daily life, and even the smallest everyday tasks can become painful reminders of the loss, creating emotional and logistical challenges. Grief can also prompt people to question life's meaning, their future, or even their will to continue – a kind of existential questioning that can be painful (Bonanno & Kaltman, 2001).

Grief can also contribute to a loss of community or social circles. Following the death of a loved one, people may decide to relocate or seek assisted-living spaces. This may necessitate them leaving behind friends, neighbors, or familiar spaces, leading to reduced social interaction and loneliness.

In the context of intense grief, some develop new eating disorders or find that pre-existing disordered eating behaviors become more severe. This happens not because of concerns about weight or appearance but because eating behaviors serve psychological and emotional functions. Lilian's story is a good example of the intersection between grief and eating disorders. Lilian is a 60-year-old woman whose second husband, John, died from a brain tumor. "I still can't believe he's gone," Lilian shared. "John was so full of life, and this came out of nowhere."

Lilian has struggled with anorexia since her late teens. She's had some periods of brief remission but had done much better in the ten years she and John were together. John's death has taken an emotional toll and changed the trajectory of Lilian's symptoms. "I think at first I was depressed," Lilian shared. "I could literally not eat. But I think now it's more about coping and control." While Lilian's eating disorder seemed to be about many of the things she described, a less conscious dynamic was Lilian's guilt and use of the eating disorder to punish herself. "When John got sick, he wanted to travel and spend time together. But I urged him to get treatment instead," Lilian said. "Despite the best hospital and treatment, he just got worse and worse. I think I was just in denial."

Lilian's eating disorder served many functions. What began as a grief-related appetite change resurfaced as a more entrenched eating disorder; by the time she reached out for help, Lilian had lost significant weight and needed an inpatient program to restabilize. The restricting was a way to numb and cope (just as binging can be a way to comfort), as well as to restore a sense of order in a world that felt out of control. Finally, Lilian's eating disorder was a form of self-punishment. Lilian felt like she didn't deserve to eat and that she'd failed John.

While not the case for Lilian, another loss-related dynamic we see involves eating disorders as an enactment of symbolic or emotional associations with food. Food is often linked with memories, rituals, and relationships. Eating (or avoiding) certain foods can become a way to stay connected to the person who died – or to avoid the pain of that connection. Emmanuelle, for example, would often binge on low-quality chocolate. As we worked to understand her eating disorder, we began to see that this was not even something she liked, but something her mother (who had died from Alzheimer's) loved. Emmanuelle's binging was a way to stay connected with her mother.

Career and financial

In a culture that values youth, ambition, and productivity, midlife career transitions can be destabilizing. Retirement, layoffs, being passed over for promotion, or competing with younger colleagues can trigger anxiety and self-doubt. For individuals whose identity is closely tied to professional success, such events can lead to a resurgence or first-time eating disorder.

Melissa is a good example of many of the challenges associated with midlife career transitions. Melissa works in pharmaceutical sales, a lifelong profession for her. Now in her 40s, "I feel like I've hit my peak – and bam! Nothing," she says. "I'm washed up." Melissa has watched as younger, more attractive colleagues are assigned bigger and more important accounts while she's making the same sales she did the prior year.

Things came to a head when her manager met with her to discuss improvement. "He wants more from me, but I'm overwhelmed. My current accounts write only so many prescriptions," she says. Melissa's only way of soothing is to eat, a pattern that she cannot escape. "The food used to help a lot," she says. "Now it only makes me feel gross. No wonder they won't give me new lines of business. I'm disgusting." To stop binging and lose some weight, Melissa has started on a prescription stimulant labelled for binge eating. She has also started working with a personal trainer, an intense workout she hopes "will make me viable again."

Competing with younger colleagues

As people age, they may start to feel less valued in workplaces that emphasize new ideas, youth, or tech-savviness. They may experience a sense of invisibility or being "past their prime." In situations like Melissa's, men and women may become increasingly dissatisfied with their bodies, especially when comparing

oneself to younger, possibly thinner or more energetic coworkers. Such feelings of inadequacy can drive extreme dieting, overexercise, or disordered eating behaviors to "measure up." Like Melissa, middle-aged workers may fear
being replaced, particularly when they see younger colleagues being promoted
or praised. Highly competitive work environments can also trigger perfectionism, which can spill into appearance and eating habits – especially if success
feels tied to how one looks.

In these situations, eating disorders can function to:

- Regain control over body, aging, or perceived loss of status.
- Boost self-esteem by fitting an ideal body image or standard of success.
- Avoid deeper fears, such as fear of aging, failure, or being left behind.
- Gain approval from peers, superiors, or even internalized societal standards.
- Create a sense of identity, especially if professional identity feels threatened.

This dynamic can be especially tough in image-conscious industries like media,
wellness, or corporate leadership, but it can show up anywhere there's pressure
to perform, appear competent, or stay competitive.

Layoffs and retirement (voluntary or involuntary)

Midlife often brings layoffs, career burnout, or a feeling of "not achieving
enough." Such events may be accompanied by economic instability and career
uncertainty – all of which can shake one's sense of security and identity.

Several studies confirm that job loss is a significant stressor associated
with adverse mental health effects such as depression (Creed & Klisch, 2005;
McKee-Ryan et al., 2005). Many people have established expectations about
when and how they will retire and their own desires for their futures. However, many workers retire earlier, and at younger ages, than they had anticipated.
Common reasons for earlier-than-anticipated retirement include having health
problems that preclude or complicate completion of work duties, workplaces
compelling an employee to take an early retirement, or leaving the workforce in
order to become a caregiver for a family member (Szinovacz & Davey, 2005).
While Troy, whom we met earlier, did not leave to care for his wife, her increasing needs created a significant lack of control and did not leave him the time or
space to adjust to retirement.

The research shows that for situations outside the control of the retiree, there
may be more of a sense of lower life satisfaction (Clarke et al., 2012), poorer
retirement adjustment (van Solinge & Henkens, 2008), and higher incidence
of depression (Falba et al., 2009). One aspect in several of these studies is that
those people who have experienced adverse work conditions may well fare better than those who have left or been laid off from jobs that are more fulfilling.

In the former case, "early exit pathways," such as early retirement packages, are a protective factor for mental health (Sjöberg, 2023).

David is a good example of the complexities. David is a 62-year-old man who worked as an investment banker. David has never married ("I was married to my job," he jokes.) and has no close friends. A fastidious and astute man, David has carefully planned for his retirement at age 65. While he has planned financially, David has secretly thought that 65 may extend into 70 and so forth; he has few interests outside of banking.

As David has aged, the demands of his job have caught up with him. "This new technology makes my life harder, not easier," he shared. David has difficulty relating to the younger professionals he meets, and lately does not enjoy his job. "To be perfectly honest," he says. "I was feeling completely burned out." Following a conversation with his manager and upon his strong urging, David has made the difficult decision to retire early.

David feels alternately angry and resigned about the decision. While part of him knows it's for the best, "I have given them my life, and now this?" He is especially angry at his manager and believes that he was encouraged to retire early because the company has hired several younger employees who are paid significantly less.

Recently, David has found himself binging on salty snacks. "I just feel so angry all the time," he says. "And useless, just useless." The binging seems to be a way to numb the anger and to manage his loss of identity.

For people who have been affected by retirement or job loss, eating disorders can serve many functions. Retirement can lead to a sudden shift in daily structure and self-identity, especially if someone strongly identified with their career. An eating disorder might serve as a way to regain a sense of control or purpose – controlling food and the body can feel like a way to exert mastery in a time of uncertainty. Like David, many people feel a shift in value or sense of usefulness after retirement. Eating behaviors might serve to manage these feelings – through either restriction (to gain a sense of self-worth) or bingeing (to fill an emotional void).

Another common function of eating disorders involves coping with emotional distress. Life transitions, such as retirement, can bring up anxiety, depression, loneliness, or other challenging emotions. Disordered eating can function as a coping mechanism to numb emotions, distract from pain, or self-soothe.

As with other areas we've discussed in this book, social isolation is a risk factor in developing eating disorders. Prior to volunteering, Troy had few connections. David was extremely isolated, and work filled the void. People who are retired often experience less social interaction, and food may become a source of comfort or structure in an otherwise unstructured day.

Retirement, layoffs, and time on one's hands may create space for earlier, unresolved issues to resurface. Someone who struggled with disordered eating earlier in life may find those behaviors returning to cope with new stressors.

Existential and emotional challenges

Finally, midlife is a time of self-reflection. While some people reflect on their lives quite positively, others may find themselves ruminating on things they have *not* achieved. They may experience a sense of time running out or may mourn the "road not taken." We have touched on many of the changes and challenges of midlife in this chapter. The passage of time, shifting identities, and a longing for the unlived life are a few of the more existential challenges that may arise at this time.

Al is a good example of the ways in which these existential concerns arise, and of the intersection with other midlife transitions. Al is 67 and has been married for much of his adult life. He and his wife, Kelly, met in the Peace Corps. "We were young and idealistic," he shared with a chuckle. "Then kids, family. I went to work for my father-in-law's insurance business. Hardly what I'd imagined when I was 20."

Now retired, Al has started to reflect on these life choices. "I only have so many years left," he said. "I'd like to do something meaningful again." Kelly, however, has different ideas and is content with retirement, helping with the grandkids, etc. Al is becoming more depressed as he looks backward and forward, and he has even contemplated suicide at times. "It's not something I'd choose, but this life feels pretty meaningless," he says. Al is stuck at a crossroads, one on which he has started to turn back to something that gave him comfort earlier in his life: food.

Al is a good example of the reflection many people go through at this time – reflecting on choices made or not made and grieving the loss of youthful ideals. Others like Diane also begin to understand, sometimes for the first time, their own mortality. "60 was a big one. I've now officially outlived both my parents," she says. "And I think, 'Who is there to take care of me when I need it?'" Diane wrestles with this question daily. Like Al, food has become a refuge of sorts. "I know it's not healthy," she says. "But nothing else stops the endless thinking."

These psychological and emotional shifts often manifest in diverse ways, including the development of midlife eating disorders, which we know are expressions of deeper internal conflict. To navigate midlife constructively, individuals must make peace with the past, embrace the present, and redefine their dreams to better align with evolving values.

Both Al and Diane used food and eating to comfort/numb and distract from their thoughts. Some related reasons for eating disorders include:

- *Regaining control.* Existential questioning can provide a loss of control. Eating behaviors can become a way to reassert control over something tangible – food, body, or routine – when other areas feel uncertain.
- *Coping with mortality.* Restriction, dieting, or excessive exercise may become symbolic efforts to maintain youth, vitality, or societal relevance.

- *Managing emotional numbness.* Disordered eating may numb existential despair, unresolved grief, or anxiety about meaning, purpose, and legacy. This is a frequent theme for midlife eating disorders.
- *Distracting from/avoiding deeper existential questions.* Preoccupation with food, calories, or weight can serve as a distraction from painful existential questions: "What is my purpose now?" "What have I accomplished?" "What happens next?" The eating disorder offers a narrow focus, shielding the individual from broader self-examination.

For further reflection and application

1 Reflect on the many ways you have changed since your early adulthood. What are some of these changes (consider interests, values, and identity changes). Be sure to consider challenges and opportunities for each.
2 Think of a midlife client you've worked with. How have some of the themes noted in this chapter applied to them? What functions do their eating disorders serve?
3 What are some common existential questions you have noted among your clients?
4 Using the information depicted in Figure 4.2, pick one area that you consider common in terms of your client population. Review the challenges and opportunities and expand on these as needed. Are there some challenges that you see more commonly? Some opportunities that you wished you'd considered with past or current clients? How can a relational framework support you in working with clients experiencing these challenges?

Clinician resource 9: life map: balancing roles and transitions

This therapy activity helps middle-aged individuals reflect on the many roles they hold, understand transitions they are going through or anticipating, and reframe these experiences through the lens of both challenges and opportunities. This activity is also good for facilitating in a group setting.

CLINICIAN RESOURCE 9: LIFE MAP: BALANCING ROLES AND TRANSITIONS

Facilitated discussion

- Facilitator briefly introduces the concept of multiple roles (e.g., parent, spouse, employee, caregiver, friend) and life transitions (e.g., children leaving home, career changes, divorce, retirement).

  - Prompt: "Midlife often comes with a balancing act – you're navigating multiple roles while experiencing or anticipating significant life changes. Today, we'll explore your current landscape through a lens of both challenge and opportunity."

Create a life map

- Client draws a circle in the middle of their paper and writes their name or "ME" inside it. From there, they branch out with lines creating categories such as:

  - Family
  - Career
  - Relationships
  - Finances
  - Personal Growth
  - Hopes/dreams
  - Community/spirituality

- Under each category, list:

  - Current roles/responsibilities
  - Any life transitions they are experiencing or anticipating
  - Specific challenges they associate with that area
  - Opportunities or strengths within those same areas

Note:

- Use one color for **challenges**
- Another for **opportunities**

Reflect and share

- Guiding questions:

    - What roles feel the most demanding right now?
    - Which roles do you most welcome?
    - Which transitions are you navigating?
    - Where do you feel stuck?
    - Where do you feel free/liberated?
    - What new possibilities might this challenge open for you?

Reframe

- Invite the client to identify:

    - One opportunity they want to expand
    - One role they might redefine in a way that aligns with who they are now
    - One continued existential question

Chapter 9

Integrative treatment of midlife eating disorders

In these chapters, we've seen the many challenges that clients experience due to midlife transitions – whether relational, body-based, or identity-based. Eating disorders in midlife continue to be underrecognized and underdiagnosed. And while they present unique clinical challenges, they also create opportunities for transformation and growth. There's nothing more inspiring than seeing someone grow and change.

Midlife eating disorders call for a nuanced, compassionate, and integrative therapeutic response. It's not enough to address symptoms, but instead we need to address individual needs. This chapter explores an integrative treatment model. That said, it is *not* meant to be a stepwise or one-size-fits-all approach. As with many eclectic approaches, it pulls from the best evidence-based models we have for treating eating disorders and allows for clinical autonomy in the same way as the Chapter Resources are meant to be adapted and individualized.

Some of the approaches I pull from include Relational Therapy, Radically Open Dialectical Behavior Therapy (RO-DBT), Intuitive Eating (IE), Health at Every Size (HAES), Acceptance and Commitment Therapy (ACT), Somatically Focused Work, Self-Compassion practices, shame resilience, and trauma-informed care. Phew! Looking at the list, it seems daunting. Client needs guide you to best practices. These approaches honor the complexity of midlife experiences and support sustainable growth and healing.

What makes treatment difficult (stigma)

In prior chapters, we've touched on the idea of stigma (weight stigma and agism in particular). Let's return to the theme of stigma, starting with a definition specific to mental health. Link and Phelan (2001) define mental health *stigma* as a powerful social process that is characterized by labeling, stereotyping, and separation. Stigma can be external, as negative comments or stereotypes (e.g., eating disorders as a white, affluent diagnosis) or internal – a person's internal judgments based on external stereotypes ("I have a teenage problem.")

DOI: 10.4324/9781032615745-10

Like other forms of discrimination, the effects of mental health stigma can be far-reaching. Let's look at several other examples. I wish that the examples were one-offs, but unfortunately, they happen far too frequently.

Cindy is a 40-year-old woman struggling with a recurrent eating disorder. While bright and motivated, she was struggling. "I tried everything," she said. "But just could not seem to stop binging and purging." Her team recommended a local partial hospital program that had a great reputation for working with binge eating. While initially reluctant, Cindy reluctantly agreed to at least give it a try.

The afternoon of the intake, I received a tearful phone call. "It was awful," Cindy shared. "From the get-go, the physician assistant I met seemed to want to argue with everything I said." The kicker was when she said to me, "How does someone your age have an eating disorder?" The damage of that statement was far-reaching, and had we not already had an established relationship, it's likely Cindy would not have reached back out.

As you think of your own caseloads, you've likely seen many examples of mental health stigma. While things are slowly changing, we still have ways to go.

Some examples of stigma include:

1   The "isms," including agism, sexism, or racism, are borne of the belief that eating disorders affect only teens and young white adult females. Older people, males, and people who are not white may all be affected.
2   Judgments, especially moral judgments. Some examples are the thought that eating disorders are about vanity ("Aren't you too old to worry about being thin?"), that eating disorders are about a need for attention or control, and that parents cannot have eating disorders ("But you have such a supportive family") or the belief that midlife eating disorders are intractable.
3   Minimization, especially as related to healthcare providers' minimization of symptoms. Weight loss is seen as positive (such as in atypical anorexia), so a lecture on weight and a prescription for a weight-loss drug are not uncommon scenarios (have you heard stories about people going to the doctor with flu symptoms and coming out with a prescription for a glucagon-like peptide-1 (GLP-1)? I have).
4   Self-stigma and shame, such as those Susan and Cindy struggle with.
5   Lack of representation in eating disorder programming, higher-level-of-care cohorts, or the media.

Stigma affects people in many ways. These include reduced help-seeking behavior, worsening symptoms due to people not seeking treatment, poor self-esteem/ shame, isolation, and healthcare inequities and biases (Corrigan et al., 2014). Stigma is probably the greatest barrier to seeking treatment, which is sad because with proper support people *can* make changes and heal from midlife eating disorders.

Susan's recovery story

Let's revisit Susan now. As a reminder, this is an early 40s biracial wife and mother whose daughters are both in college. Susan's first-time eating disorder seemed to signify a shift in identity. Her daughters were now independent, and while she could celebrate a job well done in raising them, there was a void. Susan did not have much in the way of social support or connections. The eating disorder filled the role of providing a sense of purpose and "being a friend."

In Chapter 1, Susan had (somewhat reluctantly) started to engage in therapy. The early stages were rocky. After her experience of inpatient treatment, it was difficult for her to trust anyone, and she carried a lot of shame about having a "teenage problem." There were difficult moments throughout, including a family intervention to support her but which made clear that her husband and daughters were very worried. As trust developed, Susan was able to add back some foods she'd cut out and when better nourished and more engaged in therapy. As her weight slowly increased, so did her access to a range of emotions. Grief – at her marital distance, at the perceived loss of motherhood, and at not having known her father – was a predominant theme that was not easy for her to feel. There was also anger, which was likely connected to these same factors, but which Susan projected onto the inpatient program.

We began to work through her experiences in the inpatient program, validating the difficulty of the setting and the fact that others within her church community were aware of the hospitalization. Shame was a strong theme, and one that we eventually learned did not only relate to the eating disorder. She felt shame about being the only biracial person in her school, and seemingly the only one with only one parent. Susan eventually opened up about some bullying, as well as feeling like an "outsider" in most areas of her life. Working through her shame and the early traumas was very freeing. This set the stage for her search for her father. She was eventually able to find him through Ancestry.com.

Not only did she find him but felt "like I understand myself for the first time." "It's incredible how much we share – our personalities, interests," she said. Her connection with him, and the wider family, felt like "coming home." While there was some anger about the wasted years, Susan tried to focus on the positives of those ahead. The best news: the family genetics truly had some longevity. Her father was a spry 65, and her grandfather was equally active and engaging at 85.

As Susan began to embrace her identity, she was inspired to create a Facebook group for other people searching for their roots. She enjoyed being an admin for the group and started to come out of her shell even more. Susan also joined several online eating disorder support groups and felt "understood and connected."

The final piece of the puzzle fell into place when Susan's oldest daughter became pregnant. She is eagerly awaiting her granddaughter's birth and plans to help care for her when her daughter returns to work. While Susan's eating disorder is not completely a thing of her past (she still struggles at times with body image), it's much better.

What this case (and others) tells us

As with eating disorders that occur at younger ages, working with Susan was not as simple as "just eat." In many ways, therapy with midlife eating disorders is more an art than a science, knowing when to push, when to offer a little "tough love," and when to step back and validate. We live in a culture in which midlife men and women often feel invisible or redundant. This may be due to having a body type which is different than what we see in the media, having a changing role, or coming to terms with the biological aging process.

Middle-aged people – often women, but also men and gender-diverse people – struggle with anorexia, bulimia, binge eating disorder, orthorexia, and other disordered eating patterns. Midlife eating disorders are not just superficial concerns about appearance but are expressions of deeper psychological struggles related to trauma, loss, identity shifts, and culturally reinforced disconnection from the body (Maine & Bunnell, 2008).

As we've seen in prior chapters (a reminder never hurts), contributing factors at midlife often include:

- Aging-related body changes (e.g., menopause, aging skin, weight gain, illnesses)
- An emphasis on the thin ideal, gendered body ideals
- Life transitions, caregiving, and empty nesting
- Loss, including loss of relational roles (death of partner, friends, marriage)
- History of trauma or unresolved grief
- Shame and perfectionism

Given these layered concerns, treatment must go beyond symptom reduction to include the facets that follow.

Defining recovery

I am a firm believer in allowing clients to define "recovery" for themselves. As clients have asked themselves the important question "what is recovery?" many themes have emerged. While some people (often those who are well therapized) define recovery as reaching a certain weight or refraining from eating disorder symptoms, others have defined recovery in other ways. While we've tried for a field-wide consensus statement, that's a tall order. In a more general sense, I consider recovery to encompass reaching a level of peace (or even neutrality) about one's food choices and body. A tall order indeed.

Research efforts have attempted to define recovery and have yielded more specific ideas, but like much of the total research base, definitions have been based on much younger women. The most often cited definition is that of Bardone-Cone et al. (2019). They characterize individuals as being in full recovery when they: (1) have a body mass index (BMI) over 18.5; (2) have not engaged in binge eating, purging, or fasting in the past three months; and (3) report a score on the Eating Disorder Examination – Questionnaire (EDE-Q) less than one standard deviation above community norms, indicating "normalized" eating disorder psychopathology. Individuals considered to be in partial recovery meet the first two criteria but report an EDE-Q score greater than one standard deviation above community norms.

In the spirit of the idea "recovery is in the eye of the beholder," some of the critiques of this definition include that a one-size-fits-all approach will rarely work. And while the above definition looks at symptoms, it does not look explicitly at how people manage in the world. Are they living satisfying lives aligned with their values? If they still have negative thoughts or self-beliefs, does that mean they are truly recovered? Does it capture the experience of all people with eating disorders or just a select few? This definition also does not consider the backdrop of diet culture or individual factors including aging-related changes. To remedy these concerns, let's look instead at an integrative approach that allows for nuance and encourages individuals to define recovery for themselves.

Using a trauma-aware lens

Chapter 5 introduced the connections between trauma and midlife eating disorders. So many midlife clients have a history of trauma, including unresolved losses. Successful treatment is trauma-informed treatment – treatment that prioritizes safety, choice, and collaboration. That is incredibly important for working with clients like those in Chapter 1. While trauma was not the presenting issue for any of them, all came with significant traumas in their background. For Sasha it was the trauma of her family relocating to the United States, plus the sexual assault she'd experienced; for Susan, the trauma of abandonment by her father; for Carla, the trauma of being an adult child of alcoholic parents; and for John, the rejection by his family of origin and the recent loss of his mother-in-law.

Consider these traumas in tandem, and you get a glimpse of the interconnection between trauma and eating disorders. Even when the trauma does not lead in terms of therapeutic issues, it's important to remember that eating disorders often function as coping mechanisms – attempts to manage overwhelming experiences and unmet needs. Thus, while clients with a trauma history may have flashbacks or trauma symptoms, they may present in a way that is more a sign of complex post-traumatic stress disorder (PTSD), with needs such as connection or trust. They may also demonstrate chronic dysregulation. We'll focus more on supporting these areas in subsequent sections of this chapter. For now, however, it's helpful to review elements of trauma-informed care.

We've already mentioned some key aspects of trauma-aware therapy – collaboration, safety, and choice. This is a necessity for someone with a trauma history, and it is developmentally fitting. Locked programs and those that use behavioral strategies such as level systems are inappropriate for most folks at midlife. In terms of outpatient care, there are similar concerns. Collaboration means valuing client input and shared decision-making. Safety means creating environments where people feel physically and emotionally secure. It includes having comfortable and size-appropriate seating and a space that is calm without harsh overhead lights or noise. With clients, it's important to take a collaborative rather than authoritarian stance. We are not the experts deciding what clients must or should do; rather, we are advisors, coaches, and collaborators. The third aspect, choice, references supporting a sense of control by offering options and autonomy. Trauma often involves a loss of control, so providing choices helps to restore that sense of agency. An eating disorder example may involve making the recommendation of a dietician but knowing that a client may not be ready to seek that care. It may also mean that instead of referring a client to a higher level of care, we honor the request for multiple sessions weekly. This honors the client's pace and wisdom.

Trauma-aware care also means an attitudinal shift. It means recognizing that while eating disorders have health and lifestyle consequences, they have served an important function for many clients. It's important to validate the client's survival strategies rather than pathologizing them. It's interesting to ask clients a direct question: how has your eating disorder helped you? Those who have been in other treatments may say "it hasn't," but I usually encourage them to really look at this question. Giving up an eating disorder may mean giving up an important survival strategy – albeit one that has outlasted the need.

Another important consideration for people with eating disorders and trauma is treatment that integrates body-based regulation tools. These can be found in somatic approaches, an important facet of integrative treatment.

Finally, a trauma-aware approach also avoids retraumatization in food-related or medical interventions. Jim, a nonbinary client, was forced to eat in front of a mirror so they could see firsthand just how disgusting they were. I am not going to suggest a strategy such as using mirror affirmations. Similarly, for clients who have had very negative experiences in prior higher level-of-care settings, I am going to be certain to collaborate closely with a program and assess specific trauma triggers prior to (and even if) making such a recommendation.

Trauma-informed care also means attending to relational dynamics and supporting healing in connection rather than isolation.

Healing in connection (a relational approach)

Relationships may be the single greatest healer. As you look at your own midlife clients with eating disorders, take a moment to assess the quality (not necessarily the quantity) of their relationships. Are they close and connected? More distant? Consistent and reliable? You've likely now seen that the answer to these questions is "no."

When we look at Susan's history, this certainly stands out. For Susan, it was quite a mix. As a child and adolescent, she was close to her mother and grandparents, but she felt more like an outsider within the social fabric of her peers. Despite that Susan had created a warm and loving environment for her own girls, the empty nest brought back the loneliness and the lack of other connections. Susan, and others like her, found that strong and supportive relationships – including the therapist/client relationship – are key to healing.

While that sounds simple given the case illustration, the idea that relationships and connections are healing is pretty radical. When we think about cultural values, some of the words that come to mind are separation, independence, and self-sufficiency, as pointed out by feminist psychologist Judith Jordan (Jordan, 1997). Humans, however, are fundamentally relational. Growth-fostering relationships are essential to psychological health (Jordan et al., 2004). In contrast, chronic disconnection breeds clinical concerns such as eating disorders, depression, and substance use disorders.

Societal norms often result in a suppression of people's own needs and voices. Susan's identity as "wife" and "mother" left little space for self-fulfillment. While Susan loved being a wife and mother (as do many clients), she had completely lost touch with what it was like to be Susan. In one telling session, Susan and I attempted to create a list of her needs, a suggestion that baffled her. She'd been so attuned to what her children and husband needed that she'd never really considered that she could have needs of her own. Her needs, and her voice, had become marginalized.

As a profession, there is more awareness of the role of historical trauma, particularly traumas that affect marginalized groups. As a child, Susan was often encouraged to "pass" as anything other than black. Other middle-aged biracial clients have shared similar stories. Such identity nondisclosure *is* a trauma, as is the erasure of her paternal line. Trauma, particularly interpersonal trauma, disrupts a person's ability to trust and engage in meaningful connections. Trauma creates a profound sense of isolation and disconnection from the self and others (Jordan et al., 2004). Most often, trauma occurs in the context of relationships, such as the attachment injuries Susan experienced. It makes sense that healing would also occur within relationships – starting with the therapeutic relationship.

In grad school, you may have learned about a term called "corrective relational experiences." Simply put, corrective emotional experiences are moments within a therapy when the client is met with empathy, respect, and being fully present (Miller & Stiver, 1997). As you consider these words, and perhaps recall this idea, I invite you to think back to your clinical training. My graduate program was predominantly psychodynamic – a framework that emphasized a "blank slate" therapist and clinical distance. I recall feeling acutely uncomfortable at the lack of responsiveness I sometimes experienced in interactions with professors whose physical presence was truly blank. That is the opposite of what I need for healing, and my clients seem to agree. They are seeking authentic and genuine relationships.

In treating midlife eating disorders, then, the invitation is to become an authentic partner in the healing process. This allows the therapeutic connection to become a template for other relationships. Within this safety, clients can internalize experiences of reciprocity and trust. Judith Jordan calls this a process of building "relational resilience" (Jordan, 2017).

Another way of looking at these ideas is through the lens of Ron Kurtz's Hakomi method. In my Hakomi training, I was intrigued by the idea of "nourishing experiences" and saw an immediate connection to eating disorders. Clients with eating disorders have a difficult relationship with nourishment – both literal and figurative.

Nourishing experiences refer to emotionally positive, healing interactions that directly address and meet unmet core needs from earlier in life. These experiences are designed to transform limiting core beliefs and emotional patterns formed early in life.

Many people with eating disorders hold painful core beliefs like "I am worthless" or "My needs are too much." Nourishing experiences, such as being listened to or accepted unconditionally, challenge these beliefs. How many places and spaces in life can we go and expect that the other person wants to understand our needs? This can be even more powerful if made explicit through a therapeutic statement such as "I'm here. Your needs matter to *me*." This is further strengthened by asking the client to notice what happens when they hear a nourishing statement. What do they notice in their bodies? What emotions do they experience? There is no need to respond or "do" anything. Noticing one's inner response sets the stage for the embodiment practices we discuss in the next section.

Nourishing experiences also support self-compassion. What better antidote to the self-judgment, shame, and perfectionism that come along with eating disorders?

Embodiment: coming home to the body

Another important treatment concern involves working with clients to support embodiment. As a quick reminder, *embodiment* refers to the lived experience of the body – how people perceive, inhabit, and interact with their physical forms. It is the way people experience their body not only as a biological entity but also as a source of identity, agency, and emotion (Young, 2005). These definitions point out the importance of seeing the body as a place of wisdom, safety, and "home." For most people with eating disorders, whether midlife or otherwise, the body is a place of conflict rather than safety.

When we think of this idea and the metaphor of "body-as-home," think for a moment about a household filled with conflict where people speak harshly to one another, or one in which there is inconsistent care and neglect. Perhaps you are familiar with what that's like. It's a place that most people would want to avoid, and one feels awful.

Our goal is to help people make peace with – and maybe even a friend of – their body-homes.

The opposite of embodiment is disembodiment. Sometimes we notice behavioral indications of disembodiment (for example, I've had clients who immediately grab pillows to cover their body, leaving only a head for me to talk to), or clients who hide behind a cascade of hair or those whose entire countenance radiates pain. While you can probably make the assumption that the majority of folks struggling with eating disorders are uncomfortable with their bodies, it can be helpful to have a direct conversation about the idea of embodiment.

Some questions to ask your clients to assess embodiment include:

- How often do you notice subtle changes in your body, such as feelings of tension in certain areas, or changes in breathing (including hyperventilating)?
- When engaging in walking, exercising, or moving, what do you notice in your body? What sensations do you feel?
- Can you sense where emotions reside in your body? Where do you feel your anger? Your fear? What physical sensations are you aware of (e.g., fear as a pit in the stomach, anger, a clenched jaw)?
- Do you feel "at home" in your body, or do you often feel detached from it?
- How comfortable is it to use your body to express yourself (e.g., through gestures, movement, dance, etc.)?

Any of these questions can lead to interesting and often productive conversations. I've had clients share some surprising insights. Sometimes it opens to door for them to talk about traumas. Anything clients share can be helpful as you move into embodiment practices.

As you think back to the clients in Chapter 1, you may recall Sasha and her compelling description of being "at war" with her body. Sasha's body alienation was connected to her history of trauma and a longstanding eating disorder. Other clients feel disconnected from their bodies due to shame, illness, poor body image, and weight gain. As Regina so poignantly shared in Chapter 6, "I look in the mirror and wonder who that stranger is." Both benefited from gently introducing embodiment into the therapy. For Sasha, it was replacing some of the compulsive exercise with gentle yoga. For Regina, mindful walks were what resonated most.

A path back to embodiment and safety, then, can be found through somatic practices. Somatic work is particularly important for those whose eating disorder behaviors served as ways to numb, override, or dissociate from their bodies.

Table 9.1 Somatic Goals and Strategies

Goal	Techniques
Increase awareness of interoceptive signals (emotion, hunger, fullness)	Mindfulness and mindful check-ins; scanning for hunger prior to eating, fullness following; awareness of other body cues such as thirst, fatigue; general mindfulness practices such as mindful walks and meals that include sensory components Guided imagery to label emotions and body states ("My neck tenses when I am angry")
Recognize trauma-related responses (fight, flight, freeze)	Use of window of tolerance to learn about dysregulation and identify sympathetic and parasympathetic responses; discussing breath as a component of invoking a parasympathetic response; pacing to introduce body awareness; pendulation and titration (introduce "smaller t" traumas and prepare to process "T" traumas); identifying shutdown/dissociation
Using grounding, breath, and movement to increase nervous system regulation	Grounding in nature, noticing feet on the floor (you can also add roots anchoring), 5-4-3-2-1 technique: ask clients to name five things they can see, four things they can touch, three things they can hear, two things they can smell, and one thing they can touch; breathwork, including box breathing (in 4, pause 4, out 4, pause 4); bilateral movement, including EMDR, butterfly tapping, gentle walking, dancing, and/or tapping.
Distress tolerance (ability to stay present with difficult emotions and body sensations)	DBT distress tolerance skills (riding the wave of emotions, TIP [temperature, intensity, paced breathing], self-soothing with five senses), distraction techniques, radical acceptance ("it is what it is," accept and acknowledge what you can control)

It also supports resilience in navigating age-related body changes, including menopause, illness, and body-image shifts.

Table 9.1 provides a snapshot of somatic goals and strategies to support midlife clients. There are many more, so be creative.

Self-compassion: harnessing the power of kindness to decrease shame

As we move into the next facet of integrative treatment, self-compassion, I invite each of you to pause and define this simple yet complex idea for yourselves. Some questions that come to mind are: what is self-compassion? How do we foster self-compassion? What are the barriers to self-compassion? How do shame and self-compassion intersect? And finally, why include self-compassion as an integral part of integrative treatment?

When I define self-compassion to clients, I offer that self-compassion means treating oneself with the same kindness and understanding as you would offer a friend or loved one. Our clients are some of the most compassionate people around, at least until they must be compassionate toward themselves. It's often illuminating to ask clients to keep a diary of their inner voice. While many of us have grown up in critical or perfectionistic families, as adults we can make choices about how we show up as adults. We can choose to continue to bully or demean, or we can choose to be more supportive.

If you are not familiar with Kristin Neff (2011), I highly recommend her work and use it in my work with clients. She lists three primary components of self-compassion: Self-kindness vs. Self-judgment, Common Humanity vs. Isolation, and Mindfulness vs. Over-identification. Let's break down each of these areas, beginning with kindness. And what better place to start than with acknowledging imperfection?

Clients with eating disorders often hold perfectionistic views of many facets of their lives: grades, achievement, and looks, to name a few areas. Self-compassion is about acknowledging imperfections but responding to these flaws with kindness and gentleness rather than judgment or criticism. It's also about recognizing that *everyone* experiences pain, failure, and imperfection – this is part of our shared humanity. Twelve-step programs often espouse the idea that no one is "terminally unique"; instead, we all share commonalities. Suffering is part of being human. The final component of Neff's (2011) self-compassion framework involves mindful awareness of difficult thoughts and emotions. Rather than attempting to suppress emotions, Neff (2011) encourages people to face emotions with curiosity and openness (as opposed to being swept away by strong emotions).

We have defined shame in prior sections of this book. Shame researcher Brené Brown defines shame as the intensely painful feeling or experience of believing we are flawed and unworthy of love and belonging. That inherent sense of worthlessness and not being deserving of love is part and parcel with eating disorders. I have seen that for people struggling at midlife, shame can be even more intense and pervasive. Without addressing shame, we would miss a fundamental aspect of working with eating disorders.

Clinician Resource 3 provided some helpful questions to allow clients to explore shame. Some clients will prefer to journal on these independently, and others may be open to exploring these ideas in therapy sessions. This is also a way to process shame-based experiences.

There are several ways to address shame with clients. These include creating a foundation of safety within the therapy space, helping clients recognize shame and how it manifests in thoughts, feelings, and the body, challenging shame-based beliefs, and promoting connection and vulnerability. Brown's work is particularly relevant here and encourages people to share their stories of hurt and resilience.

Of all the techniques mentioned for working with shame, self-compassion practices seem to facilitate progress. These will be new to many of our clients and will require a shift in perspective – that one is worthy of self-compassion. These practices promote kindness, humanity, and mindfulness. Table 9.2 provides some examples that are well suited for eating disorders.

Table 9.2 Self-Compassion Practices for Working with Shame

Goal	Techniques
Increase mindfulness vs. over-identification	Use mindfulness to enhance nonjudgmental awareness, observing feelings and thoughts with openness and acceptance, rather than overidentifying with them or pushing them away. Mindful self-compassion counteracts the harsh inner critic that fuels shame. Stepping outside one's usual perspective, treating oneself as you would treat a friend, with perspective and care, rather than being swept away by negative reactivity ("what would you tell a close friend?"). Guided meditations, such as Neff's Compassionate Body Scan and Affectionate Breathing, increase body compassion and enhance body neutrality.
Increase self-kindness vs. self-judgment	Write a compassionate letter acknowledging shame-based imperfections with acceptance rather than criticism. Inner child work can help clients to connect with parts of themselves that hold early shame. Soothing physical touch (such as placing one's hand over one's heart or offering a self-hug). Reframing self-talk and inner dialogue in a more compassionate voice. Self-compassion meditations (such as loving-kindness or meta meditations).
Support common humanity vs. isolation and mindfulness	Group therapy can be an effective way to highlight commonality; these shared experiences can reduce shame. Acknowledge the existence of suffering. For example, you can teach people to say "suffering is a part of life" or "other people feel this way" when facing a difficult situation. Acknowledge pain with phrases like "this is a moment of suffering" or "this hurts," to ground into the present and validate experience.

One final note here: I have seen many therapists get excited about these practices and push too hard, too fast, to work on them with clients. They are great practices. But it's also helpful to remember that our clients often fear that if they are too compassionate with themselves, they will relax some of their rigidly held eating disorder behaviors. That is likely true. While recovery can feel scary at times, letting go of one's inner bully and decreasing shame feels so much better.

Challenging – and rejecting – beliefs about weight and diet culture

Another important facet of recovery involves helping clients to challenge diet culture. While I consider the Bardone-Cone et al. (2019) definition problematic, a fact of recovery – and there is no sugarcoating it – is that recovery may mean likely weight gain. If you are struggling with that sentence, you, like many others, have likely metabolized the beliefs of diet culture.

Let's stay here for a quick review. Diet culture is a system of beliefs that equates thinness with worth, health, success, and social acceptance (Warren & Akoury, 2020; Keel & Forney, 2013). Some of the core aspects of diet culture are a societal veneration of thinness as ideal, moralizing about food ("good" and "bad" foods), and weight-based definitions of health (weight as the only indicator of being healthy). Diet culture normalizes dieting and food restriction and stigmatizes people in larger bodies. Why? Because the diet industry (including weight-loss programs, supplements, and "clean eating" trends) profits from people feeling inadequate about their bodies and continuously trying to change them. Almost all Western societies have normalized diet culture. In large part, this means normalization of eating disorders and disordered eating.

Alternatives such as IE, HAES, and body neutrality defy diet culture by promoting self-care, sustainable habits, and respect for all body types. Similarly, Cognitive Behavioral Therapy (CBT) and Dialectical Behavior Therapy (DBT) have a number of tools to support the goals of IE/HAES and reduce shame-based thinking around food and body. I'd encourage you to become familiar with these approaches and have some tools at your disposal. There are many good books, podcasts, and resources that clients can investigate.

The beliefs associated with diet culture are pervasive, so much so that people begin to adapt these beliefs as their own. Jenni Schaefer's (2014) book *Life Without Ed* popularized the idea of the eating disorder voice, the critical, often manipulative internal voice people with eating disorders often struggle with. The eating disorder voice can be highly critical, shaming people for eating certain foods or for gaining weight. It's typically controlling and full of strict ideas about food, body, or weight. It's also very persistent. Sounds familiar? That's diet culture.

Consider statements such as: "Carbs are bad. Eat that and you'll get fat." "Everyone is looking at that ice cream in your shopping cart. Put it back – now." "I'm too fat to wear a bikini. I need to cover up." "If I don't look young, I don't matter." Or "I'm only worthy if I am thin." Yes, diet culture. But diet culture masquerading as part of oneself.

Of the thoughts above, many of these can be debunked with the techniques familiar to most therapists, such as CBT's emphasis on cognitive distortions, such as black-and-white thinking, catastrophizing, and labeling. Approaches like IE (Tribole & Resch, 2020) emphasize rejecting diet culture and all that goes with it. When I think of IE, the word that comes up is "freedom." Freedom to eat when we are hungry, freedom to demand not only physical satiation but also emotional satiation (food tastes good!), and the freedom that comes with honoring (rather than punishing) one's body. I sometimes ask clients to complete this stem: "I honor my body as a source of …" Some of the words I think of (and I encourage you to do this as well) are wisdom, resilience, strength, and joy. These words imply listening to the body's signals. Hunger and fullness are natural, trustworthy processes. It also means recognizing that despite even years of mistrust, the body can be resilient and that the body can be a source of pleasure and connection.

HAES emphasizes similar principles that also allow people to challenge diet culture. As the name implies, it is a weight-inclusive approach whose research base supports the idea that "health" is not determined by body size – which is counter to many of the examples we've seen in these pages. Examples like clients seeing their primary care physicians for a headache or flu symptoms and leaving with a lecture and prescription for a GLP-1 happen frequently in my world. HAES emphasizes the need for respectful care, which is not dependent on weight or body size. It also sees food and eating as flexible, individualized eating based on hunger, satiety, and pleasure. People are taught to enjoy the very things they have been misusing. They learn that food and exercise can be enjoyable and can enhance health.

Both IE and HAES are weight-neutral approaches. Weight/body neutrality is a mindset that encourages acceptance of one's body as it is, without having to love or hate it. And we can care for our bodies independent of size, or what we've eaten the day before. How many clients share that they restrict or self-harm if they believe they have overeaten? Weight neutrality reminds us that our bodies deserve care, not punishment.

Such simple concepts – but hard sell to some clients, especially those who have internalized diet culture for many years. The biggest draw to a weight-neutral approach is its ability to reduce and quiet the obsession that comes with an eating disorder. Of all aspects of eating disorders, this is the one that most of the clients I've worked with are motivated to change. It's painful to have to listen to a constant inner litany of "You can't eat this," "You're fat, ugly," "Half is okay if you run afterward," and so forth.

While I suggest you consult the experts in each of the areas briefly outlined in this section, Table 9.3 provides some suggestions for working with body image. Izzy's story, which I'll share in the final section of this chapter (emerging strategies), also demonstrates many of these aspects.

Table 9.3 Approaches to Challenge Beliefs about Weight and Diet Culture

Approach	Strategy
Cognitive Behavioral Therapy (CBT)	**Identify and challenge diet culture thoughts:** recognize automatic negative thoughts like "I'm disgusting for eating this" and replace them with more balanced beliefs (e.g., "Food is not 'good' or 'bad'"). **Cognitive restructuring:** examine the evidence for and against diet culture rules and create alternatives (e.g., "Thinner isn't always better"). Ask clients to identify people they admire regardless of body size. **Experiments:** try fear foods or disobey the eating disorder voice, for instance.
Dialectical Behavior Therapy (DBT)	**Distress tolerance skills:** such as grounding to manage emotional discomfort without restrictive eating. **Validation:** model validation around body-image struggles and the societal pressure to conform. **Radical acceptance:** encourage acceptance of body changes and the reality that control over body size is genetically predisposed and cannot be controlled in healthy ways.
Body neutrality/IE/HAES	**Wear comfortable clothing:** choosing clothes that fit the body, not the thin ideal. **Shift focus to function over appearance:** what the body can do ("my legs carry me through the day"). **Body gratitude:** help clients develop lists of what they are grateful for ("I carried my daughter in this stomach"). **Stop body checking:** to support neutrality, support clients in stopping checking behaviors such as looking in the mirror, pinching fat, weighing, and comparing. **Exposure to diverse bodies:** encourage clients to seek out body-positive role models, like Lizzo. **Exercise for joy:** support joyful movement. **Honor hunger:** encourage clients to eat consistently and for pleasure to support satisfaction, make peace with food, and move away from diet mentality. **Shift focus from the scale:** promote trust in internal cues rather than the scale. Recognize that a number does not need to mediate self-esteem.

Challenging internalized beliefs

In the last section, we mentioned that diet culture is so pervasive that the voice of diet culture can sometimes feel like a person's own voice. Alternatively, diet culture's message may have influenced parents and peers. Some beliefs are so deeply held that they are core beliefs.

A core belief is a foundational idea about oneself, others, and the world that shapes how individuals perceive and interact with others. People form these beliefs early in life, and they can become a lens through which people view the world.

Here are some examples of core beliefs common among people with eating disorders:

- I am not good enough/enough.
- I am not lovable.
- I am a failure.
- I am flawed.
- I need to be perfect.
- It's not okay to show my emotions.
- I need to control everything (food, weight).
- I cannot trust others/be trusted.
- I am ugly (my body is hateful).

Many approaches can be helpful in addressing internalized core beliefs. I usually start there with clients, asking them to just pay attention. What stories are they telling themselves? I asked one client to take five minutes of a session to identify these thoughts and beliefs; I watched the client literally "dump" more such statements in five minutes than I could have come up with in an hour. At first, many of these statements looked like a reflection of the eating disorder voice, but it did not take long to notice that they were much deeper and more in the vein of those above.

Many of the CBT strategies we discussed in the previous section can be helpful first steps in loosening core beliefs. CBT strategies often involve helping clients to question whether such beliefs are in fact valid and whether it is advantageous to maintain that belief system. It can also include seeking evidence or experimentation. For example, if a client's cognition is "I'm a failure," they may be asked to develop a list of things that they have failed or succeeded at, or asking members of the therapy group to name their strengths.

My preferred modality for working with core beliefs is Eye Movement Desensitization and Reprocessing (Shapiro, 2017) or EMDR. EMDR is a modality that uses bilateral stimulation to help clients process and desensitize key memories that may have led to such core beliefs. EMDR is a structured protocol and comes with many tools. The EMDR Cognitions list is one and can be a great starting point for identifying core beliefs as a starting point to working on them.

Dissonance and anchoring in values

As you get to know clients, you may become aware of dissonance in their values versus those driven by the perfectionistic taskmaster some people call "Ed." Please stop for a moment and think about your own values. Some of mine are compassion, patience, responsibility, wisdom, and peace. Now pretend you have an eating disorder, or perhaps think back to a time when you did. Were you able to live life in alignment with those values? It's highly unlikely that the answer is "yes."

In recent years, ACT (Hayes et al., 2016) has gained increasing popularity. Some of the tools, such as Cognitive Defusion, Acceptance, and Present, are anchors to the here and now (great strategies to reduce rumination and support objectivity and distance). ACT allows clients to reconnect with what really matters to them outside of food and body image. ACT focuses on identifying personal values to guide behavior change. This is especially helpful at midlife when life transitions often prompt deeper self-reflection. Disordered eating may also mask deeper yearnings – values work helps uncover and meet those.

It may be helpful to share a couple of examples of anchoring in values. Linda is a 48-year-old wife and mother of a teen girl who struggles with binge eating disorder. The binging has caused some weight gain, and she is deeply ashamed of her body. She is very self-critical. While Linda can easily say that she would never talk to others the way she talks to herself, a simple values clarification exercise was helpful in helping her recognize how binge eating was misaligned with some of her core values. The exercise was a question like, "Imagine it's your 70th birthday, and your family and friends are there. What do you hope they'd say about the person you've been – not how you looked or how much you weighed, but what you stood for?"

"I'd hope that they would say I am a loving mother and wife, that I'm a genuine and authentic person, and that I've taught my daughter to respect herself," she responded. This prompted an interesting discussion about how the binge eating misaligned with her values of self-respect and authenticity. She was even able to identify some steps to move toward honoring those values. She immediately said, "I'd want to be able to show up to my party without obsessing over what I'm wearing and how I look." "I'd also want to enjoy my birthday cake instead of being in my head calculating the number of calories I'd have to restrict to compensate," she continued. These truths helped Linda to reduce her rigidity around food.

Some of these principles were also helpful for John, whose values were strongly at odds with many of his long-held values of health, balance, connection, and authenticity. "As I continued to work on my orthorexia, these conflicts became more apparent," John shared. "I hadn't realized how much of a rigid, dishonest person I'd turned into." A pivotal turning point came following a family therapy session in which his husband, Rick, became so overwhelmed that he'd started crying. "I realized that this rigid way of eating was destroying me – destroying us," John said sadly. "It was taking away my focus from what really mattered." With that turning point, John embraced food challenges in a way he had not been able to prior. He and Rick eventually moved to Key West and have been enjoying the nightlife and wonderful restaurants on the island.

Values clarification and alignment allowed John to embrace his deeply held values as motivation for recovery. Not only did John see that the eating disorder was disrupting his relationship with Rick and his connection with others, but he also embraced the idea that connection could support him in recovery. "I was finally able to let Rick in and allow him to help me," he says.

Some other values that appeal to many people and are good to highlight as people move toward recovery are compassion (including self-compassion), courage (recovery is scary), and resilience (there is an ebb and flow to recovery).

Connecting with meaning

Just as eating disorders are at odds with deeply held values, they are also at odds with spirituality. Spirituality refers to a search for meaning and purpose and often involves a connection to something larger than oneself. Brené Brown (2020) says, "Practicing spirituality brings a sense of perspective, meaning, and purpose to our lives."

People struggling with eating disorders often experience a profound disconnection from their spiritual lives. They may lose touch with religious practices and spiritual communities. They may choose to distance themselves from their spiritual selves due to feelings of unworthiness and self-rejection. This distance can reinforce their sense that they are unworthy, not deserving of love from others, including a higher power, God, or the Divine. This spiritual emptiness demands to be filled, whether through food or through obsessively focusing on weight and body. In much the way that some people resist food as nourishment, many with eating disorders also resist spiritual nourishment.

Twelve-step recovery groups have it right. Groups such as Alcoholics Anonymous focus on helping people find meaning beyond their addiction. In AA, each person defines the word "higher power," which is a shared spiritual ideology. The idea of higher power can include connection to nature, self, non-religious wisdom traditions. This shared ideology includes acknowledging powerlessness over one's addiction, examining one's morals and values, and making amends to those who have been affected by the addiction. In fact, the ultimate goal of step work is that of spiritual awakening and spreading the message of recovery to others. Thus spirituality becomes a catalyst for change.

Spirituality also supports a sense of belonging and purpose. As you think back to the many transitions of midlife, one sequela of these transitions is a lack of life purpose. For many clients, things such as illness, grief, menopause, caregiving, and aging often raise existential questions about identity, mortality, and meaning. Control, perfectionism, or body obsession can be quick fixes for connection and purpose, but they rarely truly satisfy. Instead, clients need to find belonging beyond body ideals, appearance, or productivity. Spirituality can also offer clients a different kind of nourishment – a fulfillment that makes restrictive or compulsive eating feel less appealing.

Incorporating spirituality into treatment does not mean imposing any single belief system. It means providing a space to explore existential questions and allowing clients to explore their own spirituality – whether religious, nature-based, philosophical, or relational.

When I think of spirituality, some of the goals are to:

- Reconnect with awe, wonder, or joy
- Support connection to compassion, integrity, and kindness
- Redefine worth as inner, not based on outer appearance
- Experience the body as sacred, not an object to be controlled
- Accept what is, with compassion and non-judgment

These spiritually focused values are in direct conflict with the messages of eating disorders.

Emerging treatments: the potential promise of GLP-1s and psychedelic medicines

Integrative treatment strategies can support healing and seem to work for many midlife clients. A theme throughout this book has been that there is no one-size-fits-all approach. Two emerging treatments may offer hope for clients who have not been helped by other modalities: GLP-1s and psychedelic medicines.

GLP-1s

Many of you have heard the hype about GLP-1 receptor agonists (RAs) like semaglutide (Ozempic, Wegovy) and liraglutide (Saxenda). These medications are used to manage type 2 diabetes, but anecdotal evidence and some new studies have looked at them as potential treatments for addictions and other medical conditions. Liraglutides have also been used off-label for conditions such as polycystic-ovarian syndrome and non-alcoholic fatty liver disease.

Many of us have also seen these medicines prescribed too frequently for weight loss, leading some clients down the path of weight loss and regain so familiar to eating disorder professionals. As most of us know, dieting is the most effective way to promote eating disorders. This is a conundrum, especially with emerging research on the effectiveness of GLP-1 medications in reducing alcohol and other addictive behaviors. Some of the studies in process show promising initial results for addictions, including alcohol use disorder (Farokhnia et al., 2024) and opiate abuse (Bruns et al., 2024). There has also been anecdotal evidence that these medications may support a reduction of process addiction such as compulsive gambling and shopping.

The initial study that garnered interest was published in 2024 in the *Journal of the American Medical Association* (Farokhnia et al., 2024). These researchers looked at the association between GLP-1 RAs (semaglutide and liraglutide) and the risk of alcohol-related hospitalizations. Farokhnia and colleagues were primarily interested in determining how these medicines worked on brain systems related to reward processing, stress, satiety, and cognitive functioning. Results were promising, and they recommended further study.

Psychedelic medicines

Another area of emerging interest is the possible uses of psychedelic medicines and eating disorders. While many of these treatments, including psilocybin and 3,4-methylenedioxymethamphetamine (MDMA), are investigational, one agent is currently available. Ketamine is a dissociative anesthetic and, when administered, results in psychedelic effects. Psychedelic medicines can support the recovery of eating disorders through several different mechanisms. You'll likely notice that these are like the areas of integrative treatment I've proposed in this chapter, and many of the clients I have worked with have seen benefits even in the case of more enduring eating disorders. Other researchers seem to concur (Bryson et al., 2024, Calder et al., 2023, Cuerva et al., 2024).

One of the hallmarks of eating disorders is the presence of rigid, ruminative thinking patterns. This eating disorder voice can be hard to combat. Psychedelic medicines can help loosen this rigidity and allow people to step outside of entrenched thinking patterns. They have the potential to increase psychological flexibility. This in no way happens magically – it's more a matter of the client's work during the period immediately following the medicine's administration when the brain is in a more malleable neuroplastic state. This phase of psychedelic therapy is called the integration phase, and it's then that the therapist and client work together to directly combat such thinking. For example, I ask clients to ignore and talk back to the repetitive eating disorder voice, replacing it with more compassionate statements. It's also a time when they can make shifts in behavior, such as trying foods they may have previously feared.

Ketamine and other psychedelic medicines can also support the kinds of self-compassion work we've discussed in this chapter. These medicines allow suppressed emotions to be amplified and released; they also promote enough distance to be able to allow for self-compassion. This occurs in much the same way as we see in inner child or parts work. Clients often access memories of themselves as younger and can compassionately reexperience the wounds they experienced that led to eating disorders. Sound like trauma work? It is. But unlike some forms of catharsis that can result in retraumatizing, skillful work with these medicines instead allows for healing. Psychedelic medicines can also reduce comorbid conditions such as trauma, OCD, anxiety, and depression.

Finally, these medicines can foster spiritual connection, including a sense of joy, awe, and wonder. Clients connect not only with themselves but also with the greater universe of meaning, reducing emphasis on appearance and identity as a source of worth.

You can see I'm excited about the use of these medicines, and I have invested in significant training in this area. If this is something you may be interested in incorporating into your practice, I encourage you to do so as well. You may be inspired as I share Julia's story.

Julia is a 55-year-old woman. Bright and articulate, and thoroughly therapized, she was ready for something new. She learned about ketamine when her primary therapist shared that she'd seen a presentation I offered at the Renfrew conference, and she was eager to try. She was ready to recover once and for all and was not dissuaded by the need to be active in treatment.

We started the process with preparation and psychoeducation, addressing expectations and the idea that this was not a magic bullet. In seeking "intentions" for the sessions, Julia's goal was to loosen the grip of the eating disorder voice, particularly that voice that told her she needed to restrict her food intake. "I know it's self-defeating," Julia shared. "And it has to stop. The more I starve myself, the more I binge later."

Julia had a series of eight 3-hour ketamine sessions and was actively involved in the preparation and integration. We co-created a series of compassion meditations, isolating the ED voice and replacing it with more compassionate self-statements. These meditations were part of the "swishing" phase as she would enter the ketamine session and follow-ups during the brain's open neuroplastic window. The ketamine also brought up some early memories of how this harsh voice developed in a family with multigenerational eating issues. We processed these using art, journaling prompts, and discussion.

Another important facet of the work with Julia was her own ability to connect with increased spirituality. The ketamine allowed her to relax and access a state that she had never felt somatically. She used words such as "awe" and "wonder" to describe connecting outside of herself rather than being so inwardly focused.

At the end of the ketamine series, Julia was feeling much better. She was kinder to herself, and her restrictive and binge eating had decreased significantly.

For further reflection and application

1 Reflect on the different integrative modalities within this chapter. Are there any of you'd add? Why? Identify any areas you are not currently using and consider trying them with your clients.
2 What modalities or approaches do you think may be most difficult to implement (and why)?
3 If you are a therapist who is in recovery, reflect on what factors you found most helpful in your own treatment. Which of these may be helpful to use as you create your individual treatment plans?

Clinician resource 10: a da y wit hout obsessing

The following journaling activity has been extremely helpful with clients. This can also be used as a conversation starter in sessions or even as a guided meditation. Some time and space, such as sending it home with clients, may allow even more richness and nuanced responses. They (and you) may be surprised at what emerges.

CLINICIAN RESOURCE 10: A DAY WITHOUT OBSESSING

Journaling prompt

You wake up tomorrow morning, and something feels different. The usual food noise – what to eat, how much, when, whether you "earned" it, or the need to start the newest diet or food plan – it's all quiet. Simply… not there. For once, your mind isn't preoccupied with food or calories or weight. You're just present, in your body, in your life.

Journal about what this would be like. What would you notice when food isn't the focus? What are your thoughts? What do you feel in your body? Maybe you notice the quiet, or a sense of hope, or a memory from a younger time. Whatever comes up, please capture what that experience may be like with the absence of the food obsession.

How do you move through the day? What happens when you let your hunger guide you rather than rules or old stories? What do you eat? What is it like not to label foods as "good" or "bad"? How does it feel to simply respond to your needs – to nourish rather than control?

Then, reflect on the larger picture. When you're not thinking about food all day, what are you thinking about? What fills that space? Do you notice any dreams or long-ignored desires arise when your mind is free to explore beyond the next meal?

Now take a moment to connect with your body instead of simply ignoring it. The purpose of this connection is again to just notice. What body sensations are you aware of? What emotions arise in relation to your body? Are any of these new or unfamiliar?

Finally, consider the overall experience. What surprised you? Did anything shift? What would it be like to have more days like this?

This is your chance to write honestly and without judgment. You're not writing a perfect story – just the truth of what it feels like to live one day closer to peace with food and maybe with yourself.

Appendix 1

Additional recommendations

Effective treatment of midlife eating disorders requires a developmentally sensitive individualized approach. This appendix expands on the suggestions in Chapter 9 to outline more subtle but necessary steps.

Individualized treatment

There is no one way to treat midlife eating disorders – treatment must be individualized and intersectional in nature.

- Assess for co-occurring issues: trauma, menopause, chronic illness, caregiving, loss, past trauma.
- Tailor goals to each client's needs and priorities.
- Honor client autonomy while offering accountability.

Treating the person, not just the diagnosis, is essential.

Research-informed approaches

Despite limited research on eating disorders in midlife adults, clinicians should be familiar with:

- Current studies on midlife and midlife eating disorders
- Trauma and somatic psychology literature
- Emerging studies on novel treatments
- Data showing that eating disorder recovery is possible at any age

More research is needed on effective interventions and age-specific risk factors.

Realistic images of aging and recovery

Challenging agism and the "thin ideal" is crucial in treatment.

- Use media literacy to unpack how aging is portrayed in advertising, social media, and "wellness culture"; clients are surfing, so be able to support recovery.

- Introduce diverse, realistic images of aging bodies, especially those that offer body-neutrality perspectives; this can include magazines in the waiting room or art. Consider art selections that do not have bodies or that celebrate diversity.
- Celebrate lived experience, maturity, and complexity – not just youth and appearance.

Clients may need to grieve the cultural invisibility of aging and reimagine what beauty means for them. This often means focusing on inner, rather than outer, expressions of beauty.

Education and psychoeducation

Clients and families often need education about eating disorders and aging.

- Teach the harmful effects of dieting and weight "yo-yoing."
- Explain how metabolism, hormones, and brain chemistry shift over time.
- Provide accurate resources to combat myths and stigma.

Clinicians should also continually educate themselves – and their clients – to provide care.

Developmentally appropriate treatment

Midlife clients are not adolescents in different bodies. They have different priorities (e.g., parenting, career, health), some have longer histories with their eating disorders, and they are generally more developmentally mature. Please assume that, unlike adolescents, they are going to take a proactive role in treatment.

- Align treatment with lifespan/developmental psychology models.
- Explore themes like: who am I now? What have I lost? What do I still want to become?

It is imperative that customized treatment plans acknowledge midlife and all that this lifestage brings.

More training for mental health professionals

Many clinicians are not trained to recognize or treat eating disorders in midlife and older adults. Misdiagnoses, assumptions (e.g., "You're too old for that"), and dismissal can harm clients and delay care. Stigma keeps people from seeking mental health treatment.

- Advocate for more age-inclusive education in graduate programs and continuing education.

- Train providers in trauma-informed, weight-neutral, and developmentally sensitive approaches.
- Include midlife perspectives in clinical case studies, supervision, and conference programming.

Improving provider competency reduces stigma and expands access to appropriate care.

Optimism about recovery, even for more challenging clients

Perhaps, the most radical stance is hope. Many clients believe (or have been told) it's "too late" to change. This belief can become a self-fulfilling prophecy.

- Celebrate small shifts in behavior or thoughts. Note acts of self-compassion and connection.
- Share stories and examples of midlife recovery (when appropriate).
- Hold a vision of recovery that clients may not yet see for themselves.

Clinicians should offer realistic optimism: recovery is not about perfection or returning to a prior version of oneself.

Offer integrative treatment using a team-based treatment

To be effective, recovery must be integrative. Chapter 9 offers suggestions on integrative treatment. Determine what treatment(s) will be most effective for your clients. Seek training and consultation with unfamiliar modalities.

- Include a range of modalities and approaches (Health at Every Size [HAES]/ Intuitive Eating [IE], somatic, compassion practices, relational, trauma-aware) tailored to the client's history and needs
- Create teams of professionals where indicated. Consider including dieticians, psychiatrists, and/or medical doctors trained in working with midlife eating disorders
- Seek adjunctive providers to fill knowledge or skill gaps (Eye Movement Desensitization and Reprocessing (EMDR) or somatic therapists, ketamine providers, etc.)

Bibliography

Abelsson, A., & Willman, A. (2021). Ethics and aesthetics in injection treatments with Botox and Filler. *Journal of Women & Aging, 33*(6), 583–595. https://doi.org/10.1080/08952841.2020.1730682

Aharoni Lir, S., & Ayalon, L. (2024). Beauty work or beauty care? Women's perceptions of appearance in the second half of life. *Journal of Women & Aging, 36*(3), 256–271. https://doi.org/10.1080/08952841.2024.2321668

Ahrens, C. J. C., & Ryff, C. D. (2006). Multiple roles and well-being: Sociodemographic and psychological moderators. *Sex Roles, 55*, 801–815. https://www.midus.wisc.edu/findings/pdfs/769.pdf

Aldao, A., Nolen-Hoeksema, S., & Schweizer, S. (2010). Emotion regulation strategies across psychopathology: A meta-analytic review. *Clinical Psychology Review, 30*(2), 217–237. https://doi.org/10.1016/j.cpr.2009.11.004

Amador-Patarroyo, M. J., Rodriguez-Rodriguez, A., & Montoya-Ortiz, G. (2012). How does age at onset influence the outcome of autoimmune diseases? *Autoimmune Diseases, 2012*, 251730. https://doi.org/10.1155/2012/251730

Aukerman, E. L., & Jafferany, M. (2023). The psychological consequences of androgenetic alopecia: A systematic review. *Journal of Cosmetic Dermatology, 22*(1), 89–95. https://doi.org/10.1111/jocd.14983

American Psychiatric Association. (2013). *Diagnostic and statistical manual of mental disorders* (5th ed.). American Psychiatric Publishing.

Arcelus, J., Mitchell, A. J., Wales, J., & Nielsen, S. (2011). Mortality rates in patients with anorexia nervosa and other eating disorders. A meta-analysis of 36 studies. *Archives of General Psychiatry, 68*(7), 724–731. https://doi.org/10.1001/archgenpsychiatry.2011.74

Avis, N. E., Crawford, S. L., & McKinlay, S. M. (1997). Psychosocial, behavioral, and health factors related to menopause symptomatology. *Women's Health (Hillsdale, N.J.), 3*(2), 103–120.

Awad, G. H., Norwood, C., Taylor, D. S., Martinez, M., McClain, S., Jones, B., Holman, A., & Chapman-Hilliard, C. (2015). Beauty and body image concerns among African American college women. *The Journal of Black Psychology, 41*(6), 540–564. https://doi.org/10.1177/0095798414550864

Bacon, J. L. (2017). The menopausal transition. *Obstetrics and Gynecology Clinics of North America, 44*(2), 285–296. https://doi.org/10.1016/j.ogc.2017.02.008

Baenas, I., Etxandi, M., & Fernández-Aranda, F. (2024). Medical complications in anorexia and bulimia nervosa. Complicaciones médicas en anorexia y bulimia nerviosa. *Medicina Clínica, 162*(2), 67–72. https://doi.org/10.1016/j.medcli.2023.07.028

Baker, J. H., Eisenlohr-Moul, T., Wu, Y. K., Schiller, C. E., Bulik, C. M., & Girdler, S. S. (2019). Ovarian hormones influence eating disorder symptom variability during the menopause transition: A pilot study. *Eating Behaviors*, *35*, 101337. https://doi.org/10.1016/j.eatbeh.2019.101337

Bardone-Cone, A. M., Johnson, S., Raney, T. J., Zucker, N., Watson, H. J., & Bulik, C. M. (2019). Eating disorder recovery in men: A pilot study. *The International Journal of Eating Disorders*, *52*(12), 1370–1379. https://doi.org/10.1002/eat.23153

Bardone-Cone, A. M., Wonderlich, S. A., Frost, R. O., Bulik, C. M., Mitchell, J. E., Uppala, S., & Simonich, H. (2007). Perfectionism and eating disorders: current status and future directions. *Clinical Psychology Review*, *27*(3), 384–405. https://doi.org/10.1016/j.cpr.2006.12.005

Barnes, M., Abhyankar, P., Dimova, E., & Best, C. (2020). Associations between body dissatisfaction and self-reported anxiety and depression in otherwise healthy men: A systematic review and meta-analysis. *PloS One*, *15*(2), e0229268. https://doi.org/10.1371/journal.pone.0229268

Barroso, C. S., Peters, R. J., Johnson, R. J., Kelder, S. H., & Jefferson, T. (2010). Beliefs and perceived norms concerning body image among African-American and Latino teenagers. *Journal of Health Psychology*, *15*(6), 858–870. https://doi.org/10.1177/1359105309358197

Bassett-Gunter, R., McEwan, D., & Kamarhie, A. (2017). Physical activity and body image among men and boys: A meta-analysis. *Body Image*, *22*, 114–128. https://doi.org/10.1016/j.bodyim.2017.06.007

Bath, P. A., & Deeg, D. (2005). Social engagement and health outcomes among older people: Introduction to a special section. *European Journal of Ageing*, *2*(1), 24–30. https://doi.org/10.1007/s10433-005-0019-4

Beevers, C. G., Welkowitz, L. A., & Peterman, J. S. (2016). Emotion regulation and eating disorders. In J. L. M. T. Manore (Ed.), *Nutrition and eating disorders* (pp. 125–145). Academic Press.

Bennett, E. V., Welch, K. A., & Fischer, O. J. (2024). "I tried to appreciate it in a different way": Older lesbian, bisexual, and queer women's body image and embodiment across the life course. *Body Image*, *48*, 101653. https://doi.org/10.1016/j.bodyim.2023.101653

Berent-Spillson, A., Marsh, C., Persad, C., Randolph, J., Zubieta, J. K., & Smith, Y. (2017). Metabolic and hormone influences on emotion processing during menopause. *Psychoneuroendocrinology*, *76*, 218–225. https://doi.org/10.1016/j.psyneuen.2016.08.026

Berge, J. M., Loth, K., Hanson, C., Croll-Lampert, J., & Neumark-Sztainer, D. (2012). Family life cycle transitions and the onset of eating disorders: A retrospective grounded theory approach. *Journal of Clinical Nursing*, *21*(9–10), 1355–1363. https://doi.org/10.1111/j.1365-2702.2011.03762.x

Berger, J. (2008). *Ways of seeing*. Penguin UK.

Berk, L. E. (2018). *Development through the lifespan* (7th ed.). Pearson.

Blakslee, A. (2020). The role of polyvagal theory in trauma treatment and recovery. *Journal of Trauma and Body-Based Therapies*, *15*(2), 128–145.

Blanchflower, D. G., & Oswald, A. J. (2008). Is well-being U-shaped over the life cycle?. *Social Science & Medicine (1982)*, *66*(8), 1733–1749. https://doi.org/10.1016/j.socscimed.2008.01.030

Bonanno, G. A., & Kaltman, S. (2001). The varieties of grief experience. *Clinical Psychology Review, 21*(5), 705–734. https://doi.org/10.1016/s0272-7358(00)00062-3

Boss, P. (2006). *Loss, trauma, and resilience: Therapeutic work with ambiguous loss.* W. W. Norton & Company.

Bradshaw, J. (1988). *Healing the shame that binds you.* Health Communications, Inc.

Brewerton, T. D. (2007). Posttraumatic stress disorder and eating disorders: The role of trauma in the etiology of eating disorders. *Psychiatric Clinics of North America, 30*(3), 277–294. https://doi.org/10.1016/j.psc.2007.04.002

Brown, B. (2006). Shame resilience theory: A grounded theory study on women and shame. *Families in Society, 87*(1), 43–52. https://doi.org/10.1606/1044-3894.3483

Brown, B. (2020). *The gifts of imperfection* (10th ed.). Random House.

Brown, B. (2021). *Atlas of the heart: Mapping meaningful connection and the language of human experience.* Random House.

Bruch, H. (1978). *The golden cage: The enigma of anorexia nervosa.* Harvard University Press.

Brumberg, J. J. (2000). *Fasting girls: The history of Anorexia Nervosa.* Vintage.

Bruns Vi, N., Tressler, E. H., Vendruscolo, L. F., Leggio, L., & Farokhnia, M. (2024). IUPHAR review - Glucagon-like peptide-1 (GLP-1) and substance use disorders: An emerging pharmacotherapeutic target. *Pharmacological Research, 207*, 107312. https://doi.org/10.1016/j.phrs.2024.107312

Bryson, C., Douglas, D., & Schmidt, U. (2024). Established and emerging treatments for eating disorders. *Trends in Molecular Medicine, 30*(4), 392–402. https://doi.org/10.1016/j.molmed.2024.02.009

Buckland, P., Jones, D., & Stout, P. (2018). Physical health in middle age: Prevalence and prevention. *Journal of Health and Aging, 22*(4), 358–365.

Budge, S. L., Adelson, J. L., & Howard, K. A. S. (2013). Anxiety and depression in transgender individuals: The roles of transition status, loss, social support, and coping. *Journal of Consulting and Clinical Psychology, 81*(3), 545–557. https://doi.org/10.1037/a0031774

Bulik, C. M. (2000). *Midlife eating disorders: Your journey to recovery.* Walker Books.

Bulik, C. M., Hebebrand, J., Keski-Rahkonen, A., Klump, K. L., Reichborn-Kjennerud, T., Mazzeo, S. E., & Wade, T. D. (2007). Genetic epidemiology, endophenotypes, and eating disorder classification. *The International Journal of Eating Disorders, 40*(Suppl), S52–S60. https://doi.org/10.1002/eat.20398

Bulik, C. M., Sullivan, P. F., & Kendler, K. S. (2012). Genetics of eating disorders. *Annual Review of Clinical Psychology, 8*, 165–192.

Buss, D. M. (1989). Sex differences in human mate preferences: Evolutionary hypotheses tested in 37 cultures. *Behavioral and Brain Sciences, 12*(1), 1–49. https://doi.org/10.1017/S0140525X00023992

Byrne, E., Gaffey, J., Hayden, L., Daly, A., Gallagher, P., & Dunne, S. (2023). Body image and cancer-related lymphoedema: A systematic review. *Psycho-oncology, 32*(10), 1528–1538. https://doi.org/10.1002/pon.6215

Cabral, M. C., Coelho, G. M. O., Oliveira, N., Canella, D. S., Brasil, R. L. O., Campos, T. A. M., Faerstein, E., & Bezerra, F. F. (2024). Association of body image perception and (dis)satisfaction with adiposity in adults: The Pró-Saúde study. *PloS One, 19*(6), e0304987. https://doi.org/10.1371/journal.pone.0304987

Calder, A., Mock, S., Friedli, N., Pasi, P., & Hasler, G. (2023). Psychedelics in the treatment of eating disorders: Rationale and potential mechanisms. *European Neuropsychopharmacology: The Journal of the European College of Neuropsychopharmacology, 75*, 1–14. https://doi.org/10.1016/j.euroneuro.2023.05.008

Caldwell, C. (2018). *Bodyfulness: Somatic practices for presence, empowerment, and waking up in this life.* Shambhala.

Camilleri, M. (2007). Gastroparesis: Pathophysiology and clinical management. *American Journal of Gastroenterology, 102*(4), 903–918. https://doi.org/10.1111/j.1572-0241.2007.01131.x

Cancer Research UK. (n.d.). *Age and cancer.* Cancer Research UK. Retrieved March 12, 2025, from https://www.cancerresearchuk.org/about-cancer/causes-of-cancer/age-and-cancer#:~:text=Anyone%20can%20get%20cancer%2C%20but%20cancer%20at%20a%20young%20age,people%20aged%2075%20and%20over.

Carroll, P., Tiggemann, M., & Wade, T. (1999). The role of body dissatisfaction and bingeing in the self-esteem of women with type II diabetes. *Journal of Behavioral Medicine, 22*(1), 59–74. https://doi.org/10.1023/a:1018799618864

Cash, T. F., & Smolak, L. (2011). *Body image: A handbook of theory, research, and clinical practice.* Guilford Press.

Cash, T. F. (2004). Body image: past, present, and future. *Body Image, 1*(1):1–5. https://doi.org/10.1016/S1740-1445(03)00011-1

Chandon, P., & Wansink, B. (2012). Does food marketing need to make us fat? A review and solutions. *Nutrition Reviews, 70*(10), 571–593. https://doi.org/10.1111/j.1753-4887.2012.00518.x

Chen, X., & Wang, Y. (2012). Is ideal body image related to obesity and lifestyle behaviours in African American adolescents?. *Child: Care, Health and Development, 38*(2), 219–228. https://doi.org/10.1111/j.1365-2214.2011.01227.x

Christensen, G. J. (2002). Oral care for patients with bulimia. *Journal of the American Dental Association (1939), 133*(12), 1689–1691. https://doi.org/10.14219/jada.archive.2002.0121

Chung, S. S, W. H., & Fichter, M. M. (2016). Medical complications of eating disorders. *Journal of Clinical Psychiatry, 77*(7), 921–928.

Clarke, P., Marshall, V. W., & Weir, D. (2012). Unexpected retirement from full time work after age 62: Consequences for life satisfaction in older Americans. *European Journal of Ageing, 9*(3), 207–219. https://doi.org/10.1007/s10433-012-0229-5

Cloitre, M., Garvert, D. W., Brewin, C. R., Bryant, R. A., & Maercker, A. (2013). *Expert consensus criteria for complex posttraumatic stress disorder. Journal of Traumatic Stress, 26*(6), 643–649. https://doi.org/10.1002/jts.21839

Cohn, T. J. (2017). The impact of mindfulness meditation on body image. *Journal of Counseling Psychology, 64*(4), 448–459.

Conviser, J. H., Fisher, S. D., & Mitchell, K. B. (2014). Oral care behavior after purging in a sample of women with bulimia nervosa. *Journal of the American Dental Association (1939), 145*(4), 352–354. https://doi.org/10.14219/jada.2014.5

Cooper, G. S., & Stroehla, B. C. (2003). The epidemiology of autoimmune diseases. *Autoimmunity Reviews, 2*(3), 119–125. https://doi.org/10.1016/s1568-9972(03)00006-5

Corrigan, P. W., Druss, B. G., & Perlick, D. A. (2014). The impact of mental illness stigma on seeking and participating in mental health care. *Psychological Science in the Public Interest: A Journal of the American Psychological Society, 15*(2), 37–70. https://doi.org/10.1177/1529100614531398

Creed, P. A., & Klisch, J. (2005). Future outlook and financial strain: Testing the personal agency and latent deprivation models of unemployment and well-being. *Journal of Occupational Health Psychology, 10*(3), 251–260. https://doi.org/10.1037/1076-8998.10.3.251

Cuerva, K., Spirou, D., Cuerva, A., Delaquis, C., & Raman, J. (2024). Perspectives and preliminary experiences of psychedelics for the treatment of eating disorders: A systematic scoping review. *European Eating Disorders Review: The Journal of the Eating Disorders Association, 32*(5), 980–1001. https://doi.org/10.1002/erv.3101

Cumella, E. J., & Kally, Z. (2008). Profile of 50 women with midlife-onset eating disorders. *Eating Disorders: The Journal of Treatment & Prevention, 16*(3), 193–203. https://doi.org/10.1080/10640260802016670

Cummings, S. R., & Melton, L. J. (2002). Epidemiology and outcomes of osteoporotic fractures. *Lancet, 359*(9319), 1761–1767. https://doi.org/10.1016/S0140-6736(02)08657-9

Dalenberg, C. J., Straus, E., & Carlson, E. B. (2017). Defining trauma. In S. N. Gold (Ed.), *APA handbook of trauma psychology: Foundations in knowledge* (Vol. 1, pp. 15–33). American Psychological Association.

Dalle Grave, R., Rigamonti, R., Todisco, P., Oliosi, E. (1996). Dissociation and traumatic experiences in eating disorders. *European Eating Disorders Review, 4*, 232–240.

Dalzell, H. J., & Protos, K. (2020). *A clinician's guide to gender identity and body image.* Jessica Kingsley Publishers.

Dalzell, H. J., & Protos, K, & Hunt, S. K. (2022). Eating disorders, body image, and body positivity. In A. S. Keuroghlian, J. Potter, & S. L. Reisner (Eds.), *Transgender and gender diverse health care: The Fenway Guide*. McGraw Hill. https://accessmedicine.mhmedical.com/content.aspx?bookid=3104&sectionid=259325830

Dang, L., Ananthasubramaniam, A., & Mezuk, B. (2022). Spotlight on the challenges of depression following retirement and opportunities for interventions. *Clinical Interventions in Aging, 17*, 1037–1056.

Devlin, M. J., Goldfein, J. A., & Klump, K. L. (2007). Binge eating disorder in men: A closer look at the body image and psychological factors. *International Journal of Eating Disorders, 40*(1), 93–100.

Devoe, D. J., Dimitropoulos, G., Anderson, A., Bahji, A., Flanagan, J., Soumbasis, A., Patten, S. B., Lange, T., & Paslakis, G. (2021). The prevalence of substance use disorders and substance use in anorexia nervosa: A systematic review and meta-analysis. *Journal of Eating Disorders, 9*(1), 161. https://doi.org/10.1186/s40337-021-00516-3

Dhami, L. (2021). Psychology of hair loss patients and importance of counseling. *Indian Journal of Plastic Surgery: Official Publication of the Association of Plastic Surgeons of India, 54*(4), 411–415. https://doi.org/10.1055/s-0041-1741037

Dimitrov, D., & Kroumpouzos, G. (2023). Beauty perception: A historical and contemporary review. *Clinics in Dermatology, 41*(1), 33–40. https://doi.org/10.1016/j.clindermatol.2023.02.006

Dittmar, H. (2009). How do "body perfect" ideals in the media affect women's body image and self-esteem? *Journal of Social and Clinical Psychology, 28*(1), 1 14. https://doi.org/10.1521/jscp.2009.28.1.1

Do, E. K., Cohen, S. A., & Brown, M. J. (2014). Socioeconomic and demographic factors modify the association between informal caregiving and health in the Sandwich Generation. *BMC Public Health, 14*(362). https://doi.org/10.1186/1471-2458-14-362.

Domschke, K., Stevens, S., Golik, P., & Götz, K. (2010). Interoceptive sensitivity and anxiety: The role of the insular cortex in the regulation of emotions. *Psychiatry Research, 183*(3), 137–141. https://doi.org/10.1016/j.psychres.2009.08.005

Donnelly, L. R., Clarke, L. H., Phinney, A., & MacEntee, M. I. (2016). The impact of oral health on body image and social interactions among elders in long-term care. *Gerodontology*, *33*(4), 480–489. https://doi.org/10.1111/ger.12187

Dougherty, E. N., Murphy, J., Hamlett, S., George, R., Badillo, K., Johnson, N. K., & Haedt-Matt, A. A. (2020). Emotion regulation flexibility and disordered eating. *Eating Behaviors*, *39*, 101428. https://doi.org/10.1016/j.eatbeh.2020.101428

Dovey, T. M., van der Kooij, A., & Farrow, C. V. (2008). The role of sensory sensitivity in eating disorders. *Eating Behaviors*, *9*(4), 453–460.

Ehrmann, D. A., Liljegren, M., & Birt, J. A. (2002). Endocrine dysfunction in anorexia nervosa. *Journal of Clinical Endocrinology & Metabolism*, *87*(11), 5188–5194.

Eiring, K., Wiig Hage, T., & Reas, D. L. (2021). Exploring the experience of being viewed as "not sick enough": A qualitative study of women recovered from anorexia nervosa or atypical anorexia nervosa. *Journal of Eating Disorders*, *9*, 1–10. https://doi.org/10.1186/s40337-021-00495-5

Eisenberg, M. E., & Neumark-Sztainer, D. (2010). Social norms and body image. *Eating Disorders*, *18*(1), 49–64.

Erikson, E. (1982). *The life cycle completed.* WW Norton & Company.

Erikson, E. H. (1963). *Childhood and society* (2nd ed.). Norton.

Fairburn, C. G. (2008). *Cognitive behavior therapy and eating disorders.* Guilford Press.

Fairburn, C. G., Cooper, Z., & Shafran, R. (2015). *Cognitive behavioral therapy for eating disorders: A comprehensive treatment guide.* Guilford Press.

Fairburn, C. G., & Harrison, P. J. (2003). Eating disorders. *Lancet*, *361*(9355), 407–416. https://doi.org/10.1016/S0140-6736(03)12378-1

Falba, T. A., Sindelar, J. L., & Gallo, W. T. (2009). Work expectations, realizations, and depression in older workers. *The Journal of Mental Health Policy and Economics*, *12*(4), 175–186.

Fareri, D. S., Gabard-Durnam, L., Goff, B., Flannery, J., Gee, D. G., Lumian, D. S., Caldera, C., & Tottenham, N. (2015). Normative development of ventral striatal resting state connectivity in humans. *NeuroImage*, *118*, 422–437. https://doi.org/10.1016/j.neuroimage.2015.06.022

Farokhnia, M., Lähteenvuo, M., Tiihonen, J., Solismaa, A., Tanskanen, A., Mittendorfer-Rutz, E., & Taipale, H. (2024). Repurposing semaglutide and liraglutide for alcohol use disorder. *JAMA Psychiatry*, *81*(12), 1234–1241. https://doi.org/10.1001/jamapsychiatry.2024.3599

Fichter, M. M., & Quadflieg, N. (2016). Long-term course and outcome of anorexia nervosa. *Journal of Eating Disorders*, *4*(1), 1–15.

Fikkan, J. L., & Rothblum, E. D. (2012). Is fat a feminist issue? Exploring the gendered nature of body image and weight bias. *Sex Roles*, *66*(9–10), 574–585. https://doi.org/10.1007/s11199-011-0022-5

Fink, B., & Penton-Voak, I. S. (2002). Evolutionary psychology of human mate choice. *The Evolutionary Psychology of Human Mating*, 33–58. https://www.tandfonline.com/doi/abs/10.1300/J056v18n02_05

Fischer, S. (2019). Severe and enduring anorexia nervosa: A review of the literature and clinical implications. *Eating Disorders*, *27*(5), 523–539.

Flegal, K. M., Carroll, M. D., Kit, B. K., & Ogden, C. L. (2012). Prevalence of obesity and trends in the distribution of body mass index among US adults, 1999-2010. *JAMA*, *307*(5), 491–497. https://doi.org/10.1001/jama.2012.39

Fletcher, B., Schreiber, M., & Clark, D. (2018). Cardiovascular risk and prevention in middle-aged adults. *American Journal of Preventive Medicine*, *55*(3), 296–303.

Forrester-Knauss, C., & Zemp Stutz, E. (2012). Gender differences in disordered eating and weight dissatisfaction in Swiss adults: Which factors matter?. *BMC Public Health*, *12*, 809. https://doi.org/10.1186/1471-2458-12-809

Frank, G. K. W., Shott, M. E., & DeGuzman, M. C. (2019). The neurobiology of eating disorders. *Child and Adolescent Psychiatric Clinics of North America*, *28*(4), 629–640. https://doi.org/10.1016/j.chc.2019.05.007

Fredrickson, B. L., & Roberts, T.-A. (1997). Objectification theory: Toward understanding women's lived experiences and mental health risks. *Psychology of Women Quarterly*, *21*(2), 173–206. https://doi.org/10.1111/j.1471-6402.1997.tb00108.x

Freud, S. (1953). *Three essays on the theory of sexuality* (J. Strachey, Trans.). Basic Books. (Original work published 1905)

Freud, S. (1957). *Repression*. In J. Strachey (Ed. & Trans.), *The standard edition of the complete psychological works of Sigmund Freud* (Vol. 14, pp. 141–158). Hogarth Press. (Original work published 1915)

Freud, S. (1981). Instincts and their vicissitudes. In J. Strachey (Ed. & Trans.), *The standard edition of the complete psychological works of Sigmund Freud* (Vol. 14, pp. 117–140). Hogarth Press. (Original work published 1915)

Friedman, J. S., McKenzie, S. M., & Kessler, L. A. (2017). The effects of anorexia nervosa on bone mineral density. *International Journal of Eating Disorders*, *50*(3), 234–241.

Frost, R. O., Marten, P., Lahart, C. M., & Rosenblate, R. (1990). The dimensions of perfectionism. *Cognitive Therapy and Research*, *14*(5), 449–468. https://doi.org/10.1007/BF01172967

Füstös, J., Gramann, K., Herbert, B. M., & Pollatos, O. (2013). On the embodiment of emotion regulation: Interoceptive awareness facilitates reappraisal. *Social Cognitive and Affective Neuroscience*, *8*(8), 911–917. https://doi.org/10.1093/scan/nss089

Gagne, D. A., Von Holle, A., Brownley, K. A., Runfola, C. D., Hofmeier, S., Branch, K. E., & Bulik, C. M. (2012). Eating disorder symptoms and weight and shape concerns in a large web-based convenience sample of women ages 50 and above: results of the Gender and Body Image (GABI) study. *The International Journal of Eating Disorders*, *45*(7), 832–844. https://doi.org/10.1002/eat.22030

Garner, D. M., & Garfinkel, P. E. (1980). Socio-cultural factors in the development of anorexia nervosa. *Psychological Medicine*, *10*(4), 647–656. https://doi.org/10.1017/s0033291700054945

Gart, M. S., & Gutowski, K. A. (2016). Overview of Botulinum Toxins for aesthetic uses. *Clinics in Plastic Surgery*, *43*(3), 459–471. https://doi.org/10.1016/j.cps.2016.03.003

Gaudiani, J. L., Bogetz, A., & Yager, J. (2022). Terminal anorexia nervosa: Three cases and proposed clinical characteristics. *Journal of Eating Disorders*, *10*(1), 23. https://doi.org/10.1186/s40337-022-00548-3

Gendron, T. L., & Lydecker, J. (2016). The thin-youth ideal: Should we talk about aging anxiety in relation to body image?. *International Journal of Aging & Human Development*, *82*(4), 255–270. https://doi.org/10.1177/0091415016641693

Gibson, C., O'Connor, M., White, R., Jackson, M., Baxi, S., & Halkett, G. K. B. (2021). 'I didn't even recognise myself': Survivors' experiences of altered appearance and body image distress during and after treatment for head and neck cancer. *Cancers*, *13*(15), 3893. https://doi.org/10.3390/cancers13153893

Gilbert, P. (2003). Shame, status, and social roles: A cognitive-experiential approach to understanding the role of shame in depression and anxiety. In P. Gilbert (Ed.), *The nature of shame: A psychoanalytic perspective* (pp. 109–137). Brunner-Routledge.

Gilbert, P. (2011). Shame in psychotherapy and the role of compassion focused therapy. In R. L. Dearing & J. P. Tangney (Eds.), *Shame in the therapy hour* (pp. 325–354). American Psychological Association.

Gonzalez, A., Makarov, S., & Rojas, M. (2018). Body image in autoimmune disease patients: Impact and intervention strategies. *Journal of Autoimmune Conditions, 12*(2), 95–107. https://doi.org/10.1016/j.jacc.2018.02.005

Grabe, S., Ward, L. M., & Hyde, J. S. (2008). The role of the media in body image concerns among women: A meta-analysis of experimental and correlational studies. *Psychological Bulletin, 134*(3), 460–476. https://doi.org/10.1037/0033-2909.134.3.460

Greenberg, L. S. (2002). *Emotion-focused therapy: Coaching clients to work through their feelings*. American Psychological Association.

Greeson, J. K. P., Sim, L., & Reiser, R. (2019). The role of food-related anxiety in ARFID: A systematic review of the literature. *Journal of Eating Disorders, 7*, 27.

Gregorowski, C., Seedat, S., & Jordaan, G. P. (2013). A clinical approach to the assessment and management of co-morbid eating disorders and substance use disorders. *BMC Psychiatry, 13*, 289. https://doi.org/10.1186/1471-244X-13-289

Griffiths, S., Murray, S. B., Krug, I., & McLean, S. A. (2018). The contribution of social media to body dissatisfaction, eating disorder symptoms, and anabolic steroid use among sexual minority men. *Cyberpsychology, Behavior and Social Networking, 21*(3), 149–156. https://doi.org/10.1089/cyber.2017.0375

Griffiths, S., Murray, S. B., & Touyz, S. (2013). Psychological interventions in the treatment of eating disorders at midlife. *European Eating Disorders Review, 21*(6), 430–436. https://doi.org/10.1002/erv.2256

Griffiths, S., Murray, S. B., & Touyz, S. (2015). The role of shame in the development and maintenance of eating disorders. *Clinical Psychology Review, 41*, 1–12.

Grilo, C. M., Ivezaj, V., Lydecker, J. A., & White, M. A. (2019). Toward an understanding of the distinctiveness of body-image constructs in persons categorized with overweight/obesity, bulimia nervosa, and binge-eating disorder. *Journal of psychosomatic research, 126*, 109757. https://doi.org/10.1016/j.jpsychores.2019.109757

Gross, J. J. (2002). Emotion regulation: Affective, cognitive, and social consequences. *Psychophysiology, 39*(3), 281–291. https://doi.org/10.1017/S0048577201393198

Gross, J. J., & Muñoz, R. F. (1995). Emotion regulation and mental health. *Clinical Psychology: Science and Practice, 2*(2), 151–164. https://doi.org/10.1111/j.1468-2850.1995.tb00036.x

Grucza, R. A., Norberg, K. E., & Bierut, L. J. (2007). Binge eating disorder and obesity in a community sample. *American Journal of Psychiatry, 164*(5), 845–850.

Gurung, J., Persons, P., & Kilpela, L. (2024). Body image and eating issues in midlife: A narrative review with clinical question recommendations. *Maturitas, 188*, 108068. https://doi.org/10.1016/j.maturitas.2024.108068

Harris, A. P. (2019). The beauty of blackness: Hair, body image, and black identity. *Journal of African American Studies, 23*(2), 123–137.

Hawkins, R. L., & Dovey, T. M. (2009). Sensory processing and eating behavior: Implications for understanding disordered eating. *Eating Behaviors, 10*(4), 266–272. https://doi.org/10.1016/j.eatbeh.2009.06.002

Hay, P. (2013). A longitudinal study of the prevalence and risk factors for eating disorders in the general population. *International Journal of Eating Disorders, 46*(6), 563–574.

Hay, P., & Touyz, S. (2018). Classification challenges in the field of eating disorders: can severe and enduring anorexia nervosa be better defined? *Journal of Eating Disorders, 6*, 41.

Hayes, S., Strosahl, K., & Wilson, K. (2016). *Acceptance and commitment therapy: The process of mindful change* (2nd ed.). Guilford Press.

Haynos, A. F., Wang, S. B., & Fruzzetti, A. E. (2018). Restrictive eating is associated with emotion regulation difficulties in a non-clinical sample. *Eating Disorders, 26*(1), 5–12. https://doi.org/10.1080/10640266.2018.1418264

Heider, N., Spruyt, A., & De Houwer, J. (2018). Body dissatisfaction revisited: On the importance of implicit beliefs about actual and ideal body image. *Psychologica Belgica, 57*(4), 158–173. https://doi.org/10.5334/pb.362

Herman, J. L. (1997). *Trauma and recovery: The aftermath of violence—from domestic abuse to political terror*. Basic Books.

Herman, J. L. (1992). Complex PTSD: A syndrome in survivors of prolonged and repeated trauma. *Journal of Traumatic Stress, 5*(3), 377–391. https://onlinelibrary.wiley.com/doi/10.1002/jts.2490050305

Hodgdon, B. T., Wong, J. D., & Pittman, P. S. (2023). The psychological well-being and physical health of sandwiched caregivers in the United States: A scoping review. *Families, Systems & Health, 41*(2), 240–255. https://doi.org/10.1037/fsh0000716

Hofmann, S. G. (2014). Interpersonal emotion regulation model of mood and anxiety disorders. *Cognitive Therapy and Tesearch, 38*(5), 483–492. https://doi.org/10.1007/s10608-014-9620-1

Holderness, C. C., Brooks-Gunn, J., & Warren, M. P. (1994). Co-morbidity of eating disorders and substance abuse review of the literature. *The International Journal of Eating Disorders, 16*(1), 1–34. https://doi.org/10.1002/1098-108x(199407)16:1<1::aid-eat2260160102>3.0.co;2-t

Homan, K. J., & Tylka, T. L. (2014). Appearance-based exercise motivation: A meta-analytic review. *Body Image, 11*(3), 260–271. https://doi.org/10.1016/j.bodyim.2014.04.001

Hong, S. O. (2023). Cosmetic treatment using Botulinum Toxin in the oral and maxillofacial area: A narrative review of esthetic techniques. *Toxins, 15*(2), 82. https://doi.org/10.3390/toxins15020082

Honigman, R. J., Phillips, K. A., & Castle, D. J. (2004). A review of psychosocial outcomes for patients seeking cosmetic surgery. *Plastic and reconstructive surgery, 113*(4), 1229–1237. https://doi.org/10.1097/01.prs.0000110214.88868.ca

Hooper, S. C., Kilpela, L. S., Ogubuike, V., & Becker, C. B. (2023). Fat talk, old talk, or both? Association of negative body talk with mental health, body dissatisfaction, and quality of life in men and women. *Journal of Eating Disorders, 11*(1), 77. https://doi.org/10.1186/s40337-023-00803-1

Hossein, S. A., Bahrami, M., Mohamadirizi, S., & Paknahad, Z. (2015). Investigation of eating disorders in cancer patients and its relevance with body image. *Iranian Journal of Nursing and Midwifery Research, 20*(3), 327–333.

Hsu, L. K. (2009). *Eating disorders and medical complications*. In C. G. Fairburn & K. D. Brownell (Eds.), *Eating disorders and obesity: A comprehensive handbook* (pp. 225–241). Guilford Press.

Huang, H. (2018). The rise of type 2 diabetes in middle age: A growing concern. *Journal of Clinical Endocrinology*, *103*(5), 1537–1542.

Huang, J. Y., Rojas, L. A., & McManus, D. D. (2017). Diabulimia: A dangerous disorder. *Journal of Diabetes and Its Complications*, *31*(6), 1044–1048. https://doi.org/10.1016/j.jdiacomp.2017.02.005

Hurd, L. C. (2000). Older women's body image and embodied experience: An exploration. *Journal of Women & Aging*, *12*(3–4), 77–97. https://doi.org/10.1300/J074v12n03_06

Hurtado, M. D., Saadedine, M., Kapoor, E., Shufelt, C. L., & Faubion, S. S. (2024). Weight gain in midlife women. *Current Obesity Reports*, *13*(2), 352–363. https://doi.org/10.1007/s13679-024-00555-2

Immatters. (2023, February 21). *Weighing options for mid-life women*. https://immattersacp.org/archives/2023/02/weighing-options-for-mid-life-women.htm

Infurna, F. J., Gerstorf, D., & Lachman, M. E. (2020). Midlife in the 2020s: Opportunities and challenges. *The American Psychologist*, *75*(4), 470–485. https://doi.org/10.1037/amp0000591

International Society of Aesthetic Plastic Surgery (ISAPS). Press release citing Global Survey on Aesthetic/Cosmetic Procedures (2023). Retrieved from https://www.isaps.org/discover/about-isaps/global-statistics/global-survey-2022-full-report-and-press-releases/

Ip, E. J., Doroudgar, S., Salehi, A., Salehi, F., & Najmi, M. (2023). Diabulimia: A risky trend among adults with type 1 diabetes mellitus. *Endocrine Practice*, *29*(11), 849–854. https://doi.org/10.1016/j.eprac.2023.08.001

Izydorczyk, B., Kwapniewska, A., Lizinczyk, S., & Sitnik-Warchulska, K. (2018). Psychological resilience as a protective factor for the body image in post-mastectomy women with breast cancer. *International Journal of Environmental Research and Public Health*, *15*(6), 1181. https://doi.org/10.3390/ijerph15061181

Jensen M. D. (2008). Role of body fat distribution and the metabolic complications of obesity. *The Journal of Clinical Endocrinology and Metabolism*, *93*(11 Suppl 1), S57–S63. https://doi.org/10.1210/jc.2008-1585

Johnson, F., & Wardle, J. (2005). Body image and weight control in young women: The role of diet and physical activity. *International Journal of Eating Disorders*, *37*(3), 210–216. https://doi.org/10.1002/eat.20160

Johnstone, B. M., Leino, E. V., Ager, C. R., Ferrer, H., & Fillmore, K. M. (1996). Determinants of life-course variation in the frequency of alcohol consumption: Meta-analysis of studies from the collaborative alcohol-related longitudinal project. *Journal of Studies on Alcohol*, *57*(5), 494–506. https://doi.org/10.15288/jsa.1996.57.494

Jones, H. E., Faulkner, H. R., & Losken, A. (2022). The psychological impact of aesthetic surgery: A mini-review. *Aesthetic Surgery Journal. Open Forum*, *4*, ojac077. https://doi.org/10.1093/asjof/ojac077

Jordan, J. (1997). *Women's growth in diversity: More writings from the Stone Center*. Guilford Press.

Jordan, J. (2016). *Feminist therapy and relational-cultural theory: Theory and practice*. Routledge.

Jordan, J. (2017). *Relational-cultural therapy (2nd ed.)*. American Psychological Association. https://doi.org/10.1037/0000023-000

Jordan, J., & Hinds, J. (2016). Relational-cultural theory: An overview. *American Psychologist*, *71*(6), 487–497.

Jordan, J., Hinds, J., & Hays, D. G. (2011). Relational-cultural theory and body image: Understanding relational influences on women's body image. *Journal of Counseling & Development*, *89*(2), 174–181.

Jordan, J., Walker, M., & Hartling, L. M. (Eds.). (2004). *The complexity of connection: Writings from the Stone Center's Jean Baker Miller Training Institute*. Guilford Press.

Kabat-Zinn, J. (1990). *Full catastrophe living: Using the wisdom of your body and mind to face stress, pain, and illness*. Delacorte Press.

Kambanis, P. E., Harshman, S. G., Kuhnle, M. C., Kahn, D. L., Dreier, M. J., Hauser, K., Slattery, M., Becker, K. R., Breithaupt, L., Misra, M., Micali, N., Lawson, E. A., Eddy, K. T., & Thomas, J. J. (2022). Differential comorbidity profiles in avoidant/restrictive food intake disorder and anorexia nervosa: Does age play a role?. *The International Journal of Eating Disorders*, *55*(10), 1397–1403. https://doi.org/10.1002/eat.23777

Khandpur, G. (2015). Fat and Thin Sex: Fetishised Normal and Normalised Fetish. *M/C Journal*, *18*(3). https://doi.org/10.5204/mcj.976

Kapoor, E., Collazo-Clavell, M. L., & Faubion, S. S. (2017). Weight Gain in Women at Midlife: A Concise Review of the Pathophysiology and Strategies for Management. *Mayo Clinic proceedings*, *92*(10), 1552–1558. https://doi.org/10.1016/j.mayocp.2017.08.004

Katzman, D. K. (2003). Medical complications in adolescents and adults with anorexia nervosa. *Journal of Adolescent Health*, *33*(5), 314–321.

Kaye, W. H., Bulik, C. M., Thornton, L., Barbarich, N., & Masters, K. (2004). Comorbidity of anxiety disorders with anorexia and bulimia nervosa. *Journal of Abnormal Psychology*, *113*(4), 706–713.

Kaye, W. H., Fudge, J. L., & Paulus, M. P. (2013). New insights into symptoms and neurocircuitry of anorexia nervosa. *Nature Reviews Neuroscience*, *14*(9), 584–591.

Kearney-Cooke, A. (1999). *Body image and emotional well-being: The relationship between emotions and the body*. In T. Cash & T. Pruzinsky (Eds.), *Body image: A handbook of theory, research, and clinical practice* (pp. 345–353). The Guilford Press.

Kearney-Cooke, A. (2007). The relationship between body image and self-esteem in clinical populations. *Journal of Psychotherapy Practice and Research*, *16*(3), 151–160.

Keel, P. K., & Forney, K. J. (2013). Psychosocial risk factors for eating disorders. *The International Journal of Eating Disorders*, *46*(5), 433–439. https://doi.org/10.1002/eat.22094

Keith, J. A., Midlarsky, E. (2004). Anorexia nervosa in postmenopausal women: Clinical and empirical perspectives. *Journal of Mental Health and Aging*, *10*(4), 287–299.

Kelley, C. C., Neufeld, J. M., & Musher-Eizenman, D. R. (2010). Drive for thinness and drive for muscularity: opposite ends of the continuum or separate constructs? *Body Image*, *7*(1),74–7.

Keski-Rahkonen, A. (2021). Epidemiology of binge eating disorder: Prevalence, course, comorbidity, and risk factors. *Current Opinion in Psychiatry, 34*(6), 525–531. https://doi.org/10.1097/YCO.0000000000000750

Keski-Rahkonen, A., Hoek, H. W., Susser, E. S., Linna, M. S., Sihvola, E., Raevuori, A., Bulik, C. M., Kaprio, J., & Rissanen, A. (2007). Epidemiology and course of anorexia nervosa in the community. *The American Journal of Psychiatry*, *164*(8), 1259–1265. https://doi.org/10.1176/appi.ajp.2007.06081388

Khalsa, S. S., Adolphs, R., Cameron, O. G., Critchley, H. D., Davenport, P. W., Feinstein, J. S., Feusner, J. D., Garfinkel, S. N., Lane, R. D., Mehling, W. E., Meuret,

A. E., Nemeroff, C. B., Oppenheimer, S., Petzschner, F. H., Pollatos, O., Rhudy, J. L., Schramm, L. P., Simmons, W. K., Stein, M. B., Stephan, K. E., ... Interoception Summit 2016 participants (2018). Interoception and mental health: A roadmap. *Biological Psychiatry. Cognitive Neuroscience and Neuroimaging, 3*(6), 501–513. https://doi. org/10.1016/j.bpsc.2017.12.004

Khalsa, S. S., Berner, L. A., & Anderson, L. M. (2022). Gastrointestinal interoception in eating disorders: Charting a new path. *Current Psychiatry Reports, 24*(1), 47–60. https://doi.org/10.1007/s11920-022-01318-3

Khantzian, E. J. (1997). The self-medication hypothesis of substance use disorders: A reconsideration and recent applications. *Harvard Review of Psychiatry, 4*(5), 3–9.

Khatir, M. A., Modanloo, M., Dadgari, A., Yeganeh, L. T., & Khoddam, H. (2024). Empty nest syndrome: A concept analysis. *Journal of Education and Health Promotion, 13,* 269. https://doi.org/10.4103/jehp.jehp_874_23

Kınık, M. F., Gönüllü, F. V., Vatansever, Z., & Karakaya, I. (2017). Diabulimia, a Type I diabetes mellitus-specific eating disorder. *Turk pediatri arsivi, 52*(1), 46–49. https:// doi.org/10.5152/TurkPediatriArs.2017.2366

Kilpela, L. S., Becker, C. B., Wesley, N., & Stewart, T. (2015). Body image in adult women: moving beyond the younger years. *Advances in Eating Disorders (Abingdon, England), 3*(2), 144–164. https://doi.org/10.1080/21662630.2015.1012728

Kohlberg, L. (1981). *The philosophy of moral development.* Harper & Row.

Kokoszka, A., Pacura, A., Kostecka, B., Lloyd, C. E., & Sartorius, N. (2022). Body self-esteem is related to subjective well-being, severity of depressive symptoms, BMI, glycated hemoglobin levels, and diabetes-related distress in type 2 diabetes. *PloS One, 17*(2), e0263766. https://doi.org/10.1371/journal.pone.0263766

Kołodziejczyk, A., & Pawłowski, T. (2019). Negative body image in breast cancer patients. *Advances in Clinical and Experimental Medicine: Official Organ Wroclaw Medical University, 28*(8), 1137–1142. https://doi.org/10.17219/acem/103626

Kotilahti, E., West, M., Isomaa, R., Karhunen, L., Rocks, T., & Ruusunen, A. (2020). Treatment interventions for severe and enduring eating disorders: Systematic review. *The International Journal of Eating Disorders, 53*(8), 1280–1302. https://doi.org/10.1002/ eat.23322

Krause, S., Priebe, S., & Tischer, M. (2018). Eating disorders and cancer: A comprehensive review of the literature. *European Eating Disorders Review, 26*(2), 113–121. https://doi.org/10.1002/erv.2555

Kristeller, J. L., & Wolever, R. Q. (2011). Mindfulness-based eating awareness training for treating binge eating disorder: The evidence to date. *Eating Disorders, 19*(1), 49–61.

Kristensen, K., König, H. H., & Hajek, A. (2021). The empty nest, depressive symptoms and loneliness of older parents: Prospective findings from the German Ageing Survey. *Archives of Gerontology and Geriatrics, 95,* 104425. https://doi.org/10.1016/j. archger.2021.104425

Kronenfeld, L. W., Reba-Harrelson, L., Von Holle, A., Reyes, M. L., & Bulik, C. M. (2010). Ethnic and racial differences in body size perception and satisfaction. *Body Image, 7*(2), 131–136. https://doi.org/10.1016/j.bodyim.2009.11.002

Kuk, J. L., Saunders, T. J., Davidson, L. E., & Ross, R. (2009). Age-related changes in total and regional fat distribution. *Ageing Research Reviews, 8*(4), 339–348. https:// doi.org/10.1016/j.arr.2009.06.001

Kupfer D. J. (2015). Anxiety and DSM-5. *Dialogues in Clinical Neuroscience, 17*(3), 245–246. https://doi.org/10.31887/DCNS.2015.17.3/dkupfer

Kurtz, E. (2007). *Shame & Guilt* (2nd ed.). iUniverse, Inc.

Kurtz, R. (1990). *Body-centered psychotherapy: The Hakomi method.* LifeRhythm.

Kuryłowicz, A. (2023). Estrogens in Adipose Tissue Physiology and Obesity-Related Dysfunction. *Biomedicines, 11*(3), 690. https://doi.org/10.3390/biomedicines11030690

Lachman, M. E. (2004). Development in midlife. *Annual Review of Psychology, 55,* 305–331. https://doi.org/10.1146/annurev.psych.55.090902.141521

Lachman, M. E. (2015). Mind the gap in the middle: A call to study midlife. *Research in Human Development, 12*(3–4), 327–334. https://doi.org/10.1080/15427609.2015.1068048

Lachman, M. E., & James, J. B. (1997). Multiple perspectives on midlife: Transition and stability in development. In D. P. McAdams, A. de St. Aubin, & T. P. Logan (Eds.), *Adolescent development and the life course* (pp. 345–372). University of Chicago Press.

Lachman, M. E., Teshale, S., & Agrigoroaei, S. (2015). Midlife as a pivotal period in the life course: Balancing growth and decline at the crossroads of youth and old age. *International Journal of Behavioral Development, 39*(1), 20–31. https://doi.org/10.1177/0165025414533223

Lackner, J. M., & Ray, G. (2007). *Gastrointestinal complications in eating disorders.* In C. M. Bulik (Ed.), *Handbook of eating disorders and obesity* (pp. 214–230). Guilford Press.

Lange, S. (2020). The role of shame in bulimia nervosa: A clinical perspective. *Journal of Eating Disorders, 8*(1), 1–10.

Lauriat, Tara L., and Jacqueline A. Samson, 'Endocrine Disorders Associated with Psychological/Behavioral Problems', in Phillip M. Kleespies (ed.), *The Oxford Handbook of Behavioral Emergencies and Crises*, Oxford Library of Psychology (2016; online edn, Oxford Academic, 3 Nov. 2014), https://doi.org/10.1093/oxfordhb/9780199352722.013.32, accessed 3 Sept. 2025.

Larsson, L., Degens, H., Li, M., Salviati, L., Lee, Y. I., Thompson, W., Kirkland, J. L., & Sandri, M. (2019). Sarcopenia: Aging-related loss of muscle mass and function. *Physiological Reviews, 99*(1), 427–511. https://doi.org/10.1152/physrev.00061.2017

Lavie, C. J. (2014). *The obesity paradox.* Avery.

Lee, M. R., & Sher, K. J. (2018). "Maturing out" of binge and problem drinking. *Alcohol Research: Current Reviews, 39*(1), 31–42.

Leppanen, J., Brown, D., McLinden, H., Williams, S., & Tchanturia, K. (2022). The role of emotion regulation in eating disorders: A network meta-analysis approach. *Frontiers in Psychiatry, 13,* 793094. https://doi.org/10.3389/fpsyt.2022.793094

Levine, M. P., & Murnen, S. K. (2009). "Everybody knows that mass media are/are not [pick one] a cause of eating disorders": A critical review of the evidence for a causal link between media, negative body image, and disordered eating in females. *Journal of Social and Clinical Psychology, 28*(1), 11–33. https://doi.org/10.1521/jscp.2009.28.1.1

Levine, P. A. (1997). *Waking the tiger: Healing trauma: The innate capacity to transform overwhelming experiences.* North Atlantic Books.

Levine, P. A. (2010). *In an unspoken voice: How the body releases trauma and restores goodness.* North Atlantic Books.

Levine, P. A. (2015). *Trauma and memory: Brain and body in a search for the living past.* North Atlantic Books.

Levinson, D. J. (1978). *The seasons of a man's life*. Alfred A. Knopf.

Levy, B. R., Chung, P. H., Bedford, T., & Navrazhina, K. (2014). Facebook as a site for negative age stereotypes. *The Gerontologist, 54*(2), 172–176.

Lewer, M., Bauer, A., Hartmann, A. S., & Vocks, S. (2017). Different Facets of Body Image Disturbance in Binge Eating Disorder: A Review. *Nutrients, 9*(12), 1294. https://doi.org/10.3390/nu9121294

Lilenfeld, L. R., & Kaye, W. H. (1996). The link between alcoholism and eating disorders. *Alcohol Health and Research World, 20*(2), 94–99.

Linde, K., Lehnig, F., Treml, J., Nagl, M., Stepan, H., & Kersting, A. (2024). The trajectory of body image dissatisfaction during pregnancy and postpartum and its relationship to Body-Mass-Index. *PloS One, 19*(8), e0309396. https://doi.org/10.1371/journal.pone.0309396

Linehan, M. M. (2015). *DBT® skills training handouts and worksheets* (2nd ed.). Guilford Press.

Link, B. G., & Phelan, J. C. (2001). Conceptualizing stigma. *Annual Review of Sociology, 27*, 363–385. https://doi.org/10.1146/annurev.soc.27.1.363

Liotti, G., & Gilbert, P. (2011). *The influence of attachment and trauma on the development of the self*. In L. Atkinson & P. C. G. J. (Eds.), *Handbook of attachment: Theory, research, and clinical applications* (pp. 606–623). Guilford Press.

Liran-Alper, D., & Arose, P. (2007). *Body shaping and identity toning: Body representations in commercial television*. Haim Herzog Institute for Communication, Society and Politics, Tel Aviv University. (Hebrew)

Loth, K., van den Berg, P., Eisenberg, M. E., & Neumark-Sztainer, D. (2008). Stressful life events and disordered eating behaviors: findings from Project EAT. *The Journal of Adolescent Health: Official Publication of the Society for Adolescent Medicine, 43*(5), 514–516. https://doi.org/10.1016/j.jadohealth.2008.03.007

Lovejoy, J. C., & Sainsbury, A. (2008). Sex differences in obesity and the regulation of energy balance. *Obesity Reviews, 9*(6), 697–706. https://doi.org/10.1111/j.1467-789X.2008.00526.x

Lozano-Madrid, M., Clark Bryan, D., Granero, R., Sánchez, I., Riesco, N., Mallorquí-Bagué, N., Jiménez-Murcia, S., Treasure, J., & Fernández-Aranda, F. (2020). Impulsivity, emotional dysregulation and executive function deficits could be associated with alcohol and drug abuse in eating disorders. *Journal of Clinical Medicine, 9*(6), 1936. https://doi.org/10.3390/jcm9061936

Mahajan, S., Sawant, N. S., & Mahajan, S. (2023). Depression, body image and quality of life in acne scars. *Industrial Psychiatry Journal, 32*(2), 282–287. https://doi.org/10.4103/ipj.ipj_201_22

Maine, M., & Bunnell, D. (2008). Treatment of eating disorders in midlife and beyond: A feminist relational perspective. In M. Maine, B. H. McGilley, & D. Bunnell (Eds.), *Treatment of eating disorders: Bridging the research-practice gap* (pp. 231–248). Academic Press.

Maine, M., McGilley, B. H., & Bunnell, D. (Eds.). (2020). *Treatment of eating disorders: Bridging the research-practice gap* (2nd ed.). Academic Press.

Maki, P. M., & Resnick, S. M. (2000). Hormone therapy and cognitive function. *Current Opinion in Obstetrics & Gynecology, 12*(5), 461–465. https://doi.org/10.1097/00006254-200010000-00008

Mangweth-Matzek, B., Kummer, K. K., & Hoek, H. W. (2023). Update on the epidemiology and treatment of eating disorders among older people. *Current Opinion in Psychiatry, 36*(6), 405–411. https://doi.org/10.1097/YCO.0000000000000893

Mangweth-Matzek, B., Rupp, C. I., Hausmann, A., Assmayr, K., Mariacher, E., Kemmler, G., Whitworth, A. B., & Biebl, W. (2006). Never too old for eating disorders or body dissatisfaction: a community study of elderly women. *The International Journal of Eating Disorders, 39*(7), 583–586. https://doi.org/10.1002/eat.20327

Mangweth-Matzek, B., Rupp, C. I., Vedova, S., Dunst, V., Hennecke, P., Daniaux, M., & Pope, H. G. (2021). Disorders of eating and body image during the menopausal transition: Associations with menopausal stage and with menopausal symptomatology. *Eating and Weight Disorders: EWD, 26*(8), 2763–2769. https://doi.org/10.1007/s40519-021-01141-4

Martin, S. & Strodl, E. (2023). The relationship between childhood trauma, eating behaviours, and the mediating role of metacognitive beliefs. *Appetite, 188,* https://doi.org/10.1016/j.appet.2023.106975

Masten, A. S. (2001). Ordinary magic: Resilience processes in development. *American Psychologist, 56*(3), 227–238.

Matsumoto, A., & Rodgers, R. F. (2020). A review and integrated theoretical model of the development of body image and eating disorders among midlife and aging men. *Clinical Psychology Review, 81,* 101093. https://doi.org/10.1016/j.cpr.2020.101903

Matthews, A., Connelly, M. T., & Smith, S. M. (2019). The relationship between eating disorders and cancer: A clinical review. *Journal of Clinical Psychology, 75*(7), 1224–1233. https://doi.org/10.1002/jclp.22861

Matud, M. P. (2004). Gender differences in stress and coping styles. *Personality and Individual Differences, 37*(7), 1401–1415.

Mayo Clinic. (2022). Bulimia nervosa. *Mayo Clinic.* https://www.mayoclinic.org/diseases-conditions/bulimia-nervosa/symptoms-causes/syc-20350137

Mazzocco, K., Masiero, M., Carriero, M. C., & Pravettoni, G. (2019). The role of emotions in cancer patients' decision-making. *Ecancermedicalscience, 13,* 914. https://doi.org/10.3332/ecancer.2019.914

McAdams, D. P., & de St Aubin, E. D. (1992). A theory of generativity and its assessment through self-report, behavioral acts, and narrative themes in autobiography. *Journal of Personality and Social Psychology, 62*(6), 1003.

McCabe, M. P., & Ricciardelli, L. A. (2004). Body image dissatisfaction among males across the lifespan: A review of past literature. *Journal of Psychosomatic Research, 56*(6), 675–685. https://doi.org/10.1016/S0022-3999(03)00129-6

McCormack, D., O'Keeffe, D. F., Seery, C., & Eccles, D. F. (2025). The association between body image and psychological outcomes in multiple sclerosis. A systematic review. *Multiple Sclerosis and Related Disorders, 93,* 106226. https://doi.org/10.1016/j.msard.2024.106226

McDonald, K., & Thompson, J. K. (2016). Body image and muscle dysmorphia: A review of the literature. *Psychology of Men & Masculinity, 17*(3), 315–327. https://doi.org/10.1037/a0039794

McKee-Ryan, F., Song, Z., Wanberg, C. R., & Kinicki, A. J. (2005). Psychological and physical well-being during unemployment: A meta-analytic study. *The Journal of Applied Psychology, 90*(1), 53–76. https://doi.org/10.1037/0021-9010.90.1.53

Meczekalski, B., Podfigurna-Stopa, A., & Katulski, K. (2013). Long-term consequences of anorexia nervosa. *Maturitas*, *75*(3), 215–220. https://doi.org/10.1016/j.
maturitas.2013.04.014

Medeiros de Morais, M. S., Macêdo, S. G. G. F., do Nascimento, R. A., Vieira, M. C. A.,
Moreira, M. A., da Câmara, S. M. A., Almeida, M. D. G., & Maciel, Á. C. C. (2024).
Dissatisfaction with body image and weight gain in middle-aged women: A cross sec-
tional study. *PloS One*, *19*(1), e0290380. https://doi.org/10.1371/journal.pone.0290380

Mehler, P. S., & Brown, C. (2015). Anorexia nervosa and associated medical complications. *Journal of Eating Disorders*, *3*(1), 11.

Meningaud, J. P., Benadiba, L., Servant, J. M., Herve, C., Bertrand, J. C., & Pelicier, Y.
(2003). Depression, anxiety and quality of life: Outcome 9 months after facial cosmetic surgery. *Journal of Cranio-Maxillo-Facial Surgery: Official Publication of the
European Association for Cranio-Maxillo-Facial Surgery*, *31*(1), 46–50. https://doi.
org/10.1016/s1010-5182(02)00159-2

Menzel, J. E., van den Berg, P., Melnyk, S., & Paxton, S. J. (2010). Body image and
social comparison in young adult women: The role of friends and peers. *Body Image*,
7(4), 213–220.

Merino, M., Tornero-Aguilera, J. F., Rubio-Zarapuz, A., Villanueva-Tobaldo, C. V.,
Martín-Rodríguez, A., & Clemente-Suárez, V. J. (2024). Body perceptions and psychological well-being: A review of the impact of social media and physical measure-
ments on self-esteem and mental health with a focus on body image satisfaction and its
relationship with cultural and gender factors. *Healthcare (Basel, Switzerland)*, *12*(14),
1396. https://doi.org/10.3390/healthcare12141396

Milanović, Z., Pantelić, S., Trajković, N., Sporiš, G., Kostić, R., & James, N. (2013).
Age-related decrease in physical activity and functional fitness among elderly men
and women. *Clinical Interventions in Aging*, *8*, 549–556. https://doi.org/10.2147/CIA.
S44112

Miller, A. (1979/2008). *The drama of the gifted child: The search for the true self*. Basic
Books.

Miller, J. B. (1976). *Toward a new psychology of women*. Beacon Press.

Miller, J. B., & Stiver, I. P. (1997). *The healing connection: How women form relationships in therapy and in life*. Beacon Press.

Milothridis, P., Pavlidis, L., Haidich, A. B., & Panagopoulou, E. (2016). A systematic
review of the factors predicting the interest in cosmetic plastic surgery. *Indian Journal
of Plastic Surgery: Official Publication of the Association of Plastic Surgeons of India*,
49(3), 397–402. https://doi.org/10.4103/0970-0358.197224

Misra, M., Goldstein, M. A., & Clark, M. A. (2016). Long-term outcomes in anorexia
nervosa. *Current Opinion in Psychiatry*, *29*(6), 404–410.

Misra, M., & Klibanski, A. (2014). Endocrine consequences of anorexia nervosa. *The
Lancet. Diabetes & Endocrinology*, *2*(7), 581–592. https://doi.org/10.1016/S2213-
8587(13)70180-3

Mitchell, Karen S., and Cynthia M. Bulik, 'Life course epidemiology of eating disorders',
in Karestan C. Koenen, and others (eds), *A Life Course Approach to Mental Disorders*
(Oxford, 2013; online edn, Oxford Academic, 23 Jan. 2014), https://doi.org/10.1093/
acprof:oso/9780199657018.003.0013, accessed 3 Sept. 2025.

Mitchell, K. S., Mazzeo, S. E., Schlesinger, M. R., Brewerton, T. D., & Smith, B. N.
(2012). Comorbidity of partial and subthreshold PTSD among men and women with

eating disorders in the National Comorbidity Survey-Replication Study. *International Journal of Eating Disorders*, *25*, 307–315.

Mitchison, D., Hay, P., Griffiths, S., Murray, S. B., Bentley, C., Gratwick-Sarll, K., Harrison, C., & Mond, J. (2017). Disentangling body image: the relative associations of overvaluation, dissatisfaction, and preoccupation with psychological distress and eating disorder behaviors in male and female adolescents. *International Journal of Eating Disorders*, *50*(2), 118–126.

Mitchison, D., Hay, P., Slewa-Younan, S., & Mond, J. (2014). The changing demographic profile of eating disorder behaviors in the community, *BMC Public Health*, *14*, 943–952. https://doi.org/10.1186/1471-2458-14-943

Montgomery Sklar E. (2015). Body image, weight, and self-concept in men. *American Journal of Lifestyle Medicine*, *11*(3), 252–258. https://doi.org/10.1177/1559827615594351

Moore, A. A., Giuli, L., Gould, R., Hu, P., Zhou, K., Reuben, D., Greendale, G., & Karlamangla, A. (2006). Alcohol use, comorbidity, and mortality. *Journal of the American Geriatrics Society*, *54*(5), 757–762. https://doi.org/10.1111/j.1532-5415.2006.00728.x

Morales-Sánchez, L., Luque-Ribelles, V., Gil-Olarte, P., Ruiz-González, P., & Guil, R. (2021). Enhancing self-esteem and body image of breast cancer women through interventions: A systematic review. *International Journal of Environmental Research and Public Health*, *18*(4), 1640. https://doi.org/10.3390/ijerph18041640

Morley, J. E., Perry, H. M., 3rd, Kevorkian, R. T., & Patrick, P. (2006). Comparison of screening questionnaires for the diagnosis of hypogonadism. *Maturitas*, *53*(4), 424–429. https://doi.org/10.1016/j.maturitas.2005.07.004

Mortimer, R. (2019). Pride before a fall: Shame, diagnostic crossover, and eating disorders. *Journal of Bioethical Inquiry*, *16*(3), 365–374. https://doi.org/10.1007/s11673-019-09923-3

Moskowitz, L., & Weiselberg, E. (2017). Anorexia nervosa/atypical anorexia nervosa. *Current Problems in Pediatric and Adolescent Health Care*, *47*(4), 70–84. https://doi.org/10.1016/j.cppeds.2017.02.003

Muench, F., & Morgenstern, J. (2016). Incorporating substance use treatment into trauma-focused interventions for individuals with co-occurring disorders. *Psychiatry Research*, *238*, 92–97. https://doi.org/10.1016/j.psychres.2016.02.024

Mulchandani, M., Shetty, N., & Conrad, A., (2021). Treatment of eating disorders in older people: A systematic review. *Systematic Review*, *10*, 275.

Muller, M., & Roos, A. (2015). Testosterone and abdominal fat. *Hormone and Metabolic Research*, *47*(9), 664–670. https://doi.org/10.1055/s-0035-1556255

Murray, S. B. (2008). Spirituality and body image: Implications for treatment. *Eating Disorders*, *16*(1), 67–77.

Murugan, Y., Nagarajan, P., Subrahmanyam, D., & Kattimani, S. (2022). Severity of loneliness, depression and perceived social support in adults in the empty nest stage of the family life cycle and the influence of using digital technology. *Asian Journal of Psychiatry*, *76*, 103245. https://doi.org/10.1016/j.ajp.2022.103245

Nakajima, S. (2018). Complicated grief: recent developments in diagnostic criteria and treatment. *Philosophical Transactions*, *373*. https://dx.doi.org/10.1098/rstb.2017.0273

National Alliance for Caregiving and AARP. (2020). *Caregiving in the U.S.* 2020. Washington, DC: May 2020. https://www.aarp.org/content/dam/aarp/ppi/2021/05/caregiving-in-the-united-states-50-plus. https://doi.org//10.26419/ppi.00103.022

Neff, K. (2011). *Self-compassion: The proven of being kind to yourself.* William Morrow.

Neimeyer, R. A. (Ed.). (2001). *Meaning reconstruction & the experience of loss.* American Psychological Association. https://doi.org/10.1037/10397-000

Neimeyer, R. A. (Ed.). (2012). *Techniques of grief therapy: Creative practices for counseling the bereaved.* Routledge/Taylor & Francis Group. https://doi.org/10.4324/9780203152683

Nelson, G. (2016). Osteoarthritis in older adults: Managing the pain of aging. *Geriatric Medicine, 52*(4), 437–444.

Newman, L. (1991). *SomeBody to love: A guide to loving the body you have.* Third Side Press.

Ng, R., & Indran, N. (2023). Granfluencers on TikTok: Factors linked to positive self-portrayals of older adults on social media. *PloS One, 18*(2), e0280281. https://doi.org/10.1371/journal.pone.0280281

Nguyen, M. Q., Hsu, P. W., & Dinh, T. A. (2009). Asian blepharoplasty. *Seminars in Plastic Surgery, 23*(3), 185–197. https://doi.org/10.1055/s-0029-1224798

Nitsch, A., Dlugosz, H., Gibson, D., & Mehler, P. S. (2021). Medical complications of bulimia nervosa. *Cleveland Clinic Journal of Medicine, 88*(6), 333–343. https://doi.org/10.3949/ccjm.88a.20168

North, M. S., & Fiske, S. T. (2015). Modern attitudes toward older adults in the aging world: A cross-cultural meta-analysis. *Psychological Bulletin*; Advance online publication. https://doi.org/10.1037/a0039469

Nyblade, L., Stockton, M. A., Giger, K., Bond, V., Ekstrand, M. L., Lean, R. M., Mitchell, E. M. H., Nelson, R. E., Sapag, J. C., Siraprapasiri, T., Turan, J., & Wouters, E. (2019). Stigma in health facilities: Why it matters and how we can change it. *BMC Medicine, 17*(1), 25. https://doi.org/10.1186/s12916-019-1256-2

O'Donnell, M. L., Creamer, M., & Pattison, P. (2004). Posttraumatic stress disorder and depression following trauma: Understanding comorbidity. *The American Journal of Psychiatry, 161*(8), 1390–1396. https://doi.org/10.1176/appi.ajp.161.8.1390

O'Donnell, M. L., Creamer, M., & Pattison, P. (2015). Posttraumatic stress disorder and depression: Co-occurrence and longitudinal relationships. *Journal of Abnormal Psychology, 124*(3), 875–887. https://doi.org/10.1037/abn0000067

Ogden, P., & Fisher, J. (2015). *Sensorimotor psychotherapy: Interventions for trauma and attachment.* Norton & Company

Ogden, P., Minton, K., & Pain, C. (2006). *Sensorimotor psychotherapy: Interventions for trauma and attachment.* W.W. Norton & Company.

Ogden, P., Pain, C., & Fisher, J. (2006). A sensorimotor approach to the treatment of trauma and dissociation. *The Psychiatric Clinics of North America, 29*(1), 263–xii. https://doi.org/10.1016/j.psc.2005.10.012

Papadopulos, N. A., Hodbod, M., Henrich, G., Kovacs, L., Papadopoulos, O., Herschbach, P., & Machens, H. G. (2019). The effect of blepharoplasty on our patient's quality of life, emotional stability, and self-esteem. *The Journal of Craniofacial Surgery, 30*(2), 377–383. https://doi.org/10.1097/SCS.0000000000005057

Pargament, K. I., & Mahoney, A. (2021). Spirituality: The search for the sacred. In C. R. Snyder, S. J. Lopez, L. M. Edwards, & S. C. Marques (Eds.), *The Oxford handbook of positive psychology* (3rd ed., pp. 878–891). Oxford University Press.

Pawlowski, B., Dunbar, R. I. M., & Lipowicz, A. (2000). Evolutionary psychology of human female sexuality: Cross-cultural and cross-species perspectives. *Ethology, 106*(1), 1–17. https://doi.org/10.1046/j.1439-0310.2000.00555.x

Pearl, R. L., & Puhl, R. M. (2018). Weight bias internalization and health: a systematic review. *Obesity Reviews: An Official Journal of the International Association for the Study of Obesity, 19*(8), 1141–1163. https://doi.org/10.1111/obr.12701

Peat, C. M., Peyerl, N. L., & Muehlenkamp, J. J. (2008). Body image and eating disorders in older adults: a review. *The Journal of General Psychology, 135*(4), 343–358. https://doi.org/10.3200/GENP.135.4.343-358

Peera, M., Rose, L., Kaufman, L., Zhang, E., Alkhaifi, M., & Dulmage, B. (2024). Hair loss: Alopecia fears and realities for survivors of breast cancer-a narrative review. *Annals of Palliative Medicine, 13*(5), 1235–1245. https://doi.org/10.21037/apm-24-69

Pepe, J., Body, J. J., Hadji, P., McCloskey, E., Meier, C., Obermayer-Pietsch, B., Palermo, A., Tsourdi, E., Zillikens, M. C., Langdahl, B., & Ferrari, S. (2020). Osteoporosis in premenopausal women: A clinical narrative review by the ECTS and the IOF. *The Journal of Clinical Endocrinology and Metabolism, 105*(8), dgaa306. https://doi.org/10.1210/clinem/dgaa306

Perkins, N. M., & Brausch, A. M. (2019). Body dissatisfaction and symptoms of bulimia nervosa prospectively predict suicide ideation in adolescents. *The International Journal of Eating Disorders, 52*(8), 941–949. https://doi.org/10.1002/eat.23116

Phillips K. A. (2004). Body dysmorphic disorder: recognizing and treating imagined ugliness. *World psychiatry: Official Journal of the World Psychiatric Association (WPA), 3*(1), 12–17.

Piaget, J. (1952). *The origins of intelligence in children* (M. Cook, Trans.). International Universities Press. (Original work published 1936)

Polivy, J., Herman, C. P., & Boivin, M. (2005). Eating disorders. In J. E. Maddux & B. A. Winstead (Eds.), *Psychopathology: Foundations for a contemporary understanding* (pp. 229–254). Lawrence Erlbaum Associates Publishers.

Pope, H. G., Phillips, K. A., & Olivardia, R. (2000). *The Adonis complex: The secret crisis of male body obsession*. Free Press.

Powers, M. A., Bardsley, J. K., Cypress, M., Duker, P., & Funnell, M. M. (2020). Diabetes self-management education and support in Type 1 diabetes: An updated position statement of the American Diabetes Association. *Diabetes Care, 43*(7), 1585–1595. https://doi.org/10.2337/dci20-0027

Prunty, A., Hahn, A., O'Shea, A., Edmonds, S., & Clark, M. K. (2023). Associations among enacted weight stigma, weight self-stigma, and multiple physical health outcomes, healthcare utilization, and selected health behaviors. *International Journal of Obesity (2005), 47*(1), 33–38. https://doi.org/10.1038/s41366-022-01233-w

Puhl, R. M., & Brownell, K. D. (2006). Confronting and coping with weight stigma: An investigation of overweight and obese adults. *Obesity (Silver Spring, Md.), 14*(10), 1802–1815. https://doi.org/10.1038/oby.2006.208

Puhl, R. M., & Heuer, C. A. (2009). The stigma of obesity: A review and update. *Obesity (Silver Spring, Md.), 17*(5), 941–964. https://doi.org/10.1038/oby.2008.636

Puhl, R. M., & Latner, J. D. (2007). Stigma, obesity and the health of the nation's children. *Psychological Bulletin, 133*(4), 557–580.

Raggio, G. A., Looby, S. E., Robbins, G. K., Park, E. R., Sweek, E. W., Safren, S. A., & Psaros, C. (2020). Psychosocial correlates of body image and lipodystrophy in women aging with HIV. *The Journal of the Association of Nurses in AIDS Care: JANAC, 31*(2), 157–166. https://doi.org/10.1097/JNC.0000000000000139

Reas, D. L., & Stedal, K. (2015). Eating disorders in men aged midlife and beyond. *Maturitas, 81*(2), 248–255. https://doi.org/10.1016/j.maturitas.2015.03.004

Rittenour, C. E., & Cohen, E. L. (2016). Viewing our aged selves: Age progression simulations increase young adults' aging anxiety and negative stereotypes of older adults. *International Journal of Aging & Human Development, 82*(4), 271–289. https://doi.org/10.1177/0091415016641690

Riva, G. (2018). The neuroscience of body memory: From the self through the space to the others. *Cortex; a Journal Devoted to the Study of the Nervous System and Behavior, 104*, 241–260. https://doi.org/10.1016/j.cortex.2017.07.013

Roberts, A., Cash, T. F., Feingold, A., & Johnson, B. T. (2006). Are black-white differences in females' body dissatisfaction decreasing? A meta-analytic review. *Journal of Consulting and Clinical Psychology, 74*(6), 1121–1131. https://doi.org/10.1037/0022-006X.74.6.1121

Robinson, L., Micali, N., & Misra, M. (2017). Eating disorders and bone metabolism in women. *Current Opinion in Pediatrics, 29*(4), 488–496. https://doi.org/10.1097/MOP.0000000000000508

Rodriguez, D., Larkin, M., & Wanner, S. (2020). Social isolation and stigma in eating disorder recovery: A qualitative study. *Eating Disorders, 28*(5), 529–544.

Rosenberg M. (2002). Children with gender identity issues and their parents in individual and group treatment. *Journal of the American Academy of Child and Adolescent Psychiatry, 41*(5), 619–621. https://doi.org/10.1097/00004583-200205000-00020

Rosenfield, D. (2004). *Spirituality and body image: A guide to integrating spiritual growth with health and wellness.* Reclaiming Heart Press.

Rowe, J. W., & Kahn, R. L. (1997). Successful aging. *The Gerontologist, 37*(4), 433–440. https://doi.org/10.1093/geront/37.4.433

Rubino, F., Puhl, R. M., Cummings, D. E., Eckel, R. H., Ryan, D. H., Mechanick, J. I., Nadglowski, J., Ramos Salas, X., Schauer, P. R., Twenefour, D., Apovian, C. M., Aronne, L. J., Batterham, R. L., Berthoud, H. R., Boza, C., Busetto, L., Dicker, D., De Groot, M., Eisenberg, D., Flint, S. W., … Dixon, J. B. (2020). Joint international consensus statement for ending stigma of obesity. *Nature Medicine, 26*(4), 485–497. https://doi.org/10.1038/s41591-020-0803-x

Ryan, L., Coyne, R., Heary, C., Birney, S., Crotty, M., Dunne, R., Conlan, O., & Walsh, J. C. (2023). Weight stigma experienced by patients with obesity in healthcare settings: A qualitative evidence synthesis. *Obesity Reviews: An Official Journal of the International Association for the Study of Obesity, 24*(10), e13606. https://doi.org/10.1111/obr.13606

Sabik, N. J. (2017). Is social engagement linked to body image and depression among aging women?. *Journal of Women & Aging, 29*(5), 405–416. https://doi.org/10.1080/08952841.2016.1213106

Salman, E. J., & Kabir, R. (2022). *Night eating syndrome.* [Updated 2022 September 14]. In: StatPearls [Internet]. StatPearls Publishing; 2025 January. Available from https://www.ncbi.nlm.nih.gov/books/NBK585047/

Sarwer, D. B., Whitaker, L. A., & Krugman, M. D. (2005). Cosmetic surgery and body image. *Journal of Social Issues*, *61*(2), 217–231. https://doi.org/10.1111/j.1540-4560.2005.00404.x

Schaefer, J. (2014). *Life without Ed: How one woman declared independence from her eating disorder and how you can too* (10th anniversary ed.). McGraw-Hill.

Schaefer, L. M., Burke, N. L., & Thompson, J. K. (2019). Thin-ideal internalization: How much is too much?. *Eating and Weight Disorders: EWD*, *24*(5), 933–937. https://doi.org/10.1007/s40519-018-0498-x

Schlessinger, J., Gilbert, E., Cohen, J. L., & Kaufman, J. (2017). New uses of AbobotulinumtoxinA in aesthetics. *Aesthetic Surgery Journal*, *37*(suppl_1), S45–S58. https://doi.org/10.1093/asj/sjx005

Schmahl, C., & Vermetten, E. (2019). Emotional regulation in post-traumatic stress disorder. *Psychiatric Clinics of North America*, *42*(2), 145–155. https://doi.org/10.1016/j.psc.2019.01.001

Schwartz, A. & Knipe, J. (2017). *The complex PTSD workbook: A mind-body approach for regaining control and becoming whole*. Callisto.

Schwitzer, A. M., Jarosz, P. A., & Engel, J. (2001). Emotional eating: An exploration of its associations with self-reported eating disorders, depression, and stress. *Psychology, Health & Medicine*, *6*(2), 213–222.

Shafran, R., Cooper, Z., & Fairburn, C. G. (2004). Clinical perfectionism: A cognitive-behavioral analysis. *Behaviour Research and Therapy*, *42*(11), 1265–1280. https://doi.org/10.1016/j.brat.2003.11.007

Shakeri, A., & North, M. S. (2025). The gender convergence effect in older age: A meta-analytic review comparing modern attitudes toward younger, middle-aged, and older women and men. *Psychological Bulletin*, *151*(3), 261–284. https://doi.org/10.1037/bul0000467

Shapiro, F. (2017). *Eye movement desensitization and reprocessing: Basic principles, protocols, and procedures* (3rd ed.). The Guilford Press.

Sharma, G., & Goodwin, J. (2006). Effect of aging on respiratory system physiology and immunology. *Clinical Interventions in Aging*, *1*(3), 253–260. https://doi.org/10.2147/ciia.2006.1.3.253.

Shufelt, C. L., Torbati, T., & Dutra, E. (2017). Hypothalamic amenorrhea and the long-term health consequences. *Seminars in Reproductive Medicine*, *35*(3), 256–262. https://doi.org/10.1055/s-0037-1603581

Sicari, F., Merlo, E. M., Gentile, G., Nucera, R., Portelli, M., Settineri, S., Myles, L. A. M., & Militi, A. (2023). Body image and psychological impact of dental appearance in adolescents with malocclusion: A preliminary exploratory study. *Children (Basel, Switzerland)*, *10*(10), 1691. https://doi.org/10.3390/children10101691

Siegel, D. (2001). *The developing mind: How relationships and the brain interact to shape who we are*. The Guilford Press.

Singh, D. (1993). Body shape and women's attractiveness: The critical role of waist-to-hip ratio. *Personality and Social Psychology Bulletin*, *19*(3), 288–299. https://doi.org/10.1177/0146167293193010

Siracusa, R., Paola, R. D., Cuzzocrea, S., & Impellizzeri, D. (2021). Fibromyalgia: Pathogenesis, mechanisms, diagnosis and treatment options update. *International Journal of Molecular Sciences*, *22*(8), 3891. https://doi.org/10.3390/ijms22083891

Sjöberg, O. (2023). Work-retirement transitions and mental health: A longitudinal analysis of the role of social protection generosity in 11 countries. *Scandinavian Journal of Public Health*, *51*(1), 90–97. https://doi.org/10.1177/14034948211042130

Snyder, M. (October 1974). Self-monitoring of expressive behavior. *Journal of Personality and Social Psychology*, *30*(4), 526–537. https://doi.org/10.1037/h0037039

Song, K., Lee, J., Lee, S., Jeon, S., Lee, H. S., Kim, H. S., & Chae, H. W. (2023). Height and subjective body image are associated with suicide ideation among Korean adolescents. *Frontiers in Psychiatry*, *14*, 1172940. https://doi.org/10.3389/fpsyt.2023.1172940

Sörensen, S., Missell, R. L., Eustice-Corwin, A., & Otieno, D. A. (2021). Perspectives on aging-related preparation. *Journal of Elder Policy*, *1*(2), 10.18278/jep.1.2.7. https://doi.org/10.18278/jep.1.2.7

Southward, M. W., Christensen, K. A., Fettich, K. C., Weissman, J., Berona, J., & Chen, E. Y. (2014). Loneliness mediates the relationship between emotion dysregulation and bulimia nervosa/binge eating disorder psychopathology in a clinical sample. *Eating and Weight Disorders: EWD*, *19*(4), 509–513. https://doi.org/10.1007/s40519-013-0083-2

Spiegel, D. A., & Kelly, S. A. (2005). A review of binge eating disorder in men: Risk factors and treatment options. *Journal of Men's Health and Gender*, *2*(2), 124–129.

Steinberg, D., & Katz, D. (2009). The genetic basis of human obesity. *Obesity Reviews*, *10*(2), 130–142. https://doi.org/10.1111/j.1467-789X.2008.00519.x

Steiner-Adair, C. (2001). *Full circle: A guide to healthy eating and emotional well-being for women in midlife and beyond*. HarperCollins.

Stewart, T., Joyce, P. R., & McIntosh, V. V. (2020). Pharmacotherapy in eating disorders: A critical review. *The Australian and New Zealand Journal of Psychiatry*, *54*(2), 104–113.

Stice, E. (2002). Risk and maintenance factors for eating pathology: A meta-analytic review. *Psychological Bulletin*, *128*, 825–848.

Streatfeild, J., Hickson, J., Austin, S. B., Hutcheson, R., Kandel, J. S., Lampert, J. G., Myers, E. M., Richmond, T. K., Samnaliev, M., Velasquez, K., Weissman, R. S., & Pezzullo, L. (2021). Social and economic cost of eating disorders in the United States: Evidence to inform policy action. *The International Journal of Eating Disorders*, *54*(5), 851–868. https://doi.org/10.1002/eat.23486

Strober, M., Freeman, R., & Morrell, W. (1997). The long-term course of severe anorexia nervosa in adolescents: survival analysis of recovery, relapse, and outcome predictors over 10-15 years in a prospective study. *The International Journal of Eating Disorders*, *22*(4), 339–360. https://doi.org/10.1002/(sici)1098-108x(199712)22:4<339::aid-eat1>3.0.co;2-n

Stroebe, M., Schut, H., & Boerner, K. (2017). Models of coping with bereavement: An updated overview. *Estudios de Psicología*, *38*(3), 582–607. https://doi.org/10.1080/02109395.2017.1340055

Substance Abuse and Mental Health Services Administration. (2014). *SAMHSA's concept of trauma and guidance for a trauma-informed approach* (HHS Publication No. (SMA) No. 14–4884).

Sullivan, P. F. (1995). Mortality in anorexia nervosa. *The American Journal of Psychiatry*, *152*(7), 1073–1074.

Surrey, J. L. (1991). The "self-in-relation": A theory of women's development. In J. M. Miller (Ed.), *The healing power of emotion: Affective neuroscience, development & clinical practice* (pp. 116–136). Routledge.

Meneguzzo, P., Zuccaretti, D., Tenconi, E., & Favaro, A. (2024). Transgender body image: Weight dissatisfaction, objectification & identity - Complex interplay explored via matched group. *International Journal of Clinical and Health Psychology: IJCHP*, *24*(1), 100441. https://doi.org/10.1016/j.ijchp.2024.100441

Szinovacz, M. E., & Davey, A. (2005). Predictors of perceptions of involuntary retirement. *The Gerontologist*, *45*(1), 36–47. https://doi.org/10.1093/geront/45.1.36

Tagay, S., Schlottbohm, E., Reyes-Rodriguez, M. L., Repic, N., & Senf, W. (2014). Eating disorders, trauma, PTSD, and psychosocial resources. *Eating disorders*, *22*(1), 33–49. https://doi.org/10.1080/10640266.2014.857517

Talumaa, B., Brown, A., Batterham, R. L., & Kalea, A. Z. (2022). Effective strategies in ending weight stigma in healthcare. *Obesity Reviews: An Official Journal of the International Association for the Study of Obesity*, *23*(10), e13494. https://doi.org/10.1111/obr.13494

Tangney, J. P., & Dearing, R. L. (2002). *Shame and guilt*. The Guilford Press.

Tedeschi, R. G., & Calhoun, L. G. (2004). Posttraumatic growth: Conceptual foundations and empirical evidence. *Psychological Inquiry*, *15*(1), 1–18.

Thomas, H. N., Hamm, M., Borrero, S., Hess, R., & Thurston, R. C. (2019). Body image, attractiveness, and sexual satisfaction among midlife women: A qualitative study. *Journal of Women's Health (2002)*, *28*(1), 100–106. https://doi.org/10.1089/jwh.2018.7107

Thompson, J. K., & Stice, E. (2001). Thin-ideal internalization: Mounting evidencce for a new risk factor for body-image disturbance and eating pathology. *Current Directions in Psychological Science*, *10*(5), 181–183. https://doi.org/10.1111/1467-8721.00144

Tiggemann, M. (2004). Body image across the adult life span: stability and change. *Body Image, 1*(1), 29–41.

Tiggemann, M., & Lynch, J. (2001). Body image across the life span in adult women: The role of self-objectification. *Developmental Psychology*, *37*(2), 197–205. https://doi.org/10.1037/0012-1649.37.2.243

Tiggemann, M., & Slater, A. (2014). NetGirls: The Internet, Facebook, and body image concern in adolescent girls. *International Journal of Eating Disorders*, *47*(6), 630–643. https://doi.org/10.1002/eat.22314

Tod, D., Edwards, C., & Cranswick, I. (2016). Muscle dysmorphia: current insights. *Psychology Research and Behavior Management*, *9*, 179–188. https://doi.org/10.2147/PRBM.S97404

Toma, C. L., & Hancock, J. (2016). Looks and lies: The role of physical attractiveness in online dating. *Cyberpsychology, Behavior, and Social Networking*, *19*(9), 618–624. https://doi.org/10.1089/cyber.2016.0247

Treasure, J., Cardi, V., Leppanen, J., & Turton, R. (2015). New treatment approaches for severe and enduring eating disorders. *Physiology & Behavior*, *152*(Pt B), 456–465. https://doi.org/10.1016/j.physbeh.2015.06.007

Treasure, J., Claudino, A. M., & Zucker, N. (2010). Eating disorders. *Lancet (London, England)*, *375*(9714), 583–593. https://doi.org/10.1016/S0140-6736(09)61748-7

Tribole, E., & Resch, E. (2020). *Intuitive eating: A revolutionary anti-diet approach* (4th ed.). St. Martin's Essentials.

Troop, N. A., & Redshaw, C. (2012). General shame and bodily shame in eating disorders: a 2.5-year longitudinal study. *European Eating Disorders Review: The Journal of the Eating Disorders Association*, *20*(5), 373–378. https://doi.org/10.1002/erv.2160

Tull, M. T., Gratz, K. L., & Gunderson, J. G. (2012). The relationship between emotional dysregulation and posttraumatic stress disorder in a sample of women with substance use disorders. *Journal of Traumatic Stress*, *25*(3), 313–321. https://doi.org/10.1002/jts.21713

Tylka, T. L., & Wood-Barcalow, N. L. (2015). The body satisfaction scale: A new measure of self-objectification and its relationship to body image and self-esteem. *Journal of Social and Clinical Psychology*, *34*(8), 672–689. https://doi.org/10.1016/j.bodyim.2015.04.001

van den Berg, P., Paxton, S. J., Keery, H., Wall, M., Guo, J., & Neumark-Sztainer, D. (2007). Body dissatisfaction and body comparison with media images in males and females. *Body Image*, *4*(3), 257–268. https://doi.org/10.1016/j.bodyim.2007.04.003

van der Kolk, B. A. (2014). *The body keeps the score: Brain, mind, and body in the healing of trauma*. Viking.

van der Kolk, B. (2015). *The body keeps the score: Brain, mind and body in the healing of trauma*. Penguin Books.

van Solinge, H., & Henkens, K. (2008). Adjustment to and satisfaction with retirement: Two of a kind?. *Psychology and Aging*, *23*(2), 422–434. https://doi.org/10.1037/0882-7974.23.2.422

Vartanian, L. R., & Dey, S. (2013). Self-concept clarity, thin-ideal internalization, and appearance-related social comparison as predictors of body dissatisfaction. *Body Image*, *10*(4), 495–500. https://doi.org/10.1016/j.bodyim.2013.05.004

Vincent, C., Bodnaruc, A. M., Prud'homme, D., Olson, V., & Giroux, I. (2023). Associations between menopause and body image: A systematic review. *Women's Health (London, England)*, *19*, 17455057231209536. https://doi.org/10.1177/17455057231209536

Vidaña, A. G., Forbush, K. T., Barnhart, E. L., Mildrum Chana, S., Chapa, D. A. N., Richson, B., & Thomeczek, M. L. (2020). Impact of trauma in childhood and adulthood on eating-disorder symptoms. *Eating Behaviors*, *39*, 101426. https://doi.org/10.1016/j.eatbeh.2020.101426

von Soest, T., Kvalem, I. L., Roald, H. E., & Skolleborg, K. C. (2009). The effects of cosmetic surgery on body image, self-esteem, and psychological problems. *Journal of Plastic, Reconstructive & Aesthetic Surgery: JPRAS*, *62*(10), 1238–1244. https://doi.org/10.1016/j.bjps.2007.12.093

von Soest, T., Kvalem, I. L., Skolleborg, K. C., & Roald, H. E. (2006). Psychosocial factors predicting the motivation to undergo cosmetic surgery. *Plastic and Reconstructive Surgery*, *117*(1), 51–64. https://doi.org/10.1097/01.prs.0000194902.89912.f1

van Solinge, H., & Henkens, K. (2008). Adjustment to and satisfaction with retirement: Two of a kind? *Psychology and Aging*, *23*(2), 422–434. https://doi.org/10.1037/0882-7974.23.2.422

Warren, C. S., & Akoury, L. M. (2020). Emphasizing the "cultural" in sociocultural: A systematic review of research on thin-ideal internalization, acculturation, and eating pathology in US ethnic minorities. *Psychology Research and Behavior Management*, *13*, 319–330. https://doi.org/10.2147/PRBM.S204274

Wasserman, A. M., Mathias, C. W., Hill-Kapturczak, N., Karns-Wright, T. E., & Dougherty, D. M. (2020). The development of impulsivity and sensation seeking: Associations with substance use among at-risk adolescents. *Journal of Research on Adolescence:*

The Official Journal of the Society for Research on Adolescence, *30*(4), 1051–1066. https://doi.org/10.1111/jora.12579

Watters, S., & Higgins, A. (2024). Muscle dysmorphia: An under-recognised aspect of body dissatisfaction in men. *British Journal of Nursing (Mark Allen Publishing)*, *33*(12), 584–588. https://doi.org/10.12968/bjon.2023.0176

Webb, J. R. (2021). *Understanding forgiveness and addiction: Theory, research, and clinical application*. Routledge.

Webb, J. R., & Boye, C. M. (2024). Self-forgiveness and self-condemnation in the context of addictive behavior and suicidal behavior. *Substance Abuse and Rehabilitation*, *15*, 21–30. https://doi.org/10.2147/SAR.S396964

Westbury, S., Oyebode, O., van Rens, T., & Barber, T. M. (2023). Obesity stigma: Causes, consequences, and potential solutions. *Current Obesity Reports*, *12*(1), 10–23. https://doi.org/10.1007/s13679-023-00495-3

Westwood, S. (2023). "It's the not being seen that is most tiresome": Older women, invisibility and social (in)justice. *Journal of Women & Aging*, *35*(6), 557–572. https://doi.org/10.1080/08952841.2023.2197658

Wildes, J. E., Ringham, R. M., & Marcus, M. D. (2010). Emotion avoidance in patients with anorexia nervosa: Initial test of a functional model. *The International Journal of Eating Disorders*, *43*(5), 398–404. https://doi.org/10.1002/eat.20730

Williams, L., Gurung, J., Persons, P., & Kilpela, L. (2024). Body image and eating issues in midlife: A narrative review with clinical question recommendations. *Maturitas*, *188*, 108068. https://doi.org/10.1016/j.maturitas.2024.108068

Wilfred, S. A., Becker, C. B., Kanzler, K. E., Musi, N., Espinoza, S. E., & Kilpela, L. S. (2021). Binge eating among older women: Prevalence rates and health correlates across three independent samples. *Journal of Eating Disorders*, *9*, 132. https://doi.org/10.1186/s40337-021-00484-8

Wilson, S., Benning, S. D., & Racine, S. E. (2022). Examining relationships among thin-ideal internalization, eating pathology, and motivational reactions to high- and low-calorie food. *Appetite*, *178*, 106258. https://doi.org/10.1016/j.appet.2022.106258

Winick, C. (1962). Maturing out of narcotic addiction. *Bulletin on Narcotics*, *14*, 1–7.

Wolf, N. (2013). *The Beauty Myth: How images of beauty are used against women*. Random House.

Wonderlich, S. A., & Crosby, R. D. (2009). Eating disorders in the workplace: A review of occupational outcomes and interventions. *International Journal of Eating Disorders*, *42*(1), 61–70.

Woodyatt, L., Wenzel, M., & Griffin, B. J. (Eds.). (2017). *Handbook of the psychology of self-forgiveness* (pp. 2–28). Springer International Publishing.

Wooten, W., Laubaucher, C., George, G. C., Heyn, S., & Herringa, R. J. (2022). The impact of childhood maltreatment on adaptive emotion regulation strategies. *Child Abuse & Neglect*, *125*, 105494. https://doi.org/10.1016/j.chiabu.2022.105494

Xiang, L., Low, A. H. L., Leung, Y. Y., Fong, W., Gandhi, M., Yoon, S., Lau, T. C., Koh, D. R., & Thumboo, J. (2021). Interval between symptom onset and diagnosis among patients with autoimmune rheumatic diseases in a multi-ethnic Asian population. *International Journal of Rheumatic Diseases*, *24*(8), 1061–1070. https://doi.org/10.1111/1756-185X.14165

Young, I. M. (2005). *On female body experience: "Throwing like a girl" and other essays*. Oxford University Press.

Zanarini, M. C., Frankenburg, F. R., & Hennen, J. (2004). The role of personality disorders in the development of eating disorders. *Journal of Personality Disorders, 18*(4), 401–410.

Zhang, X., Pennell, M. L., Bernardo, B. M., Clark, J., Krok-Schoen, J. L., Focht, B. C., Crane, T. E., Shadyab, A. H., & Paskett, E. D. (2021). Body image, physical activity and psychological health in older female cancer survivors. *Journal of Geriatric Oncology, 12*(7), 1059–1067. https://doi.org/10.1016/j.jgo.2021.04.007

Index

For Product Safety Concerns and Information please contact our EU
representative GPSR@taylorandfrancis.com
Taylor & Francis Verlag GmbH, Kaufingerstraße 24, 80331 München, Germany

www.ingramcontent.com/pod-product-compliance
Lightning Source LLC
Chambersburg PA
CBHW050649280326
41932CB00015B/2842